Thank you for picking up my book. Your support means a lot, and I hope you find the read both enjoyable and insightful. Beyond being an author, my work extends into research and consultancy within organizational behavior and leadership. I engage with a broad spectrum of clients, from individuals to larger teams and organizations, offering guidance in leadership development.

For a deeper dive into my professional background and consulting philosophy, several websites are available. There, you'll also find my contact details. I'm eager to hear your thoughts on the book or discuss potential collaboration in leadership coaching.

Discover more about my work and other publications related to leadership and organizational behavior at my personal website, https://thomaspatrickhuber.com.

Learn about my specific approach to leadership coaching and consulting at https://elevateus.ch, the official website of my company.

Lastly, in case you want to reach out to me directly please send me an email at thomaspatrick@mac.com.

I appreciate your support in purchasing this book and look forward to connecting with you.

Wishing you an enlightening journey,

Thomas P Huber, PhD, MS ECS

Preface

In the preface to "Depth Leadership: Navigating the Unconscious in Executive Coaching," I embark on a journey to bridge two worlds that, at first glance, may seem distinct yet are intrinsically connected: the world of leadership and the realm of psychology. This book is born out of a profound belief in the transformative power of understanding the unconscious mind in shaping leaders who are not only effective but truly exemplary. My journey into these interconnected disciplines has been both a professional pursuit and a personal passion, reflecting decades of exploration, learning, and application.

The genesis of this book lies in the countless hours spent coaching executives, where I observed a recurring theme: the most significant hurdles to leadership excellence often stem from beneath the surface, from the unseen depths of the unconscious mind. These experiences led me to delve deeper into psychoanalytic theory, seeking tools and insights that could unlock new dimensions of leadership development. What I discovered was a rich tapestry of concepts that, when applied to executive coaching, could facilitate profound personal growth and transformation.

"Depth Leadership" is designed to serve as a guide for those who aspire to excel in leadership by navigating the complexities of the human psyche. It's written for executive coaches, leaders, and anyone intrigued by the intersection of psychology and leadership. Through this book, I aim to demystify the psychoanalytic approach, making it accessible and applicable to the challenges and opportunities faced by today's leaders. Each chapter weaves together theory, practical insights, and case studies, providing a comprehensive framework for understanding and applying psychoanalytic principles in leadership contexts.

This work also reflects a personal journey of discovery and transformation. In writing this book, I have revisited my own experiences, challenges, and breakthroughs, both as a coach and as a leader. Sharing these reflections, I hope to offer not just a methodology but a testament to the profound impact that a deep understanding of the unconscious can have on leadership effectiveness and personal fulfillment.

The book is structured to progressively deepen the reader's understanding, starting with foundational psychoanalytic concepts, moving through their application in understanding leadership dynamics, and culminating in practical strategies for executive coaching. It is my hope that readers will emerge from this journey with a new perspective on leadership and a toolkit for fostering depth, insight, and transformation in themselves and those they lead or coach.

As you turn these pages, I invite you to embark on this journey with an open mind and a curious heart. "Depth Leadership" is not just a book; it is an invitation to explore the uncharted territories of your own leadership potential, guided by the insights of psychoanalytic theory. Together, we will discover the depths beneath the surface of leadership, finding in those depths the keys to extraordinary leadership transformation.

Thomas P Huber, PhD, MS ECS

Lugano, 2024

Introduction to Depth Leadership

This introductory chapter sets the stage for the journey into "Depth Leadership: Navigating the Unconscious in Executive Coaching." It outlines the book's aims, scope, and the pivotal intersection between psychoanalytic theory and leadership coaching. This chapter is designed to prepare readers for a transformative exploration of how deep psychological insights can revolutionize leadership and coaching practices.

The primary aim of this book is to offer an insightful guide that bridges the rich, complex world of psychoanalytic concepts with the dynamic, challenging realm of executive leadership coaching. At its core, this book is designed to illuminate how deep psychological insights—rooted in the traditions and discoveries of psychoanalysis—can significantly enhance leadership effectiveness and foster profound personal growth among leaders.

Leadership, in its essence, is not merely about strategies, decision-making, or organizational skills; it is fundamentally about people—understanding them, motivating them, and guiding them towards a shared vision. This understanding extends beyond the conscious to the unconscious, where the roots of many thoughts, feelings, and behaviors lie. By integrating psychoanalytic concepts into executive leadership coaching, this book aims to equip leaders and coaches with the tools to explore these depths, offering pathways to more authentic, emotionally intelligent, and effective leadership.

The journey into one's psychological underpinnings can be both challenging and rewarding. It requires courage, openness, and a willingness to confront aspects of oneself that are often hidden. However, the rewards—increased self-awareness, improved interpersonal relationships, and the ability to navigate the complexities of leadership with greater ease and confidence—are immeasurable. Through a psychoanalytic lens, leaders can gain insights into their motivations, fears, and unconscious biases, leading to transformative personal and professional development.

This manuscript serves as a practical resource, providing concrete strategies, techniques, and case studies that demonstrate the application of psychoanalytic principles in real-world leadership scenarios. From understanding the dynamics of power and authority to navigating the challenges of imposter syndrome and leadership anxieties, the book addresses a wide range of topics that are crucial for today's leaders.

The purpose of this book is to create a dialogue between psychoanalysis and executive coaching, enriching the practice of leadership development with depth psychology's nuanced understanding of the human psyche. By doing so, it aspires to contribute to the cultivation of leaders who are not only successful in achieving their organizational goals but are also insightful, reflective, and attuned to the psychological dimensions of leadership and human relations.

We embark on a comprehensive exploration that bridges the nuanced world of psychoanalytic theory with the dynamic challenges of executive leadership coaching. It is designed to cater to a diverse audience, including executive coaches, organizational leaders, HR professionals, and anyone intrigued by the intersection of psychology and leadership. The scope of this book spans from foundational psychoanalytic theories, through their application in understanding leadership dynamics, to offering practical strategies for executive coaching.

Our exploration begins with an introduction to psychoanalysis, delving into its historical origins and key figures such as Freud, Jung, and Klein. This sets the groundwork for understanding fundamental concepts like the unconscious, defense mechanisms, transference, and countertransference, alongside the psychoanalytic model of the mind's structure (id, ego, superego) and its relevance to personality development and behavior.

The application of psychoanalytic theory in understanding leadership dynamics covers how these principles provide insights into leadership as a psychological phenomenon. This includes the unconscious factors influencing leadership styles and effectiveness, and the complex dynamics between leaders and followers. The discussion extends to navigating power and authority, analyzing the psychoanalytic underpinnings within leadership contexts, and offering insights on how leaders can manage these complexities.

Practical strategies for executive coaching are then presented, offering techniques and tools for coaches to apply psychoanalytic principles in their practice. This encompasses listening with a "third ear," interpreting unconscious communication, and using psychoanalytic insights to tackle common leadership challenges such as enhancing emotional intelligence, overcoming imposter syndrome, and managing leadership anxieties. Detailed case studies illustrate the transformative application of these concepts in real-world coaching scenarios.

The exploration also addresses the ethical considerations in integrating psychoanalytic approaches into executive coaching, highlighting the importance of confidentiality and the depth of psychological exploration. The significance of ongoing learning, supervision, and self-reflection for coaches adopting these approaches is emphasized, ensuring they remain effective, ethical, and attuned to the needs of coachees.

By covering these areas, the book aims to provide a rich understanding of how psychoanalytic theory can deepen leadership development and executive coaching, offering readers theoretical insights alongside practical tools and strategies for professional growth and effective leadership.

Leadership in contemporary contexts is an ever-evolving concept, reflecting the complex and dynamic landscapes of today's organizations. Unlike traditional views that often-depicted leadership as a static set of characteristics or a one-size-fits-all approach, modern perspectives recognize leadership as a multifaceted and fluid practice. This shift acknowledges the rapid changes in global markets, technological advancements, and the increasing emphasis on diversity, equity, and inclusion within the workplace.

Today's leaders are expected to navigate a multitude of challenges, from managing remote teams spread across different time zones to fostering innovation in highly competitive environments. Leadership now requires a delicate balance between decisiveness and flexibility, allowing leaders to adapt strategies as situations evolve. The contemporary leader is also seen as a catalyst for change, not only driving organizational goals but also championing social responsibility and ethical practices.

The influence of digital transformation on leadership cannot be overstated. Leaders must leverage technology to enhance decision-making and productivity yet remain vigilant about the digital divide and the human aspects of their teams. Emotional intelligence has emerged as a critical competency, enabling leaders to connect with their teams, understand diverse perspectives, and build inclusive cultures that attract and retain talent.

The concept of leadership has expanded beyond individual roles to include collective leadership practices. This approach recognizes the value of distributed leadership within teams, where leadership responsibilities are shared to harness diverse skills and foster a sense of ownership and engagement among team members.

The evolving nature of leadership also reflects a shift towards more authentic and vulnerable leadership styles. Leaders are encouraged to show their humanity, share their failures as learning opportunities, and build trust through transparency. This authenticity helps to create a more relatable and inspiring vision that motivates teams to strive towards common goals.

Defining leadership in contemporary contexts involves understanding it as a dynamic and adaptive process that responds to the complexities of the modern organizational environment. It demands a blend of strategic foresight, technological savvy, emotional intelligence, and a commitment to ethical and inclusive practices. As organizations continue to evolve, so too will the definitions and expectations of leadership, requiring ongoing learning and adaptation from those who aspire to lead effectively in the 21st century.

Psychoanalysis, with its deep exploration of the human psyche, offers profound insights into the intricacies of leadership behaviors and relationships. By introducing basic psychoanalytic concepts such as the unconscious, defense mechanisms, and transference, we can uncover the underlying psychological forces that shape leadership dynamics. These concepts not only enhance our understanding of leadership but also offer pathways to more effective and emotionally intelligent leadership practices.

- The Unconscious: Central to psychoanalytic theory is the concept of the unconscious mind, which houses thoughts, memories, and desires not readily accessible to the conscious mind but that significantly influence behaviors and decisions. In the context of leadership, the unconscious can drive a leader's reactions, biases, and decision-making processes in ways they may not be fully aware of. Recognizing the influence of the unconscious can help leaders understand the deeper motivations behind their actions and the actions of others, leading to more reflective and informed leadership approaches.

- Defense Mechanisms: These are unconscious psychological strategies employed by individuals to protect themselves from anxiety-arising thoughts and feelings. Leaders, like all individuals, may unconsciously use defense mechanisms such as denial, projection, or rationalization to cope with stress, criticism, or conflict. Understanding these mechanisms can help leaders become more aware of how they might be distorting reality or shifting responsibility, thereby fostering a more open, authentic, and adaptive leadership style.

- Transference: This concept refers to the redirection of feelings and desires from one person to another, particularly in the context of relationships that resemble significant past relationships. In leadership, transference can manifest when employees project feelings associated with parental figures or past authority figures onto a leader. This dynamic can deeply influence the leader-follower relationship, affecting communication, trust, and authority dynamics. Leaders aware of transference can better navigate these emotional undercurrents, leading to healthier, more productive relationships.

The relevance of psychoanalysis to leadership lies in its ability to illuminate the unseen aspects of leadership behavior and relationships. By applying psychoanalytic concepts, leaders can achieve a deeper self-awareness and understanding of their teams, enabling them to address unconscious biases, manage emotional reactions more effectively, and cultivate a leadership style that resonates on a more personal and impactful level. Ultimately, psychoanalytic insights can empower leaders to navigate the complex human dimensions of organizational life with greater empathy, clarity, and effectiveness.

The historical intersection between psychoanalysis and leadership theories reveals a rich tapestry of ideas and insights that have significantly influenced our understanding of leadership. This intersection is marked by the pioneering work of several key figures and developments that have bridged the depth of psychoanalytic thought with the practical concerns of leadership and organizational behavior.

1. Sigmund Freud and the Foundations of Psychoanalytic Theory: Freud's exploration of the unconscious mind laid the groundwork for subsequent applications of psychoanalytic concepts to leadership. His theories on personality structures (id, ego, and superego) and defense mechanisms provide a

framework for understanding the psychological complexities of leaders and their followers.

2. Carl Jung and Archetypes: Jung's work on psychological archetypes and the collective unconscious introduced the idea that certain leadership personas, such as the hero or the wise old man, resonate universally. Jung's concepts have been applied to leadership to understand how leaders embody these archetypes and how they can influence organizational culture and follower perceptions.

3. Erik Erikson and Psychosocial Development: Erikson's stages of psychosocial development, which extend from childhood through adulthood, offer insights into the challenges and growth opportunities that shape leaders throughout their lives. His theory suggests that successful navigation of these stages can lead to qualities essential for effective leadership, such as trust, integrity, and wisdom.

4. Wilfred Bion and Group Dynamics: Bion's work on group dynamics in the mid-20th century directly linked psychoanalytic concepts with organizational and leadership studies. His insights into basic assumption theory and the emotional experiences of groups have influenced leadership theories that address the unconscious processes within teams and organizations.

5. Kurt Lewin and Leadership Styles: Although not a psychoanalyst himself, Lewin's research in the 1930s and 1940s on leadership styles and group dynamics was influenced by psychoanalytic ideas. His categorization of leadership styles (autocratic, democratic, and laissez-faire) and his force field analysis model incorporated psychological principles in understanding organizational change.

6. Manfred Kets de Vries: A contemporary figure, Kets de Vries combines psychoanalytic concepts with management and leadership, exploring the dark side of leadership, the dynamics of leadership teams, and the role of personality disorders in

organizational life. His work underscores the importance of emotional health and psychological insight in effective leadership.

The integration of psychoanalytic theory into leadership studies has evolved over time, influenced by changes in both fields. Initially, the focus was on the individual leader's psychology and its impact on decision-making and leadership style. Over time, the scope broadened to include the psychological dynamics of groups and organizations, the emotional underpinnings of leadership relationships, and the role of unconscious processes in organizational life.

This historical intersection continues to enrich leadership theories by providing deeper insights into the human element of organizational leadership. By understanding the psychological foundations of behavior, leaders can better navigate the complexities of modern organizational life, fostering environments that promote growth, innovation, and resilience.

Psychoanalytic coaching is a reflective and exploratory process that stands apart from other coaching approaches through its deep focus on the unconscious aspects of an individual's psyche. This method integrates principles and techniques from psychoanalytic theory to help individuals gain profound personal and professional development. Unlike traditional coaching methods that may prioritize goal setting, skill development, and conscious thought processes, psychoanalytic coaching delves into the less visible, often overlooked aspects of an individual's inner world. It aims to uncover the unconscious motivations, conflicts, and defense mechanisms that shape behavior and interpersonal dynamics.

At the heart of psychoanalytic coaching is the exploration of the unconscious, including examining dreams, slips of the tongue, and recurring patterns of behavior to reveal underlying psychological drivers. This approach uniquely addresses and utilizes the dynamics of transference, where clients project onto their coaches feelings and attitudes held towards significant others, and countertransference, the coach's emotional response to the client's transference. These phenomena are seen as valuable sources of information about the client's relational patterns and inner world.

Psychoanalytic coaching involves a deeper level of psychological exploration than typically found in other coaching methods. It seeks to understand the root causes of behaviors and emotional responses, aiming for a comprehensive understanding of the individual's psychological landscape. This approach places special emphasis on emotional experiences and relational issues, recognizing these as critical elements in personal and professional development. It often involves exploring past relationships and experiences to understand their impact on current functioning.

Unlike many coaching approaches that aim for immediate performance improvements or goal achievement, psychoanalytic coaching focuses on long-term personality and behavioral changes. It strives for a fundamental transformation in the individual's self-awareness, emotional intelligence, and relational capacities, offering a path to more authentic, effective, and fulfilling ways of living and leading. Though not therapy, psychoanalytic coaching shares some therapeutic elements, such as the emphasis on healing and growth. Coaches trained in psychoanalytic techniques are adept at creating a safe, confidential space where clients can explore sensitive or difficult issues, facilitating a unique and powerful approach to development that goes beyond surface-level changes to achieve deep, lasting transformation.

The influence of unconscious thoughts and feelings on leadership is profound, permeating aspects of decision-making, communication, and relationship-building in ways that leaders themselves may not fully recognize. The realm of the unconscious, with its hidden desires, fears, and memories, plays a critical role in shaping a leader's behavior and interactions with others. This unseen force can guide a leader towards certain decisions, influence their way of communicating, and affect their ability to forge strong relationships within their team and organization.

In decision-making, a leader's unconscious biases and preferences often surface, steering choices in directions that may not always align with rational analysis or conscious intentions. These biases, rooted in past experiences and emotional memories, can lead to patterns of decision-making that favor certain outcomes over others, sometimes to the detriment of objectivity and fairness. Recognizing and understanding these unconscious influences can help leaders make more balanced and inclusive decisions.

Communication is another area where the unconscious exerts its influence. The way leaders express themselves, the words they choose, and the emotions they convey can all be shaped by unconscious factors. For instance, a leader might unconsciously project their own feelings of insecurity or aggression onto their communication style, impacting how messages are received and interpreted by others. By becoming aware of these underlying drivers, leaders can learn to communicate more effectively, ensuring their messages align with their conscious intentions and foster a positive organizational culture.

The building and maintenance of relationships are also significantly affected by unconscious dynamics. The phenomena of transference and countertransference, where leaders and followers project onto each other feelings and attitudes from past significant relationships, can deeply influence the nature of their interactions. Leaders might unknowingly replicate patterns from previous authority relationships, affecting their ability to connect with and inspire their teams. Similarly, unresolved conflicts and emotional wounds from a leader's past can hinder their capacity to trust and be vulnerable, essential components of authentic and meaningful relationships.

Understanding and addressing these unconscious influences require leaders to engage in deep self-reflection and possibly seek psychoanalytic coaching or support. By bringing these unconscious elements into consciousness, leaders can gain greater control over their behaviors and choices, leading to more thoughtful decision-making, clearer and more authentic communication, and stronger, more constructive relationships.

This journey into the unconscious not only enhances leadership effectiveness but also contributes to personal growth and self-awareness, making it a valuable endeavor for any leader committed to their development and the well-being of their organization.

Integrating psychoanalytic insights into leadership development offers a myriad of advantages that transcend conventional training and development paradigms. At the forefront of these benefits is enhanced self-awareness, a critical component of effective leadership. By delving into the unconscious aspects of their psyche, leaders can uncover hidden motivations, fears, and biases that influence their behavior and decision-making processes. This deeper understanding of oneself not only fosters greater self-control and decision-making clarity but also encourages a more authentic leadership style, as leaders become more attuned to their true values and motivations.

Emotional intelligence, another crucial benefit of psychoanalytic insight, is significantly enriched as leaders become more aware of their own emotional states and how these emotions affect their interactions with others. The psychoanalytic exploration helps leaders recognize and regulate their emotional responses, leading to improved management of stress, conflict, and challenging interpersonal dynamics. Furthermore, this heightened emotional awareness enables leaders to better empathize with their team members, understanding their motivations, concerns, and emotional responses with greater nuance. This empathy not only strengthens the leader's capacity to motivate and inspire but also fosters a more supportive and cohesive team environment.

The impact of psychoanalytic insights extends into the realm of relational dynamics within organizations. By understanding the unconscious processes that underpin relationships, such as transference and projection, leaders can navigate the complex web of interpersonal relations with greater skill. This awareness allows for the identification and resolution of unconscious conflicts and patterns that may hinder effective collaboration and trust within teams. Leaders equipped with psychoanalytic insights are better positioned to create a positive organizational culture that values open communication, mutual respect, and psychological safety.

Psychoanalytic insight encourages a reflective practice among leaders, promoting a continuous learning mindset that is open to feedback and self-improvement. This reflective practice not only enhances personal growth but also models a culture of introspection and adaptability within the organization.

The integration of psychoanalytic insights into leadership development offers profound benefits that can transform leadership effectiveness. Enhanced self-awareness improved emotional intelligence, and more sophisticated relational dynamics are just a few of the advantages that contribute to more insightful, empathetic, and adaptive leadership. These benefits not only elevate the individual leader's capabilities but also have a ripple effect throughout the organization, promoting a more engaged, motivated, and resilient workforce.

In this book, we explore a series of compelling case studies that showcase the transformative impact of psychoanalytic approaches on leadership coaching and development. These narratives not only provide insights into the practical application of psychoanalytic principles but also illuminate the profound changes experienced by leaders who engage deeply with their unconscious motivations and dynamics.

One case study features a tech startup CEO who, despite her company's rapid growth, found herself grappling with decision paralysis and a pervasive sense of imposter syndrome. Psychoanalytic coaching sessions uncovered that her fears were rooted in early childhood experiences of being overshadowed by a highly successful sibling. By addressing these deep-seated feelings of inadequacy, she was able to gain confidence in her leadership abilities, leading to more decisive and assertive decision-making.

Another example involves a senior executive from a global financial services firm who exhibited a pattern of aggressive behavior towards colleagues, undermining team cohesion and performance. Through the psychoanalytic exploration of his interpersonal relationships, it was revealed that his aggression stemmed from an unconscious identification with a competitive family dynamic. This insight enabled him to understand and modify his behavior, fostering a more collaborative and supportive team environment.

A third case study delves into the experiences of a nonprofit organization leader who faced challenges in motivating her team. Psychoanalytic coaching helped her realize that her difficulty in expressing vulnerability and acknowledging her own needs was creating a barrier to genuine connections with her team members. By working through these issues, she was able to cultivate a leadership style characterized by empathy and openness, significantly enhancing team morale and engagement.

These case studies, among others presented in the book, demonstrate the versatility and depth of psychoanalytic approaches in addressing a wide range of leadership challenges. From overcoming personal insecurities and behavioral patterns to enhancing interpersonal relationships and team dynamics, psychoanalytic coaching offers leaders a pathway to not only achieve professional growth but also embark on a journey of personal transformation. Through these narratives, readers will gain a clearer understanding of how psychoanalytic principles can be applied in diverse leadership contexts, leading to more effective, self-aware, and emotionally intelligent leadership.

The integration of psychoanalytic theory into leadership contexts opens up a realm of practical applications that can profoundly influence both individual leaders and their organizations. This approach goes beyond the surface level of leadership skills and strategies, delving into the deeper psychological underpinnings that drive behavior, decision-making, and interpersonal dynamics. By setting the stage for a deeper exploration in subsequent chapters, we begin to unravel how psychoanalytic concepts can be applied in real-world leadership scenarios, offering a pathway to more nuanced, effective, and transformative leadership practices.

Psychoanalytic theory, with its focus on understanding the unconscious aspects of the mind, provides leaders with insights into their own motivations, fears, and desires, as well as those of their followers. This deeper self-awareness can lead to significant improvements in leadership effectiveness, including enhanced decision-making capabilities that take into account not just the logical but also the emotional dimensions of business challenges. Leaders become better equipped to navigate the complexities of organizational life, managing stress and conflict with greater ease and fostering a positive, productive work environment.

The psychoanalytic approach to leadership emphasizes the importance of emotional intelligence, which includes skills such as empathy, self-regulation, and the ability to motivate and inspire others. By understanding and managing their own emotional responses, and by recognizing and addressing the emotional needs of their teams, leaders can build stronger, more resilient organizations that are capable of thriving in the face of change and adversity.

The practical applications of psychoanalytic theory also extend to the realm of interpersonal relationships and team dynamics. By exploring the unconscious factors that influence how leaders and followers interact, such as transference and countertransference, leaders can work towards creating more authentic and constructive relationships. This can lead to improved communication, increased trust, and a stronger sense of community within the team or organization.

Psychoanalytic principles can be applied to address specific leadership challenges, such as overcoming resistance to change, dealing with power dynamics, and navigating the emotional landscape of leadership transitions. Through case studies and examples, subsequent chapters will delve into these applications, providing leaders with concrete strategies and tools to apply psychoanalytic insights in their leadership practice.

The practical applications of psychoanalytic theory in leadership contexts offer a powerful framework for developing more insightful, emotionally intelligent, and effective leaders. By exploring these applications in depth, this book aims to equip current and aspiring leaders with the knowledge and skills needed to lead with greater awareness, empathy, and resilience, ultimately contributing to the creation of more humane and effective organizations.

This journey takes the reader on an enlightening journey through the integration of psychoanalytic theory with executive leadership coaching, offering a comprehensive exploration of how deep psychological insights can transform leadership practices. Through a structured progression of themes, the book unfolds in a way that builds understanding and practical application step by step.

We begin with an introduction to the aims and scope of the book, setting the stage for a deep dive into the psychoanalytic principles and their relevance to leadership development. This foundational section lays the groundwork for understanding the complex interplay between the unconscious mind and leadership behaviors.

Subsequent chapters delve into the core concepts of psychoanalytic theory, including the unconscious, defense mechanisms, transference, and countertransference. Here, readers gain insights into the psychological underpinnings that influence personal development and interpersonal dynamics, providing a lens through which leadership can be re-examined.

We then transitions to exploring the application of these psychoanalytic concepts in understanding leadership dynamics. It examines the impact of unconscious processes on leadership styles, decision-making, and the leader-follower relationship, offering a new perspective on navigating the challenges of leadership.

Practical strategies for executive coaching form the next part of the book, where psychoanalytic principles are translated into concrete tools and techniques for leadership development. This section includes guidance on listening with a third ear, interpreting unconscious communication, and managing resistance and defense mechanisms, among other strategies.

Case studies and examples bring the theoretical concepts and practical applications to life, illustrating the transformative impact of psychoanalytic approaches on leaders and their organizations. These narratives provide real-world context and demonstrate how psychoanalytic coaching can address a wide range of leadership challenges.

The final chapters focus on the design and implementation of psychoanalytically informed coaching programs, addressing ethical considerations and the importance of supervision and continuing professional development for coaches. This section ensures that readers are equipped with the knowledge to ethically and effectively integrate psychoanalytic principles into their coaching practice.

Our exploration concludes with a reflection on the future of psychoanalytic approaches in leadership development, contemplating the evolving landscape of leadership and the ongoing relevance of psychoanalytic insights in fostering more insightful, empathetic, and effective leaders. Through this chapter-by-chapter journey, the book offers readers a comprehensive understanding of psychoanalytic theory and its application in executive leadership coaching, providing a rich toolkit for personal and professional transformation.

Through this book, readers can embark on a profound journey of discovery and transformation, gaining valuable insights into the intricate relationship between psychoanalytic theory and executive leadership coaching. As they navigate through the chapters, they will uncover a wealth of knowledge and practical strategies that promise to enhance their understanding of leadership and personal development.

One of the key learnings readers can anticipate is a deeper insight into their own leadership style. By engaging with psychoanalytic concepts, readers will learn to recognize the unconscious motivations, biases, and emotional underpinnings that influence their approach to leadership. This heightened self-awareness will empower them to adapt and refine their leadership practices in ways that are more aligned with their values and goals, leading to more authentic and effective leadership.

Understanding unconscious processes forms another cornerstone of the book's teachings. Readers will explore the hidden aspects of the psyche, including the dynamics of the unconscious mind, defense mechanisms, and the phenomena of transference and countertransference. This exploration will equip leaders with the tools to better understand themselves and their followers, fostering stronger, more empathetic relationships and a more cohesive organizational culture.

The book provides practical strategies for applying psychoanalytic principles in coaching scenarios. From listening with a 'third ear' to interpreting unconscious communication and managing resistance, readers will learn how to utilize psychoanalytic techniques to facilitate deep, transformative change in those they lead or coach. These strategies not only enhance the coaching process but also contribute to the development of leaders who are more self-aware, emotionally intelligent, and capable of navigating the complexities of modern organizational life.

In addition to personal and professional growth, the book offers guidance on designing psychoanalytically informed coaching programs, addressing ethical considerations, and emphasizing the importance of ongoing supervision and professional development. This comprehensive approach ensures that readers are well-prepared to integrate psychoanalytic insights into their coaching practice ethically and effectively.

Readers can expect to have gained a profound understanding of how psychoanalytic theory can enrich leadership development. They will be equipped with the knowledge and skills to explore the depths of their own and others' psychological landscapes, leading to more insightful, empathetic, and adaptive leadership. This journey promises not only to transform their approach to leadership and coaching but also to offer a pathway to more fulfilling personal and professional lives.

As readers embark on the journey through this book, they are invited to approach its contents with an openness to introspection and personal discovery. The integration of psychoanalytic principles into the realm of leadership coaching is not merely an academic exercise; it is an invitation to explore the deeper aspects of oneself and the impact these have on one's leadership and interpersonal relationships. This exploration requires courage, as it involves confronting aspects of the self that are often hidden from conscious awareness, yet it promises substantial rewards in terms of personal growth and enhanced leadership effectiveness.

Our work here is designed to serve as a guide, leading readers through the complex landscape of the unconscious mind and its influence on leadership behaviors and decisions. To fully benefit from this journey, readers are encouraged to embrace vulnerability and curiosity, allowing themselves to question long-held beliefs and behaviors. This process of self-reflection is fundamental to unlocking the transformative potential of psychoanalytic coaching, offering insights that can lead to profound changes in how one leads and relates to others.

Personal discovery is a central theme of the book, with each chapter offering new perspectives and insights that challenge the reader to think deeply about their motivations, fears, and desires. By engaging with the material in a reflective manner, readers can begin to uncover the unconscious dynamics that shape their leadership style, opening up new possibilities for change and growth.

We emphasize the importance of ongoing growth and development, suggesting that the journey of self-discovery and improvement is a continuous one. Readers are encouraged to view the insights gained from the book not as a final destination but as stepping stones on a broader path of personal and professional development. This perspective fosters a mindset of lifelong learning and adaptability, which are crucial qualities for effective leadership in today's ever-changing world.

This work offers more than just a set of theories and practices; it offers a pathway to deeper self-awareness and emotional intelligence, which are foundational to authentic and impactful leadership. By approaching the book with an openness to introspection and personal discovery, readers can embark on a transformative journey that not only enhances their capabilities as leaders but also enriches their personal lives and relationships. This journey of reflection and growth is an invaluable opportunity to develop into the kind of leader who inspires, motivates, and brings out the best in those they lead.

Reading this book marks the commencement of a transformative journey that ventures deep into the realms of leadership and the unconscious mind, promising a dual path of professional enhancement and profound personal growth. This journey invites you to explore the intricate layers of your psyche and leadership practice, offering a unique opportunity to uncover and harness the full potential of your leadership capabilities.

As you navigate through the pages, you'll be guided through a process of self-discovery that challenges you to confront and understand the unseen forces that drive your thoughts, behaviors, and interactions with others. This exploration is not just about enhancing your skills as a leader; it's about embarking on a profound journey of personal transformation that will change the way you see yourself, your relationships, and your role within the larger tapestry of your professional life.

Our exploration serves as a bridge between the rich, introspective world of psychoanalytic theory and the dynamic, often challenging reality of leadership. By integrating these seemingly disparate domains, you'll gain access to a deeper understanding of what it means to lead with authenticity, empathy, and effectiveness. The insights and strategies presented will equip you with the tools to navigate the complexities of modern leadership with greater awareness and adaptability.

This journey is about more than just acquiring knowledge; it's about engaging in a process of reflection and growth that will challenge you to evolve in ways you may not have imagined. As you delve into the psychoanalytic concepts and their applications to leadership, you'll be encouraged to reflect on your own experiences, motivations, and challenges. This reflective practice is key to unlocking the transformative potential of the book, allowing you to emerge as a more insightful, emotionally intelligent leader capable of fostering a positive impact on those around you.

The voyage promises to extend beyond professional development, offering insights and growth opportunities that enrich your personal life. By understanding the unconscious dynamics that influence your behavior and relationships, you'll gain a new level of self-awareness and emotional intelligence that enhances your interactions both within and outside the workplace.

Embarking on this journey through the book is the beginning of an ongoing process of learning, reflection, and growth. It is an invitation to transform not only your leadership practice but also your understanding of yourself and your place in the world. This transformative journey promises to be both challenging and rewarding, leading to a deeper, more authentic expression of leadership and a richer, more fulfilling personal and professional life.

Part I: Foundations of Psychoanalytic Theory

We start by embarking on an exploration of psychoanalytic theory within the leadership coaching and development sphere, this book unfolds a comprehensive narrative that delves into the profound impact of the unconscious on leadership behaviors, decision-making processes, and interpersonal dynamics. It begins with the foundational principles of psychoanalytic theory, offering a lens through which to view the intricacies of human behavior and personality in leadership roles.

The journey begins by tracing the historical context and development of psychoanalysis, from its revolutionary inception in the late 19th and early 20th centuries to its contemporary applications and broader impact on culture, art, and society. This exploration reveals how psychoanalytic thought has evolved over time, highlighting its enduring influence beyond the clinical setting.

Key figures in psychoanalysis, such as Sigmund Freud, Carl Jung, and Melanie Klein, emerge as pivotal in shaping the theory, with their work laying the groundwork for understanding the unconscious, psychosexual development stages, and the dynamics of early childhood experiences that shape adult behavior and personality. This section introduces readers to these seminal contributors and their foundational concepts, setting the stage for a deeper understanding of psychoanalytic principles.

The narrative then delves into the fundamental concepts of psychoanalysis, including the unconscious mind, defense mechanisms, and psychosexual stages of development, offering insights into the role of the unconscious in shaping our thoughts, behaviors, and emotions. The significance of dreams and the phenomena of transference and countertransference are examined, reflecting the projection of past feelings onto present interactions and their relevance in leadership coaching.

Bridging psychoanalytic theory with leadership coaching, the discussion extends to how an understanding of the unconscious, defense mechanisms, and transference phenomena can enhance coaching effectiveness and leadership development. The potential of psychoanalytic concepts to address common leadership challenges, such as decision-making, conflict resolution, and team dynamics, is introduced, paving the way for more detailed exploration in subsequent chapters.

Deepening the exploration of psychoanalytic theory, this section offers an in-depth look at the unconscious mind and defense mechanisms, detailing techniques for accessing the unconscious and providing a comprehensive overview of defense mechanisms and their implications for leadership behaviors. The exploration of transference is expanded into leadership and coaching contexts, highlighting the importance of recognizing and managing these dynamics to enhance self-awareness and supervision.

Practical applications of psychoanalytic concepts in both psychotherapy and leadership coaching are elaborated upon, demonstrating how insights into leader-follower dynamics, emotional intelligence, and interpersonal relationships can be enhanced. Real-life case studies illustrate the transformative impact of psychoanalytic principles on leadership development and coaching.

Through this narrative, readers are invited on a transformative journey into the depths of leadership and the unconscious mind, promising both professional enhancement and personal growth. This exploration not only illuminates the complexities of human behavior and personality in leadership but also offers a pathway to more insightful, empathetic, and effective leadership practices, setting the stage for a comprehensive understanding of psychoanalytic theory and its practical applications in leadership coaching.

Chapter 2, titled "Getting Deeper Into Psychoanalysis," serves as a pivotal deep dive into the foundational theories and concepts that underpin psychoanalytic thought. This chapter is dedicated to exploring the intricate layers of psychoanalytic theory, offering readers a comprehensive understanding of its principles, the historical context of its development, and its key figures.

This second chapter aims to equip readers with a solid grounding in the fundamental concepts of psychoanalysis, such as the unconscious mind, defense mechanisms, transference, and countertransference, and their relevance to understanding human behavior and thought processes. By delving into the historical evolution of psychoanalysis, from Freud's initial formulations to the contributions of later theorists like Jung, Klein, and Winnicott, the chapter traces the trajectory of psychoanalytic thought and its diversification over time.

This exploration is not just academic; it's profoundly practical. The chapter illustrates how psychoanalytic concepts can be applied to the challenges of leadership and personal development, providing insights into the psychological underpinnings of leadership behaviors, decision-making, and interpersonal dynamics. Through a detailed examination of the theory and practice of psychoanalysis, readers will gain a deeper appreciation of how this rich theoretical framework can inform and enhance the practice of leadership coaching.

"Getting Deeper Into Psychoanalysis" sets the stage for the subsequent chapters, laying a theoretical foundation that will inform the book's approach to integrating psychoanalytic principles into leadership development. It promises to be an enlightening journey into the depths of psychoanalytic theory, offering readers the tools and insights needed to explore the unconscious aspects of leadership and personal growth. This chapter is an essential read for anyone seeking to understand the complex interplay between psychoanalysis and leadership, providing a robust framework for the practical application of psychoanalytic principles in executive coaching.

Chapter 3, titled "Psychoanalytic Understanding of Personality," builds on the foundational knowledge established in the previous chapter by delving into the psychoanalytic perspective on personality structure and development. This chapter is crucial for understanding how individual differences in leadership styles, decision-making processes, and interpersonal relations can be comprehensively understood through the lens of psychoanalytic theory.

Here our aim is to unpack the complex dynamics of the human psyche as conceptualized by psychoanalysis, focusing on the structure of the mind, including the roles of the id, ego, and superego, and how these entities interact to shape personality. It explores the stages of psychosexual development, highlighting how each stage contributes to the formation of personality traits and potential areas of conflict that may impact an individual's behavior and interactions.

This chapter examines the concept of neuroses and character traits from a psychoanalytic viewpoint, discussing how unresolved conflicts and defense mechanisms contribute to the development of neurotic patterns and characteristic behaviors. By providing a deep dive into these aspects, the chapter offers valuable insights into understanding the underlying psychological factors that influence leadership behavior and effectiveness.

Through a detailed exploration of psychoanalytic theories of personality, readers will gain a deeper appreciation of how these theories can be applied to leadership development and coaching. The chapter not only enriches the reader's understanding of the psychological underpinnings of personality but also demonstrates how psychoanalytic insights can be utilized to foster personal growth and enhance leadership capabilities.

Chapter 3 is an essential chapter for anyone interested in the intersection of psychoanalysis and leadership. It sets the groundwork for applying psychoanalytic concepts to real-world leadership challenges, offering a nuanced understanding of personality that is critical for effective leadership coaching. This chapter ensures that readers are well-equipped with the theoretical knowledge necessary to explore the depths of personality from a psychoanalytic perspective, paving the way for the practical application of these insights in leadership and personal development.

Chapter 1: Foundational Aspects of Psychoanalytic Theory

Historical Context and Development

The emergence of psychoanalysis in the late 19th and early 20th centuries marked a revolutionary pivot in the understanding of the human mind, fundamentally altering perceptions of mental health, consciousness, and the depths of human psychology. This period, characterized by rapid industrialization and scientific discovery, provided fertile ground for questioning traditional views of the mind and its disorders. At the heart of this revolution was Sigmund Freud, a Viennese neurologist whose observations and insights laid the foundational stones of psychoanalytic theory.

Freud's pioneering work began with his study of hysteria and neuroses, leading him to propose the existence of an unconscious mind—a repository of feelings, thoughts, and desires inaccessible to the individual's conscious awareness yet exerting a profound influence on behavior. This concept of the unconscious challenged the prevailing Cartesian notion of the conscious mind as the sole arbiter of human psychology.

Psychoanalysis introduced several key concepts that offered new insights into the workings of the mind. Among these were the ideas of repression, where unacceptable or painful thoughts and feelings are pushed into the unconscious, and the defense mechanisms, strategies employed by the ego to protect the individual from psychological distress. Freud's theory of psychosexual development further elaborated on how early life experiences shape personality and behavior patterns in adulthood.

The therapeutic aspect of psychoanalysis, characterized by techniques such as free association, dream analysis, and the interpretation of slips of the tongue, provided a method for accessing and understanding the contents of the unconscious. This approach to therapy was revolutionary, offering a pathway to mental wellness that involved uncovering and addressing the root causes of psychological distress rather than merely treating symptoms.

The impact of psychoanalysis extended far beyond the clinical setting, influencing art, literature, and social theory. It offered a new language for discussing human motivation, desire, and conflict, and its implications were felt in the exploration of themes such as identity, sexuality, and power dynamics in cultural and societal contexts.

As psychoanalysis evolved, it also faced criticism and underwent divisions, leading to the development of various schools of thought within the psychoanalytic tradition. Figures such as Carl Jung, Alfred Adler, and Melanie Klein expanded and, in some cases, diverged from Freudian theory, contributing their own insights and theories about the unconscious, archetypes, and object relations.

The origins of psychoanalysis in the late 19th and early 20th centuries represent a seminal moment in the history of psychology, offering a complex, nuanced approach to understanding the human mind that continues to influence and inform contemporary thought on mental health, therapy, and human behavior.

The evolution of psychoanalytic theory from its inception in the late 19th and early 20th centuries to its contemporary applications demonstrates a fascinating journey of expansion, diversification, and adaptation. Initially founded by Sigmund Freud as a method to treat mental disorders, psychoanalysis has grown into a broad field influencing various aspects of psychology, culture, and even the understanding of social phenomena. This evolution is marked by significant shifts in focus and methodology, reflecting the theory's adaptability to new insights and societal changes.

Following Freud's foundational work, which centered on the unconscious mind, psychosexual development, and the interpretation of dreams, psychoanalysis began to diversify as his colleagues and successors offered new perspectives. Carl Jung, one of Freud's most prominent contemporaries, introduced the concept of the collective unconscious and archetypes, broadening the scope of psychoanalysis to include spiritual and mythical dimensions of the human psyche. Jung's divergence from Freud's theories marked one of the first major expansions of psychoanalytic thought, emphasizing universal psychological patterns over Freud's focus on individual sexual and aggressive drives.

Melanie Klein further contributed to the evolution of psychoanalysis with her work on object relations theory, shifting the focus to how early relationships with primary caregivers shape the psyche. Klein's emphasis on the importance of infancy and childhood experiences introduced a new area of psychoanalytic exploration and therapeutic intervention, highlighting the role of internalized relationships in psychological development.

The mid-20th century saw the emergence of ego psychology, spearheaded by Anna Freud and Heinz Hartmann, which emphasized the role of the ego in mediating between the demands of the id, the superego, and the external world. This shift towards a more functional analysis of the mind underscored the adaptability and resilience of the ego, focusing on its capacity for defense, adaptation, and reality-testing.

In the latter half of the 20th century and into the 21st century, psychoanalytic theory has continued to evolve, incorporating insights from neuroscience, attachment theory, and feminist psychology. Contemporary psychoanalysis often emphasizes relational aspects, exploring how interpersonal relationships influence psychological development and functioning. The relational turn in psychoanalysis has led to a greater focus on the therapeutic relationship itself as a central element of the healing process.

Modern psychoanalytic thought has expanded its applications beyond individual therapy to include group dynamics, organizational behavior, and cultural analysis. Psychoanalytic concepts are used to understand phenomena such as leadership styles, corporate culture, and societal structures, demonstrating the theory's versatility and enduring relevance. Methodologically, contemporary psychoanalytic practice has adapted to diverse clinical needs, incorporating shorter-term therapies and more direct interventions alongside traditional long-term analysis. This flexibility reflects a broader understanding of psychoanalytic principles and their application in varied contexts, from clinical settings to everyday life challenges.

Throughout its evolution, psychoanalytic theory has retained its core commitment to exploring the depths of the human mind, while continually adapting to incorporate new insights and address changing societal needs. This dynamic process of growth and change ensures that psychoanalysis remains a vital and relevant field, offering profound insights into the complexities of human behavior and mental health.

Psychoanalysis has had a profound impact on culture, art, and society, extending its influence far beyond the clinical setting where it originated. The introduction of psychoanalytic concepts by Sigmund Freud and his followers provided a new lens through which to understand human behavior, motivations, and relationships, fundamentally altering the way individuals perceive themselves and the world around them. This influence is evident across a wide range of cultural and societal domains, from literature and cinema to philosophy and critical theory.

In literature, psychoanalytic theory has been used as a tool for literary analysis, allowing critics and readers alike to explore the psychological depths of characters and narratives. Authors such as Virginia Woolf, James Joyce, and Franz Kafka have incorporated psychoanalytic themes into their works, exploring the complexities of the human psyche and the unconscious forces that drive behavior. Similarly, the Surrealist movement in art, led by figures like Salvador Dalí and André Breton, drew heavily on psychoanalytic ideas, seeking to unlock the creative potential of the unconscious mind through dream imagery and free association techniques.

Cinema, too, has been deeply influenced by psychoanalytic concepts, with filmmakers using the medium to explore themes of identity, desire, and repression. Alfred Hitchcock, Ingmar Bergman, and Federico Fellini, among others, have created films that delve into the psychological motivations of their characters, often employing symbols and narrative structures that reflect psychoanalytic theories of the mind.

Beyond art and literature, psychoanalysis has impacted philosophical and critical thought, contributing to the development of critical theory and influencing thinkers associated with the Frankfurt School, such as Herbert Marcuse and Theodor Adorno. These theorists have applied psychoanalytic concepts to critique society and culture, exploring the ways in which unconscious processes are implicated in social dynamics, ideology, and power relations.

Psychoanalysis has also played a significant role in shaping contemporary discussions around identity, gender, and sexuality. The work of Sigmund Freud on sexual development and the Oedipus complex laid the groundwork for later theorists, including Jacques Lacan and Judith Butler, to explore the construction of gender and sexual identity. This has contributed to a deeper understanding of the fluidity of identity and the psychological underpinnings of gender roles and norms.

Psychoanalytic theory has influenced the field of education, particularly in understanding the emotional and psychological needs of children and the dynamics of learning and development. It has provided insights into the importance of early childhood experiences, the emotional aspects of teacher-student relationships, and the unconscious factors that can influence learning outcomes.

In the broader societal context, psychoanalysis has contributed to the understanding of mass psychology, group dynamics, and cultural phenomena. By examining the ways in which unconscious desires and fears manifest in society, psychoanalysis offers a unique perspective on the motivations behind social movements, political ideologies, and cultural trends. The impact of psychoanalysis on culture, art, and society demonstrates the theory's far-reaching relevance and its ability to provide deep insights into the human condition. By exploring the unconscious dimensions of human experience, psychoanalysis continues to enrich our understanding of creativity, identity, and the complex web of social and psychological forces that shape our world.

Key Figures in Psychoanalysis

Sigmund Freud, the father of psychoanalysis, made foundational contributions to the field that have profoundly influenced our understanding of the human mind. His innovative theories on the unconscious, psychosexual development, and the Oedipus complex laid the groundwork for psychoanalytic thought, offering insights into the complex processes that underlie human behavior and mental processes.

- The Unconscious: Freud's concept of the unconscious is perhaps his most significant contribution to psychological theory. He posited that much of human behavior is influenced by thoughts, memories, and desires that lie outside of conscious awareness. These unconscious forces can manifest in dreams, slips of the tongue (Freudian slips), and neurotic symptoms, revealing the hidden content of the psyche. Freud developed techniques such as free association and dream analysis to explore the unconscious, allowing individuals to access and understand these buried aspects of their mind.

- Psychosexual Development: Freud introduced the theory of psychosexual development, which suggests that human development occurs in a series of stages centered around erogenous zones. These stages are the oral, anal, phallic, latency, and genital stages. According to Freud, experiences during these stages have a lasting impact on an individual's personality and behavior. Conflicts or fixations at any stage can result in psychological issues in adulthood. This theory highlighted the importance of early childhood experiences and the sexual nature of human development, concepts that were revolutionary and controversial at the time.

- The Oedipus Complex: Within the phallic stage of psychosexual development, Freud described the Oedipus complex, a child's unconscious sexual desire for the opposite-sex parent and jealousy toward the same-sex parent. This complex plays a critical role in the development of the superego and the resolution of the complex, according to Freud, is essential for healthy psychological development. The Oedipus complex introduced the idea that family dynamics and early childhood relationships are central to the formation of personality and the development of neuroses.

Freud's work established psychoanalysis as a discipline concerned with the exploration of the unconscious mind and its influence on human behavior. His theories challenged existing notions of consciousness and rationality, introducing the idea that human beings are driven by forces beyond their conscious control. Despite criticism and the evolution of psychoanalytic theory beyond Freud's original ideas, his contributions remain central to the field. Freud's work has not only shaped psychoanalysis but has also left a lasting impact on literature, art, culture, and how society understands and discusses mental health and human sexuality.

Carl Jung, a Swiss psychiatrist and psychoanalyst, initially collaborated with Sigmund Freud but eventually diverged from Freudian psychoanalysis, developing his own theories that significantly expanded the scope of psychoanalytic thought. Jung's contributions, including the concepts of the collective unconscious, archetypes, and individuation, have had a profound impact on psychology, offering a unique perspective on the human psyche and its development.

- The Collective Unconscious: One of Jung's most revolutionary ideas is the concept of the collective unconscious, a layer of the unconscious mind shared among beings of the same species. Jung proposed that this collective unconscious is the repository of latent memories and experiences inherited from our ancestors. Unlike Freud, who focused on personal experiences and repressed memories shaping the individual unconscious, Jung introduced the notion that there are universal, inherited elements that form the basis of human psychological processes.

- Archetypes: Closely related to the collective unconscious are archetypes, which Jung described as universal, primordial symbols and images that reside in the collective unconscious. Archetypes are the psychic counterpart of instinct and manifest in individuals through dreams, fantasies, and delusions. Some of the most well-known archetypes include the Persona (the social mask one wears in public), the Shadow (the unconscious aspect of the personality which the conscious ego does not identify in itself), the Anima and Animus (the unconscious feminine side in men and the masculine tendencies in women, respectively), and the Self (the unification of consciousness and unconsciousness in an individual, representing the psyche as a whole).

- Individuation: Jung's theory of individuation represents the process of self-realization and development towards wholeness. Individuation involves the integration of conscious and unconscious elements of the psyche, leading to the development of a unique, balanced personality. This process requires recognizing and reconciling opposites within the psyche, including reconciling one's conscious identity with the shadow. Individuation is central to Jung's understanding of psychological growth and is seen as the ultimate goal of human development.

Jung's divergence from Freud centered around several key disagreements, including the role of sexuality in psychological development and the nature of the unconscious. Jung's work introduced a more mystical and spiritual dimension to psychoanalysis, emphasizing the search for meaning and the exploration of the spiritual aspects of human life as central to psychological well-being.

Jung's contributions to psychoanalysis have had a lasting impact, influencing not only the field of psychology but also areas such as literature, religion, and cultural studies. His theories on the collective unconscious and archetypes have provided a framework for understanding the shared symbols and myths that permeate cultures, while his concept of individuation offers a path toward personal development and fulfillment. Jung's work established analytical psychology as a distinct approach to understanding the human mind, complementing and expanding upon Freudian psychoanalysis.

Melanie Klein, a pioneering figure in the field of psychoanalysis, made significant contributions through her work on object relations theory, fundamentally altering the understanding of early childhood development and its lasting impact on adult behavior. Klein's theories diverged from the traditional Freudian emphasis on psychosexual stages, instead focusing on the relationships and emotional bonds between children and their primary caregivers, which she termed "objects."

- Object Relations Theory: Klein's object relations theory posits that the internalization of early relationships, particularly with the mother or primary caregiver, forms the foundation of an individual's emotional life and personality. She introduced the concept that infants project their feelings onto these "objects" and then internalize the objects along with the projected feelings, creating complex internal psychic structures. This process begins in infancy, a standpoint that marked a departure from the emphasis on later childhood stages in Freudian theory.

Klein's work underscored the significance of the earliest experiences of attachment, separation, and the interplay of fantasy and reality in the formation of the psyche. She identified the early "good" and "bad" object experiences as critical to the development of the ego and the capacity to manage one's own emotions and relationships with others.

- Phantasy and Play Technique: Klein was innovative in her methodological approach to understanding the inner worlds of children. She developed the play technique as a means of communication and analysis with children, recognizing play as the child's natural medium of expression. Through the analysis of play, Klein was able to explore the unconscious fantasies (or "phantasies" as she spelled it to differentiate between unconscious fantasy and daydreaming) and anxieties of children, revealing insights into their emotional and psychological states.

- Paranoid-Schizoid and Depressive Positions: Among Klein's key theoretical contributions are the concepts of the paranoid-schizoid and depressive positions. The paranoid-schizoid position, occurring in the first few months of life, is characterized by the splitting of the external world into "good" and "bad" parts as a defense mechanism. The depressive position follows, where the infant begins to integrate these split images, leading to a more nuanced understanding of self and others. The successful navigation of these positions is crucial for psychological development and affects an individual's ability to form healthy relationships in adulthood.

Klein's work on object relations theory has profound implications for understanding adult behavior. The early internalized relationships and the mechanisms developed to cope with early anxieties can manifest in adult life, influencing interpersonal relationships, emotional regulation, and even the propensity for certain psychological disorders. Klein's insights into the impact of early object relations on adult behavior have contributed to the development of psychoanalytic psychotherapy techniques focused on addressing these deep-seated patterns.

Melanie Klein's contributions to psychoanalysis, particularly her work on object relations theory, have had a lasting impact on the field, providing a deeper understanding of the importance of early childhood experiences and their influence on adult psychology. Her pioneering work continues to inform clinical practice, psychoanalytic theory, and our broader understanding of human development and behavior.

Psychoanalytic theory has been enriched and diversified by the contributions of several influential figures beyond its founder, Sigmund Freud. These theorists, including Anna Freud, Donald Winnicott, and Jacques Lacan, have introduced new dimensions to psychoanalytic thought, each bringing unique perspectives and expanding the theory's applications.

Anna Freud, the youngest daughter of Sigmund Freud, made substantial contributions to psychoanalysis with her work in child psychology and defense mechanisms. Building on her father's foundations, she focused on the ways children cope with anxiety and conflict, elaborating on the defense mechanisms people use to protect the ego. Her seminal work, "The Ego and the Mechanisms of Defence," laid the groundwork for ego psychology and emphasized the importance of the ego's role in managing internal and external pressures. Anna Freud's dedication to understanding children also led her to apply psychoanalytic principles in educational and therapeutic settings, pioneering the field of child psychoanalysis.

Donald Winnicott was a British pediatrician and psychoanalyst known for his work on the mother-child relationship, transitional objects, and the concept of the "good enough" mother. Winnicott introduced the idea of the "holding environment," emphasizing the importance of a nurturing setting in which a child's emotional and developmental needs are met. He also explored the role of transitional objects, such as blankets or stuffed animals, in a child's development, viewing them as crucial to the process of becoming independent and developing a sense of self. Winnicott's theories on true self and false self-further contributed to understanding how early relationships affect the authenticity of personal expression.

Jacques Lacan, a French psychoanalyst, is best known for his reinterpretations of Freud's work through the lenses of structuralism, linguistics, and philosophy. Lacan emphasized the role of language in the unconscious, proposing that the unconscious is structured like a language. His concept of the "mirror stage" describes a crucial phase in a child's development when they begin to recognize their reflection as themselves, which he argued forms the basis of the ego. Lacan's work is characterized by its theoretical complexity and has influenced various fields, including critical theory, literary studies, and feminist theory. His seminars and writings have contributed to a revitalization of psychoanalytic theory in the mid-20th century, emphasizing the symbolic and imaginary dimensions of human psychology.

These figures, among others, have significantly contributed to the development and diversification of psychoanalytic theory. Each has introduced new concepts and perspectives, expanding the scope of psychoanalysis beyond its original formulations. Their work has deepened the understanding of human psychology, influencing both clinical practice and theoretical exploration in psychoanalysis and beyond.

Fundamental Concepts of Psychoanalysis

The concept of the unconscious mind is central to psychoanalytic theory, representing one of the most revolutionary ideas introduced by Sigmund Freud and further developed by subsequent psychoanalysts. This concept posits that much of our mental life, including desires, memories, and motivations, operates outside of our conscious awareness. The unconscious mind influences our thoughts, feelings, and behaviors in profound ways, often without our direct knowledge, acting as a reservoir for content that is hidden from our immediate perception.

According to psychoanalytic theory, the unconscious mind contains elements that have been repressed or are otherwise inaccessible to the conscious mind due to their potentially distressing nature or conflict with societal norms. These elements can include repressed memories, primal desires, and unresolved conflicts from childhood. Despite being hidden, these unconscious aspects exert a significant influence on our psychological well-being, our decisions, and the way we relate to others.

The existence of the unconscious mind challenges the notion of complete self-awareness and rational control over one's actions and thoughts. It suggests that understanding human behavior and psychological distress requires delving into these hidden realms. Psychoanalytic therapy, therefore, involves techniques designed to bring unconscious material into consciousness, allowing individuals to confront and understand these hidden aspects of their psyche. Methods such as dream analysis, free association, and the interpretation of slips of the tongue (Freudian slips) are used to bridge the gap between the conscious and unconscious mind, offering insights into the underlying dynamics that shape an individual's mental life.

The unconscious mind's central role in psychoanalytic theory underscores the complexity of human psychology, emphasizing that a comprehensive understanding of oneself and others goes beyond what is immediately visible or known. By exploring the depths of the unconscious, psychoanalytic theory opens up pathways for profound personal insight and psychological change, offering a richer, more nuanced understanding of the forces that drive human behavior.

Sigmund Freud's theory of psychosexual stages of development is a cornerstone of his psychoanalytic theory, offering a framework for understanding how early experiences influence personality development. According to Freud, personality develops through a series of stages during childhood, each characterized by the erogenous zone that is the focus of a child's psychosexual energy. The way these stages are navigated plays a crucial role in shaping an individual's adult personality, behaviors, and preferences.

The first stage, the oral stage, occurs from birth to about 18 months. During this period, the mouth is the primary focus of libidinal energy, and satisfaction is obtained through oral activities such as sucking and eating. Freud believed that issues unresolved during the oral stage could lead to oral fixation in adulthood, manifesting as behaviors associated with dependency or aggression.

Following the oral stage is the anal stage, from about 18 months to three years, where the focus of libidinal energy shifts to the anus. During this stage, children experience pleasure from controlling bladder and bowel movements. Freud suggested that conflicts unresolved during this stage could lead to an anal-retentive personality, characterized by obsessiveness and stinginess, or an anal-expulsive personality, seen as disorderly and destructive.

The phallic stage, occurring from ages three to six, is marked by the libidinal energy concentrating on the genital area. Freud introduced the concepts of the Oedipus complex in boys and the Electra complex in girls during this stage, theorizing that children experience unconscious sexual desires for the opposite-sex parent and view the same-sex parent as a rival. Successful navigation of this stage is critical for the development of a healthy adult identity and sexuality.

The latency stage follows, spanning the period of six years to puberty. During this stage, Freud believed that psychosexual development pauses, and children focus on social interactions, learning, and hobbies. The sexual and aggressive drives are sublimated into socially acceptable activities.

The final stage, the genital stage, begins at puberty and continues into adulthood. Here, the sexual energy is directed towards heterosexual pleasure rather than self-pleasure, marking the mature stage of sexual development. Freud posited that successful resolution of earlier conflicts allows for the development of a well-balanced and mature personality.

Freud's theory of psychosexual stages highlights the enduring impact of early experiences on personality development. He argued that unresolved conflicts in any of the stages could lead to fixation, influencing an individual's future behavior and interactions. While some aspects of Freud's theory have been critiqued and modified over time, the concept that early childhood experiences have a lasting effect on personality development remains influential in both psychoanalytic theory and broader psychological thought.

Dream analysis holds a central place in psychoanalytic theory, serving as a crucial method for exploring the unconscious mind. Sigmund Freud, the father of psychoanalysis, posited that dreams are the "royal road to the unconscious," providing a direct pathway to the hidden desires, thoughts, and conflicts that reside outside of conscious awareness. Through the analysis of dreams, psychoanalysts can decipher the complex language of the unconscious, revealing insights into an individual's innermost psychological workings.

Freud's approach to dream analysis is founded on the distinction between manifest content and latent content. The manifest content of a dream refers to the actual storyline or imagery experienced by the dreamer—what one remembers upon waking. This content, however, is often symbolic and can be seen as a facade that disguises the true meaning of the dream.

The latent content represents the hidden, unconscious wishes and thoughts that the dream seeks to express. According to Freud, the latent content is often related to repressed desires or unresolved conflicts, which are too threatening or painful to confront directly in waking life. Therefore, the unconscious mind disguises these forbidden thoughts and desires through the process of dreamwork, transforming them into the less direct and more acceptable form of manifest content.

Dreamwork involves several mechanisms, including condensation (combining multiple ideas or images into a single dream symbol), displacement (shifting emotional significance from a distressing object or idea to a less threatening one), and symbolization (using symbols to represent unconscious thoughts or desires). Through these processes, the unconscious mind crafts dreams that can safely express forbidden desires and unresolved conflicts.

Analyzing dreams, therefore, requires unraveling the symbolic language of the manifest content to access the latent content and the unconscious thoughts it conceals. This process can illuminate aspects of the psyche that are inaccessible through other means, offering valuable insights into the individual's emotional state, underlying motivations, and psychological conflicts.

Dream analysis remains a significant aspect of psychoanalytic practice, reflecting the enduring belief in the importance of the unconscious in shaping human behavior and experience. By providing a window into the unconscious, dream analysis offers a unique and powerful tool for understanding the complexities of the human mind and facilitating psychological insight and growth.

Introducing Transference and Countertransference

Transference is a fundamental concept in psychoanalysis that involves the projection of feelings, desires, and expectations from past relationships onto the therapist in a psychoanalytic setting. This phenomenon occurs when individuals unconsciously redirect emotions and attitudes originally felt in significant early relationships toward their therapist. Transference is rooted in the idea that individuals tend to repeat patterns of behavior and emotional responses developed in childhood, particularly in the context of influential relationships with parents or other primary caregivers.

The relevance of transference extends beyond the therapeutic relationship to encompass client-coach dynamics in various settings, including leadership coaching and personal development. In these contexts, clients may unconsciously project onto their coaches feelings of trust, dependency, admiration, or resentment that are actually remnants of past relationships. Such projections can significantly influence the coaching process, affecting how clients perceive feedback, advice, and the overall coaching relationship.

Understanding transference is crucial for therapists and coaches alike, as it offers valuable insights into the client's internal world, including unresolved conflicts, unmet needs, and relational patterns. Recognizing and interpreting transference allows coaches to better understand the underlying issues that may be impacting a client's behavior and decision-making processes. Moreover, it can reveal how past experiences shape a client's expectations and interactions in the present, providing a richer context for personal and professional development work.

In psychoanalytic therapy, working through transference is considered essential for achieving insight and emotional growth. By exploring and resolving the transferred feelings and conflicts, individuals can gain a deeper understanding of themselves and their relationships, leading to more authentic and fulfilling interactions. Similarly, in coaching, effectively managing transference can enhance the coach-client relationship, facilitating a more productive and transformative coaching experience.

Transference underscores the importance of the emotional and relational aspects of coaching and therapy, highlighting the need for coaches and therapists to be aware of their own responses and the dynamics at play. By navigating transference with sensitivity and insight, professionals can support their clients in achieving greater self-awareness, resolving past conflicts, and moving toward their goals with increased clarity and confidence.

Countertransference refers to the emotional reactions and responses that therapists or coaches experience towards their clients' transference. This concept is grounded in the understanding that therapists and coaches, despite their training and professionalism, are not immune to the influence of their own unconscious feelings, biases, and past experiences. When clients project their feelings, desires, and expectations onto their therapists or coaches, it can evoke personal reactions that, if unrecognized, may impact the effectiveness of the therapeutic or coaching relationship.

The phenomenon of countertransference was initially viewed as an obstacle to the therapeutic process, suggesting that the therapist's personal reactions could cloud professional judgment and interfere with the client's treatment. However, over time, the understanding of countertransference has evolved. It is now recognized as a valuable tool that, when managed properly, can provide deep insights into the client's internal world and the dynamics of the therapeutic or coaching relationship. Recognizing and managing countertransference is crucial for several reasons. Firstly, it allows therapists and coaches to maintain professional boundaries and objectivity, ensuring that their personal emotions and experiences do not unduly influence the therapeutic process. By reflecting on their own reactions, professionals can distinguish between their own issues and those of their clients, facilitating a clearer understanding of the client's needs and experiences.

Secondly, countertransference can serve as a diagnostic tool, offering clues about the client's relational patterns, unconscious conflicts, and emotional states. For example, if a therapist feels an unusual degree of irritation or protectiveness towards a client, it may indicate specific dynamics at play that are worth exploring. By carefully examining their own reactions, therapists and coaches can gain valuable insights that guide the therapeutic or coaching interventions. Moreover, addressing countertransference openly and thoughtfully can enhance the therapeutic alliance or coaching relationship. It demonstrates the therapist's or coach's commitment to self-awareness and personal growth, modeling for clients the importance of introspection and emotional regulation. When managed effectively, countertransference can contribute to a more authentic, empathetic, and productive relationship between the professional and the client.

Countertransference is an integral aspect of the therapeutic and coaching processes, reflecting the complex interplay of emotions and projections that characterize these relationships. Recognizing and managing countertransference reactions is essential for maintaining professionalism, leveraging insights into the client's psyche, and fostering a supportive and effective therapeutic or coaching environment. Through ongoing self-reflection and supervision, therapists and coaches can navigate these dynamics skillfully, contributing to positive outcomes for their clients.

The Relevance of Psychoanalytic Concepts to Leadership and Coaching

Applying psychoanalytic insights to leadership coaching offers a rich framework for enhancing coaching effectiveness and leadership development. By bridging psychoanalytic theory with the practicalities of leadership, coaches and leaders can delve into the deeper psychological processes that influence behavior, decision-making, and interpersonal dynamics in the workplace. An understanding of the unconscious, defense mechanisms, and transference phenomena provides a comprehensive approach to addressing the complexities of leadership and organizational life.

The unconscious mind, with its repository of repressed desires, unresolved conflicts, and automatic thought processes, plays a significant role in shaping a leader's actions and reactions. By exploring these unconscious influences, leaders can gain insights into their motivations, fears, and biases that may be affecting their leadership style and decision-making. Leadership coaching that incorporates psychoanalytic insights encourages leaders to become more self-aware, enabling them to recognize and address unconscious patterns that may be hindering their effectiveness.

Defense mechanisms, such as denial, projection, and rationalization, serve as protective strategies that shield individuals from anxiety and perceived threats. In the context of leadership, these mechanisms can manifest in ways that distort reality, impair judgment, or obstruct constructive feedback. Coaches equipped with psychoanalytic knowledge can help leaders identify and understand their use of defense mechanisms, fostering a more open and reflective approach to challenges and feedback. This awareness allows leaders to develop more adaptive coping strategies, enhancing their resilience and emotional intelligence.

Transference phenomena, where leaders and followers unconsciously project feelings and expectations from past significant relationships onto each other, can significantly impact the dynamics within teams and organizations. Understanding transference can help leaders recognize the emotional undercurrents of their relationships with team members, allowing for more empathetic and effective communication. It also enables leaders to navigate the complexities of authority, dependency, and conflict with greater nuance and sensitivity.

Incorporating psychoanalytic insights into leadership coaching offers a holistic approach to leadership development. It not only addresses the observable aspects of leadership behavior but also engages with the deeper psychological dimensions that underlie these behaviors. This approach fosters a more integrated form of leadership development, where leaders are encouraged to explore and integrate aspects of their personality and emotional life into their leadership practice.

The application of psychoanalytic theory to leadership coaching enriches the coaching process and leadership development journey. It provides leaders with the tools to engage in profound personal growth, leading to more authentic, emotionally intelligent, and effective leadership. Through this deepened understanding of themselves and their relationships, leaders are better equipped to create positive and lasting impacts within their organizations.

Psychoanalytic approaches offer insightful perspectives into addressing common leadership challenges, including decision-making, conflict resolution, and team dynamics. By applying psychoanalytic concepts, leaders and coaches can uncover the deeper psychological underpinnings of these challenges, providing a more nuanced understanding and innovative solutions.

In the realm of decision-making, psychoanalytic insights into the unconscious mind can illuminate the hidden motivations and fears that influence a leader's choices. Understanding the role of unconscious biases and emotional drives allows leaders to reflect critically on their decision-making processes, striving for choices that are not only rational but also emotionally and ethically sound. This introspective approach can lead to more balanced and thoughtful decisions, mitigating the risk of being swayed by unacknowledged personal biases or unresolved psychological conflicts.

Conflict resolution benefits significantly from a psychoanalytic approach by addressing not just the surface disagreements but also the underlying emotional currents that fuel conflicts. Recognizing the projections and transference phenomena at play can help leaders and teams understand the deeper relational dynamics contributing to discord. By facilitating open discussions that acknowledge these underlying issues, leaders can foster a culture of empathy and understanding, leading to more effective and lasting resolutions.

Team dynamics are profoundly influenced by the unconscious processes within and between team members, including shared anxieties, collective defense mechanisms, and group identities. Psychoanalytic concepts such as group psychology and the notion of the collective unconscious provide a framework for understanding these dynamics. Leaders who are attuned to these aspects can better manage team morale, motivation, and cohesion. They can identify and address the unconscious fears and desires that may be hindering team performance, fostering a healthier and more productive team environment.

Psychoanalytic methods emphasize the importance of the leader's self-awareness and emotional intelligence. By engaging in their own psychoanalytic exploration, leaders can become more attuned to their emotional responses, defense mechanisms, and the impact of their unconscious on their leadership style. This self-awareness is crucial for modeling emotional intelligence, fostering trust, and building strong relationships within the team.

Incorporating psychoanalytic concepts into leadership practices offers a powerful tool for addressing common leadership challenges. It encourages a deeper exploration of the psychological dimensions of leadership, leading to more effective, empathetic, and insightful leadership practices. Through this approach, leaders can navigate the complexities of decision-making, conflict resolution, and team dynamics with greater awareness and skill, enhancing both their personal development and their team's performance.

Conclusion

As we wrap up the first chapter of our exploration into psychoanalytic theory and its profound impact on understanding human psychology, we have laid a solid foundation for the deep dive that awaits us in the subsequent chapters. This initial journey has illuminated the intricate workings of the human mind through the lens of psychoanalysis, providing us with valuable insights into the unconscious processes that shape our thoughts, behaviors, and emotions.

We've explored the historical origins of psychoanalysis, tracing its development from the revolutionary ideas of Sigmund Freud to the contributions of his successors, who expanded and diversified the theory. This historical context sets the stage for a deeper understanding of the complex and often hidden aspects of human psychology that psychoanalytic theory seeks to uncover.

The discussion of key psychoanalytic concepts such as the unconscious, defense mechanisms, and the seminal theories of transference and countertransference has introduced us to the mechanisms through which individuals navigate their inner and outer worlds. These concepts not only enrich our understanding of psychotherapy but also offer practical applications in everyday life, leadership, and executive coaching, highlighting the versatility and relevance of psychoanalytic theory across various domains.

This chapter has underscored the enduring value of psychoanalytic principles in facilitating a deeper comprehension of human behavior, enhancing emotional intelligence, and improving interpersonal relationships. As we move forward, the groundwork laid here will enable us to delve further into the application of these principles in therapy, leadership, and beyond, exploring how they can be leveraged to foster personal growth, emotional healing, and effective change. Chapter 1 has opened the door to the fascinating world of psychoanalysis, inviting us to explore the depths of the human psyche. As we continue our journey, we are encouraged to reflect on the insights gained and to remain open to the profound transformations that understanding psychoanalytic theory can bring to our professional practices and personal lives. The exploration of psychoanalysis is not just an academic endeavor but a journey towards greater self-awareness and understanding, offering tools for navigating the complexities of the human condition with empathy and insight.

Chapter 2: Getting Deeper Into Psychoanalysis

As we venture further into the intricate landscape of psychoanalysis, Chapter 2 aims to deepen our understanding of its core principles and their profound implications for comprehending human behavior. At the heart of psychoanalytic theory lie the concepts of the unconscious, defense mechanisms, transference, and countertransference—elements that offer a window into the unseen forces shaping our thoughts, feelings, and actions. This chapter will explore these fundamental concepts, unraveling the complex tapestry of the human psyche and highlighting their significance not only in psychotherapy but also in the realms of leadership and executive coaching.

The unconscious mind, a cornerstone of psychoanalytic thought, serves as the vast, hidden repository of desires, fears, and memories that escape conscious awareness yet influence every facet of our behavior. Understanding the unconscious opens up avenues for exploring the deeper motivations behind our actions, providing insights that are crucial for personal growth and development. We will delve into the mechanisms by which the unconscious exerts its influence, examining how it can both propel us forward and hold us back.

Defense mechanisms, the unconscious strategies we employ to protect ourselves from psychological discomfort, offer another lens through which to view human behavior. By identifying and understanding these mechanisms, we can begin to see beyond the immediate reactions to the underlying fears and conflicts driving them. This understanding is invaluable in psychotherapy, where unraveling these defenses can lead to breakthroughs in treatment, and in leadership coaching, where it can foster greater emotional intelligence and resilience.

Transference and countertransference introduce the dynamic interplay between individuals in therapeutic and coaching relationships. Transference, the projection of feelings and expectations from past relationships onto the therapist or coach, reveals how past experiences continue to shape our present interactions. Countertransference, in turn, reflects the emotional response of the therapist or coach to the client's transference, offering critical insights into the therapeutic process and the coaching dynamic. Recognizing and managing these phenomena can dramatically enhance the effectiveness of therapy and coaching, facilitating deeper connections and more meaningful change.

This chapter will not only elucidate these psychoanalytic concepts but also illustrate their practical applications. Through a psychoanalytic lens, we will explore how an understanding of the unconscious, defense mechanisms, transference, and countertransference can illuminate the complexities of human behavior. In the context of leadership and executive coaching, these insights become tools for unlocking potential, resolving conflicts, and fostering an environment of growth and development. Join us as we dive deeper into psychoanalysis, uncovering the layers of the human mind and their implications for understanding ourselves and leading others.

The Unconscious

The concept of the unconscious, as proposed by Sigmund Freud, marks a pivotal moment in the history of psychology, introducing a revolutionary perspective on the workings of the human mind. Freud conceptualized the unconscious as a vast, hidden reservoir that holds thoughts, memories, and desires which are not accessible to our conscious awareness. Despite being out of the direct purview of consciousness, these repressed elements exert a profound influence on an individual's behaviors and emotions, often determining the underlying motivations for actions that might otherwise seem inexplicable.

Freud's theory posits that much of our mental activity is, in fact, unconscious. This includes primitive instincts, socially unacceptable desires, painful memories, and intense emotions that have been suppressed due to their potential to cause psychological distress. According to Freud, the mind employs various defense mechanisms, such as repression, to keep these unsettling thoughts and feelings out of consciousness. However, they do not vanish and can emerge in disguised forms, manifesting through dreams, slips of the tongue, and symptoms of neurosis.

The significance of the unconscious in psychoanalytic theory cannot be overstated. It challenges the notion of complete self-awareness and rational control, suggesting instead that individuals are often driven by forces beyond their conscious understanding. This insight has profound implications for psychotherapy, as it implies that lasting change and self-understanding require exploring and integrating these unconscious elements into consciousness. Through therapeutic techniques like free association and dream analysis, psychoanalysis aims to uncover the hidden content of the unconscious, allowing individuals to confront and work through their repressed issues.

Freud's concept of the unconscious has transcended psychotherapy, influencing various domains including art, literature, and cultural studies. It has provided a framework for exploring the depth of human creativity, the complexities of character and narrative, and the underpinnings of cultural phenomena. In leadership and executive coaching, an understanding of the unconscious offers invaluable insights into organizational dynamics, decision-making processes, and interpersonal relationships. Recognizing the impact of unconscious factors can lead to more empathetic, effective leadership practices, as leaders become more attuned to their own motivations and the unconscious influences affecting their teams.

Freud's theory of the unconscious has opened up new pathways for understanding the human condition, offering a lens through which to view the intricate interplay between conscious and unconscious forces that shape our lives. By acknowledging the power of the unconscious, psychoanalysis provides a means to deeper self-knowledge, emotional healing, and personal growth.

Sigmund Freud's psychoanalytic theory introduced a nuanced model of the mind, delineating it into three primary layers: the conscious, preconscious, and unconscious. Each of these layers plays a critical role in the functioning of the mind, housing different types of thoughts, memories, and desires that influence our behavior and emotional life. Understanding the interaction among these layers is essential for grasping the complexity of human psychology as posited by Freud.

The conscious mind represents the tip of the iceberg; it comprises thoughts, sensations, and experiences of which we are aware at any given moment. It is the aspect of our mental processing that we can think and talk about rationally. For example, reading this text involves your conscious mind, as you are directly aware of and focusing on the material.

Beneath the conscious mind lies the preconscious, a layer that contains information not currently in the forefront of the mind but can easily be brought into consciousness. The preconscious acts as a sort of repository for memories and knowledge that you are not actively thinking about but can readily access when needed. An example of preconscious content might be your home address or a memory from a recent vacation; you are not constantly thinking about this information, but you can recall it without effort when required.

The unconscious mind, the deepest layer, is a vast and elusive domain that holds repressed desires, traumatic memories, and fundamental drives that are inaccessible to the conscious mind due to their potentially disturbing or socially unacceptable nature. The content of the unconscious mind exerts a significant influence on behavior and emotions, often in ways that individuals are not aware of. For instance, a forgotten traumatic event from childhood might shape an individual's relationships or emotional responses in adulthood, despite the individual having no conscious memory of the event.

The interaction between these layers is dynamic and continuous. The unconscious mind influences the conscious through mechanisms like dreams and Freudian slips, where repressed or unresolved issues surface indirectly. For example, a Freudian slip might occur when you accidentally use one word in place of another, revealing an unconscious thought or desire. Similarly, dreams often symbolize unconscious conflicts or wishes, providing insights into the unseen aspects of the psyche.

Freud believed that the goal of psychoanalytic therapy was to bring unconscious content into consciousness, thereby allowing individuals to confront and work through their repressed issues. This process involves navigating the preconscious, using techniques such as free association and dream analysis to access and interpret the material hidden in the unconscious.

Understanding the layers of the conscious, preconscious, and unconscious mind illuminates the intricate workings of human psychology and the complex interplay between different levels of awareness. This framework not only provides a basis for psychoanalytic therapy but also offers profound insights into the nature of human thought, emotion, and behavior.

Psychoanalytic theory posits that accessing the unconscious is essential for understanding the deeper, often hidden, motivations behind thoughts, feelings, and behaviors. Sigmund Freud and his successors developed several innovative methods to explore the unconscious, each providing unique insights into the complex landscape of the human psyche. Among these methods, dream analysis, free association, and slips of the tongue (commonly known as Freudian slips) stand out as fundamental techniques for uncovering the content and dynamics of the unconscious.

Dream Analysis is one of the most iconic psychoanalytic techniques, grounded in Freud's belief that dreams are the "royal road to the unconscious." Dreams, according to Freud, are manifestations of repressed desires, unresolved conflicts, and unconscious wishes. Through dream analysis, individuals can decode the symbolic language of dreams to uncover the latent content—the underlying, hidden psychological meanings—masked by the manifest content, which is the dream as remembered upon waking. For example, a dream about flying might be interpreted as a symbol of a desire for freedom or escape from constraints, revealing unconscious wishes or anxieties.

Free Association is another key method, inviting individuals to verbalize thoughts, words, or images as they come to mind, without censorship or judgment. This technique allows for a spontaneous flow of consciousness that can bypass the defenses of the ego, leading to the emergence of material from the unconscious. The psychoanalyst listens carefully to these associations, looking for patterns or emotional responses that might indicate underlying unconscious processes. For instance, if a person repeatedly returns to thoughts about authority figures while engaging in free association, it might suggest unresolved issues related to power and dependency.

Slips of the Tongue, or Freudian slips, provide yet another avenue for accessing the unconscious. Freud posited that these verbal mishaps are not mere accidents but meaningful expressions of unconscious thoughts or desires that the individual might be trying to repress. For example, saying "I'm so tired of this place" instead of "I'm so thrilled about this place" might inadvertently reveal true feelings about a situation. Analyzing these slips can offer insights into the speaker's real attitudes and emotions that they might not be fully aware of or willing to acknowledge.

Each of these methods—dream analysis, free association, and slips of the tongue—serves as a powerful tool for exploring the unconscious, offering glimpses into the inner workings of the mind that are not accessible through more direct or conscious means. By employing these techniques within psychoanalytic therapy or even in self-reflection, individuals can uncover the underlying motives, conflicts, and desires that shape their psychological landscape, facilitating a deeper understanding of themselves and paving the way for personal growth and healing.

Defense Mechanisms

Defense mechanisms are unconscious psychological strategies employed by individuals to cope with reality and preserve a sense of self-image when faced with thoughts, feelings, or experiences that are too difficult or unacceptable to confront directly. These mechanisms function as filters through which emotional distress, anxiety, and internal conflicts are managed and mitigated, allowing individuals to maintain psychological stability and self-esteem.

The nature of defense mechanisms is largely automatic and unconscious, meaning that individuals typically do not decide to engage them deliberately; rather, they are spontaneously activated in response to perceived threats to the ego. These threats might include fear of criticism, feelings of guilt, conflicts between desires and societal norms, or any situation that challenges an individual's sense of self or perceived control over their environment.

Defense mechanisms vary widely in their sophistication and adaptiveness. Some mechanisms, such as repression (pushing unacceptable thoughts out of conscious awareness) or denial (refusing to acknowledge reality), might serve immediate protective functions but can ultimately hinder emotional growth and reality testing. Others, like sublimation (channeling unacceptable impulses into socially acceptable activities) or humor (using comedy to express uncomfortable feelings), are considered more mature and adaptive, as they not only manage distress but also contribute to positive outcomes for the individual.

Despite their protective function, overreliance on defense mechanisms can lead to maladaptive behaviors and interfere with an individual's ability to deal with reality effectively, potentially impacting relationships, work, and overall mental health. Psychoanalytic therapy often involves exploring these unconscious coping strategies, bringing them into consciousness, and working through the underlying issues they mask. This process can help individuals develop healthier ways of dealing with stress and emotional pain, leading to more authentic and fulfilling lives.

Defense mechanisms are unconscious processes employed by the ego to protect the individual from anxiety and psychological distress. These mechanisms operate on a spectrum from primitive to mature, affecting how individuals perceive and interact with the world. A comprehensive understanding of these mechanisms includes recognizing their diversity and their implications for behavior and mental health.

Repression is considered the cornerstone of defense mechanisms. It involves unconsciously blocking unacceptable thoughts, feelings, or impulses from entering consciousness. Repression serves as a foundation for many other defense mechanisms, acting to keep disturbing or threatening content out of awareness. For instance, a person who has experienced trauma might repress memories of the event, thereby diminishing immediate distress but potentially leading to long-term psychological consequences.

Denial involves refusing to acknowledge the reality of a painful or threatening situation. It's a mechanism that allows an individual to avoid facing uncomfortable truths by rejecting their existence. For example, someone with a substance abuse problem might deny having an addiction, despite clear evidence to the contrary.

Projection occurs when individuals attribute their own unacceptable thoughts, feelings, or motives to another person. By projecting these qualities onto others, they can deny their existence within themselves while still acknowledging them in the external world. For example, a person who is hostile might accuse others of being hostile towards them.

Displacement involves shifting emotional reactions from the original source of distress to a safer or more acceptable target. This mechanism can reduce anxiety or discomfort by allowing the expression of feelings in a less threatening context. For example, an employee angry at their boss might displace that anger onto a family member at home.

Regression is a retreat to an earlier stage of development in the face of stress or conflict, where individuals adopt more childlike behaviors or coping strategies. Regression can manifest as dependency, withdrawal, or adopting previously outgrown behaviors, such as temper tantrums in adults facing overwhelming anxiety.

Sublimation is considered one of the most adaptive defense mechanisms. It involves channeling unacceptable impulses or emotions into socially acceptable or even productive activities. For example, someone with aggressive tendencies might take up a sport that allows for the expression of aggression in a controlled and socially sanctioned way.

Rationalization involves justifying behaviors or feelings with logical, acceptable explanations, often to hide the real reasons or motivations. This mechanism allows individuals to maintain their self-esteem by explaining away failures, disappointments, or misdeeds in a way that preserves their sense of self-worth. For example, a student who fails an exam might rationalize the failure by blaming the teacher for poor instruction rather than acknowledging their lack of preparation.

Understanding these defense mechanisms provides valuable insights into the ways individuals navigate emotional distress and conflict. Recognizing and addressing maladaptive defense mechanisms in psychotherapy can lead to healthier coping strategies and more authentic living, as individuals learn to confront rather than avoid their psychological challenges.

To illuminate the practical implications of defense mechanisms, let's consider some cases and examples that showcase how these unconscious processes manifest in everyday situations, psychotherapy, and leadership contexts.

Case 1: Repression in Leadership

John, a dedicated manager, often finds himself inexplicably irritable in meetings discussing team performance. Unbeknownst to him, he represses memories of being harshly criticized in his early career. This repression surfaces as a defensive irritability, aimed at protecting himself from perceived threats to his competence. In psychotherapy, exploring these repressed memories helps John understand his reactions, fostering a more composed and empathetic approach to team management.

Case 2: Denial in Personal Health

Emma has recently been advised to adopt a healthier lifestyle following a minor health scare. Despite the clear advice from her doctor, she continues her old habits, claiming she feels "just fine." Emma's denial serves as a shield against the anxiety of acknowledging her vulnerability. This case illustrates how denial can hinder individuals from taking necessary actions for their well-being, a topic often explored in therapeutic settings to encourage more adaptive coping strategies.

Case 3: Projection in Workplace Conflict

Alex, a project leader, frequently accuses his team members of not being committed enough to the project. However, it's Alex who feels insecure about his own dedication and projects these feelings onto his team. Recognizing this projection can be a breakthrough moment in therapy, helping Alex to address his insecurities directly. In leadership, such insight can transform team dynamics, fostering a more supportive and understanding environment.

Case 4: Displacement in Family Dynamics

After a particularly stressful week at work, where she felt powerless against her superiors, Sara comes home and snaps at her children for minor misbehaviors. Sara's displacement of frustration reflects a misdirection of emotions from a source of stress to a less threatening target. Therapy can help Sara develop awareness of this pattern, encouraging healthier emotional expression and improving family relationships.

Case 5: Regression Under Stress

During a critical negotiation, Michael, a seasoned executive, unexpectedly resorts to shouting and stubbornly refusing compromise, behaviors uncharacteristic of his usual diplomatic approach. This regression under stress reveals a fallback to more primitive, childlike defense mechanisms. Psychotherapy can assist Michael in understanding and managing stress-induced regression, enhancing his leadership effectiveness.

Case 6: Sublimation in Creative Pursuits

Lena, facing unresolved anger towards a colleague, channels her emotional energy into painting, a hobby she finds deeply fulfilling. This sublimation not only helps Lena cope with her anger healthily but also enriches her personal life and creative expression. Such examples can be discussed in therapy as positive strategies for dealing with negative emotions.

Case 7: Rationalization in Career Setbacks

Tom, who was passed over for a promotion, convinces himself that the job would have been too demanding and that he is better off without the added stress. While this rationalization helps Tom cope with disappointment, it may prevent him from addressing the real reasons behind the setback. In both therapeutic and coaching settings, uncovering and challenging such rationalizations can pave the way for personal and professional growth.

These cases highlight the diversity of defense mechanisms and their impact on personal development, relationships, and leadership. By recognizing and addressing these unconscious strategies, individuals can foster greater self-awareness, emotional resilience, and interpersonal effectiveness.

Transference

Transference is a fundamental psychoanalytic concept that describes the process by which unconscious feelings, desires, and expectations from past relationships are transferred onto another person, typically occurring within the therapeutic setting where patients project these emotions onto their therapists. Originating from the work of Sigmund Freud, transference is understood as a replication of past relationships in the present, allowing unresolved conflicts and dynamics from earlier life stages to be played out with the therapist.

The development of the concept of transference is closely linked to Freud's broader exploration of the unconscious mind and the mechanisms by which it influences conscious thoughts and behaviors. Freud observed that patients often related to him not purely based on his actions as a therapist but influenced by their own internal models of other relationships. This observation led to the recognition that the emotional bonds and conflicts patients experienced with significant figures in their past, particularly parents or primary caregivers, were being re-enacted in the therapeutic relationship.

Transference is not merely a repetition of the past but serves as a window into the patient's inner world, revealing the patterns, desires, and defenses that structure their relationships. It provides invaluable insights into the patient's psyche, offering a live representation of how they relate to others and the emotional baggage they carry into interactions. By working through these transferences in therapy, patients can gain insight into their unconscious motivations, heal past wounds, and develop healthier ways of relating to themselves and others.

The recognition and management of transference are central to the psychoanalytic process, allowing the therapist to use the therapeutic relationship as a corrective emotional experience. Therapists aim to understand and interpret the transference dynamics, gently guiding patients to recognize these projections and the historical roots behind them. Through this process, therapy facilitates not just a re-examination of past relationships but also the potential for emotional growth and change in the present.

Transference also extends beyond the psychotherapeutic setting, occurring in various interpersonal relationships, including those in the workplace, friendships, and romantic partnerships. In these contexts, understanding transference can improve interpersonal dynamics and self-awareness, highlighting the universal relevance of this psychoanalytic concept to human relationships and personal development.

Transference, a cornerstone of psychoanalytic therapy, manifests in various forms, each carrying its own implications for the therapeutic relationship. The recognition and management of these different types of transference are crucial for facilitating effective therapy and achieving therapeutic goals. The primary types of transference encountered in therapy include positive, negative, and erotic transference, each reflecting different aspects of the patient's unconscious feelings and desires.

Positive Transference occurs when a patient projects positive feelings, such as love, admiration, or idealization, onto the therapist. These feelings are often rooted in the patient's past relationships with significant figures whom they viewed as caring or nurturing. While positive transference can facilitate a strong therapeutic alliance by fostering trust and cooperation, it may also hinder therapy if the patient's idealization prevents them from seeing the therapist as a real person with limitations. Recognizing and gently challenging these idealizations can help patients develop a more realistic view of others and themselves.

Negative Transference involves the projection of negative emotions, such as anger, disappointment, or resentment, onto the therapist. These feelings typically stem from past experiences of hurt, neglect, or mistreatment by important figures in the patient's life. Negative transference can pose challenges to the therapeutic process, as it may lead to resistance, conflict, or even termination of therapy. However, it also presents a valuable opportunity to explore and work through difficult emotions and relational patterns in a safe and supportive environment.

Erotic Transference is characterized by the patient developing romantic or sexual feelings towards the therapist. These feelings often arise from unconscious desires or unmet needs being directed toward the therapist as a substitute for significant others.

Erotic transference can be particularly challenging to navigate, as it may create discomfort or confusion within the therapeutic relationship. Handling erotic transference with sensitivity and professionalism is crucial, focusing on understanding its underlying roots and helping the patient explore these feelings without acting on them.

Each type of transference has a significant impact on the therapeutic relationship, offering unique insights into the patient's inner world and relational dynamics. Therapists must be attuned to the presence and nature of transference, using their understanding of these dynamics to guide the therapeutic process. By addressing transference directly and thoughtfully, therapists can help patients gain insight into their unconscious patterns, heal from past relational wounds, and develop healthier ways of relating to themselves and others.

Transference, in all its forms, underscores the complexity of human relationships and the profound influence of our pasts on our present interactions. In psychotherapy, navigating transference is essential for facilitating deep psychological change, underscoring the importance of the therapist's awareness, sensitivity, and skill in managing these dynamics.

Transference, while traditionally discussed within the context of psychotherapy, plays a significant role in leadership and coaching contexts as well. In these settings, the dynamics of transference can significantly impact the relationships between leaders and followers or coaches and clients, influencing outcomes, effectiveness, and the overall climate of the interaction. Understanding transference in these contexts offers valuable insights into the emotional undercurrents that shape these relationships, providing opportunities for deeper connection and more effective leadership and coaching practices.

In leadership, transference can manifest when followers unconsciously project feelings, attitudes, and expectations from significant past relationships onto a leader. These projections may be based on experiences with parental figures, previous leaders, or other authority figures, affecting how followers perceive and interact with the leader. Positive transference might result in idealization of the leader, where followers attribute extraordinary capabilities or qualities to the leader, potentially overlooking their flaws or the realities of the situation. Conversely, negative transference can lead to undue criticism or resistance, where the leader is seen through the lens of past negative experiences with authority figures, regardless of the leader's actual behaviors or intentions.

This dynamic can challenge leaders to navigate complex emotional landscapes, requiring them to recognize and manage not only their own reactions but also the projections placed upon them by followers. Leaders aware of the potential for transference can strive to create a more authentic and open environment, encouraging realistic perceptions and healthy professional relationships. This awareness also enables leaders to address their own countertransference issues—how their reactions to followers' projections might influence their leadership style and decisions.

In coaching, transference plays a similarly critical role, as clients may project onto their coaches feelings and expectations rooted in past relationships. A client might see the coach as a nurturing figure, projecting feelings of trust and safety that facilitate openness and vulnerability. Alternatively, a client might project past experiences of judgment or rejection onto the coach, hindering the development of a trusting coaching relationship. Recognizing these dynamics allows coaches to better understand the client's responses and tailor their approach to support the client's growth and development effectively.

Managing transference in coaching involves creating a space where clients feel seen and understood, beyond the projections they may bring into the relationship. It also requires coaches to be mindful of their own responses to clients, ensuring that their guidance remains centered on the client's needs and goals rather than being influenced by countertransference.

In both leadership and coaching, the awareness and management of transference and countertransference dynamics are essential for fostering productive, healthy relationships. By acknowledging and addressing these unconscious processes, leaders and coaches can enhance their effectiveness, facilitating personal and professional growth in those they lead or support. This understanding underscores the complexity of human relationships and the importance of emotional intelligence in leadership and coaching roles.

Countertransference

Countertransference is defined as the therapist's or coach's emotional entanglement with the client's transference, encompassing both conscious and unconscious reactions to the feelings, attitudes, and behaviors that the client projects onto them. This concept, originating in psychoanalytic theory, highlights the therapist's or coach's internal response to the dynamics of transference, where the emotional baggage, unresolved conflicts, and unmet needs of the client trigger personal reactions in the professional. Countertransference was initially viewed as a hindrance to the therapeutic process, indicating that the therapist's unresolved issues might interfere with their objectivity and effectiveness. However, over time, the understanding of countertransference has evolved to recognize its valuable role in therapy and coaching.

The importance of countertransference lies in its potential as a diagnostic and therapeutic tool. When therapists or coaches are aware of and can reflect on their emotional reactions to clients, they gain insights into the client's psychological state and the nature of the therapeutic or coaching relationship. This self-awareness allows professionals to distinguish between their own emotional responses and the client's issues, facilitating a clearer understanding of the client's needs and how best to address them.

Acknowledging and managing countertransference is crucial for maintaining the integrity of the therapeutic or coaching relationship. It ensures that the professional's personal issues do not unduly influence the process, allowing for a safe, supportive environment in which the client can explore their thoughts and feelings. In therapy, countertransference can reveal the therapist's blind spots or areas of sensitivity, which, when explored, can enhance their empathetic engagement with the client and inform more effective therapeutic interventions.

In coaching, particularly in contexts such as executive or leadership coaching, countertransference can inform the coach's understanding of the client's relational dynamics, leadership style, and emotional triggers. By recognizing their reactions to a client's transference, coaches can better navigate the coaching relationship, providing targeted support that addresses the client's underlying emotional and psychological challenges.

Countertransference is a complex phenomenon that, when recognized and managed appropriately, enriches the therapeutic and coaching processes. It underscores the reciprocal nature of the professional-client relationship, where the emotional exchanges and projections offer valuable pathways for insight, healing, and growth.

Recognizing and managing countertransference is essential for maintaining the efficacy and integrity of therapeutic and coaching relationships. It demands a high level of self-awareness and ongoing professional development from therapists and coaches. Here are strategies to recognize and manage countertransference, emphasizing the critical roles of self-awareness and supervision:

Strategies for Recognizing Countertransference

1. Reflective Practice: Regular self-reflection is key to recognizing one's emotional responses and biases. Therapists and coaches can develop this through journaling about their feelings after sessions, exploring any strong emotional reactions or patterns that emerge in relation to certain clients.

2. Self-Awareness Exercises: Engaging in mindfulness and meditation can enhance self-awareness, helping professionals

notice their emotional reactions more acutely and differentiate between their own emotions and those of their clients.

3. Education and Training: Continuous learning about countertransference, including its manifestations and theoretical underpinnings, equips professionals with the knowledge to identify when their reactions might be influencing their professional judgment.

4. Peer Consultation: Regular discussions with peers can provide valuable perspectives, helping therapists and coaches identify instances of countertransference they might not have recognized on their own.

Strategies for Managing Countertransference

1. Supervision: Seeking regular supervision is perhaps the most effective strategy for managing countertransference. Supervisors can offer objective insights into the therapist's or coach's emotional reactions, helping them understand and work through these responses constructively.

2. Personal Therapy: For therapists and coaches, engaging in their own therapy can be instrumental in addressing personal issues that might contribute to countertransference. This personal work can prevent their unresolved conflicts from impacting their professional relationships.

3. Boundary Setting: Maintaining clear professional boundaries helps in managing countertransference by creating a safe, structured space for the therapeutic or coaching relationship. This includes being mindful of time, space, self-disclosure, and the balance of power in the relationship.

4. Developing Coping Strategies: Building a repertoire of coping strategies, such as stress management techniques, can help professionals manage their emotional responses more effectively, reducing the impact of countertransference on their work.

5. Professional Development Workshops: Participating in workshops and training sessions focused on countertransference can provide practical tools and strategies for dealing with these emotional reactions in a professional context.

The importance of recognizing and managing countertransference cannot be overstated. It not only safeguards the integrity of the therapeutic or coaching process but also supports the personal and professional growth of the therapist or coach. By addressing countertransference proactively, therapists and coaches can foster a therapeutic environment that promotes genuine understanding, emotional safety, and effective intervention, ultimately enhancing the well-being and development of their clients.

Understanding and utilizing countertransference not only helps therapists and coaches manage their own emotional responses but also serves as a powerful tool for gaining valuable insights into the client's or coachee's emotional state and relational dynamics. When recognized and interpreted skillfully, countertransference becomes a window into the unconscious processes and unspoken emotions of the client, enhancing the depth and effectiveness of the therapeutic or coaching engagement.

Countertransference reactions can mirror the client's typical ways of relating to others, revealing patterns that might not be immediately apparent through verbal communication alone. For example, a therapist feeling inexplicably criticized or undervalued by a client might reflect the client's underlying relational dynamic of provoking rejection or criticism from others. Such insights can guide the therapeutic process, allowing for targeted interventions that address these relational patterns.

Emotional responses elicited in the therapist or coach can signal unmet emotional needs or unresolved conflicts in the client. A feeling of overprotectiveness towards a client, for instance, might indicate the client's unexpressed need for safety and validation. Recognizing these needs through countertransference enables professionals to tailor their approach, providing the support or confrontation necessary to facilitate growth and healing.

Countertransference, when managed appropriately, can deepen the empathetic connection between the therapist or coach and the client. By consciously reflecting on their emotional reactions, professionals can better attune to the client's emotional experience, fostering a relationship characterized by genuine understanding and compassion. This empathetic attunement is crucial for building trust and safety, foundational elements of effective therapy and coaching.

Countertransference can be particularly illuminating in situations where the client exhibits resistance or employs defense mechanisms. A therapist's feelings of frustration or impotence in the face of a client's resistance can reflect the client's own feelings towards their problems or the therapeutic process. Acknowledging and exploring these countertransference feelings can uncover new ways to engage the client and navigate their defenses.

Insights gained from countertransference can inform specific therapeutic interventions, making them more resonant and impactful for the client. For example, understanding a recurring pattern of feeling dismissed or ignored by the client can lead the therapist to explore themes of invisibility or neglect in the client's life, opening up new areas for therapeutic exploration.

To effectively utilize countertransference as a tool, therapists and coaches must engage in continuous self-reflection and seek supervision to ensure their interpretations are grounded in the client's reality rather than their own projections. This careful, reflective approach to countertransference not only mitigates the risk of boundary violations or ethical concerns but also enriches the therapeutic or coaching relationship, offering profound opportunities for insight, growth, and transformation.

Practical Applications of Fundamental Concepts

In the realm of psychotherapy, the ideas and concepts derived from psychoanalytic theory are intricately woven into practices that facilitate insight, emotional healing, and behavior change. Through engaging with the unconscious, analyzing defense mechanisms, and navigating the nuanced dynamics of transference and countertransference, psychotherapy delves deep into the client's inner world, catalyzing profound personal transformation.

Exploration of the unconscious forms the cornerstone of psychotherapeutic work, utilizing techniques such as dream analysis and free association to unearth repressed desires, unresolved conflicts, and traumatic memories. This journey into the unconscious brings these obscured elements into the light of consciousness, allowing clients to face and understand the root causes of their distress. Such revelations can dismantle long-standing psychological barriers, offering clients a path to reconcile internal conflicts and embrace new, healthier ways of relating to themselves and the world around them.

Defense mechanisms, those unconscious operations designed to shield the individual from psychological discomfort, are meticulously examined within the therapeutic setting. Therapists guide clients in recognizing their own patterns of defense, from denial and projection to rationalization, revealing how these strategies may perpetuate their issues, constrict their emotional experiences, or impair their relationships. Awareness of these patterns paves the way for the adoption of more adaptive coping mechanisms, enhancing clients' capacity for emotional regulation and resilience.

The interplay of transference and countertransference is another fertile ground for therapeutic intervention. The emotional projections that clients cast onto their therapists serve as a reflective surface, mirroring the client's historical relationships and present relational tendencies. Addressing these projections within therapy allows clients to heal from past relational traumas and cultivate a more secure sense of self. Concurrently, therapists' awareness and management of their own countertransference reactions are essential for maintaining the objectivity and effectiveness of the therapy. By tuning into their emotional responses to clients, therapists can better empathize and connect, strengthening the therapeutic bond.

Central to psychotherapy is the facilitation of insight, guiding clients to a deeper understanding of their motivations, behaviors, and the underpinnings of their distress. Coupled with the emotional processing of past hurts, this journey towards insight promotes profound emotional healing. Clients are supported in navigating through pain, grief, and anger in a secure environment, leading to emotional renewal and liberation.

Ultimately, the goal of psychotherapy is to encourage sustainable behavior change. Armed with newfound insights and having worked through deep-seated conflicts, clients are better positioned to make informed choices in their actions and interactions. Psychotherapy supports clients in exploring new behaviors, engaging in healthier relational dynamics, and implementing coping strategies that reflect their true values and aspirations. This comprehensive approach does not merely alleviate psychological suffering but enriches clients' lives, enabling them to live with greater authenticity and fulfillment.

The application of psychoanalytic concepts in leadership development and executive coaching provides a profound framework for understanding and enhancing the dynamics of leadership and management. By incorporating insights into the unconscious, defense mechanisms, and the phenomena of transference and countertransference, leaders and coaches can navigate the complex emotional and psychological landscapes of the workplace, leading to more effective leadership and healthier organizational cultures.

Understanding leader-follower dynamics through a psychoanalytic lens involves recognizing how unconscious factors influence these relationships. Leaders may unknowingly project their own unresolved issues onto followers, while followers may transfer feelings related to past authority figures onto leaders. This awareness allows leaders to navigate these dynamics more consciously, fostering a deeper understanding of their team's motivations and responses. It enables leaders to address and mitigate potential conflicts arising from these unconscious projections, thereby enhancing team cohesion and effectiveness.

Emotional intelligence, a critical component of effective leadership, can also be significantly developed through the insights provided by psychoanalytic concepts. Emotional intelligence involves self-awareness, self-regulation, empathy, motivation, and social skills—all areas that can be enhanced by understanding one's own unconscious motivations and defense mechanisms. By exploring their own psychological underpinnings, leaders can improve their capacity to manage their emotions, respond to stress more adaptively, and empathize with the emotional states of others. This not only benefits the individual leader but also sets a tone of emotional openness and authenticity within the organization.

Improving interpersonal relationships is another area where psychoanalytic concepts have a substantial impact. The exploration of transference and countertransference dynamics can illuminate the emotional currents running beneath workplace interactions, offering insights into the sometimes-complex relationships between leaders and their teams or between colleagues. Leaders who are attuned to these dynamics can better manage their reactions and interactions, creating a work environment that values understanding and respects the psychological well-being of all members.

Executive coaching that incorporates psychoanalytic principles can facilitate profound personal and professional growth for leaders. By creating a space for leaders to reflect on their unconscious motivations, fears, and desires, coaches can guide them towards greater self-awareness and emotional maturity. This process helps leaders identify and overcome personal barriers to effective leadership, such as unresolved conflicts, maladaptive behavior patterns, or limiting beliefs rooted in past experiences.

The integration of psychoanalytic concepts into leadership development and executive coaching offers valuable tools for understanding and improving leader-follower dynamics, enhancing emotional intelligence, and fostering healthier interpersonal relationships. This approach not only aids in the personal growth of leaders but also contributes to the development of more empathetic, responsive, and effective leadership styles, ultimately benefiting the entire organization.

Case Study 1: Therapeutic Context - Uncovering Repressed Memories

Emily, a 30-year-old client, presented with symptoms of anxiety and depression, struggling with interpersonal relationships and a pervasive sense of unfulfillment. Despite a successful career, she felt disconnected from her emotions and others. During therapy, through the use of free association and dream analysis, Emily began to recall and discuss memories of being emotionally neglected by her parents during her childhood. These repressed memories, once surfaced, helped Emily and her therapist understand the root of her emotional detachment and fear of intimacy. Recognizing these repressed experiences allowed Emily to work through her feelings of abandonment and develop healthier relationships. The therapy facilitated a process where Emily could grieve her lost childhood and start building a more authentic connection with her emotions and others. This case highlights the significance of uncovering and addressing unconscious material to heal emotional wounds and improve mental health.

Case Study 2: Leadership Context - Projection and Team Dynamics

Michael, a team leader in a tech company, often criticized his team for lack of initiative and creativity. Despite his efforts, the team's morale was low, and productivity suffered. Through executive coaching, Michael explored his feelings and discovered he was projecting his insecurities about his own creativity onto his team. This insight came from reflecting on his reactions to team meetings and feedback sessions, where he recognized his disproportionate frustration. Understanding this projection allowed Michael to address his own fears and change his approach to leadership. He started encouraging open communication and creativity by expressing confidence in his team's abilities and providing supportive feedback. This shift improved team morale and productivity, showcasing how leaders can transform team dynamics by becoming aware of and managing their projections.

Case Study 3: Psychotherapy - Navigating Countertransference

Background: Dr. Smith, a seasoned psychotherapist, found herself feeling unusually frustrated and hopeless with a new client, John, who was dealing with severe depression and resistance to therapy. Dr. Smith engaged in supervision to explore her feelings, recognizing that John's hopelessness mirrored her unresolved feelings about a family member's struggle with depression. This countertransference was affecting her ability to maintain therapeutic neutrality and optimism. By acknowledging and working through her countertransference, Dr. Smith regained her therapeutic stance, providing John with the empathetic support and persistence he needed. This case illustrates the importance of therapists managing their emotional reactions to maintain effectiveness and support their clients' healing processes.

These case studies exemplify the profound impact of understanding and working with the unconscious, defense mechanisms, transference, and countertransference in both therapeutic and leadership contexts. They demonstrate how deep psychological insights can lead to significant personal and professional growth, improved interpersonal relationships, and more effective leadership.

Conclusion

This chapter has delved into the rich and complex landscape of psychoanalytic theory, exploring its foundational concepts and their profound implications for understanding human behavior and psychology. Through the exploration of the unconscious, defense mechanisms, transference, and countertransference, we have seen how psychoanalytic principles offer invaluable insights into the depths of the human psyche, revealing the intricate and often unconscious processes that underlie our thoughts, feelings, and actions.

The unconscious mind, with its repository of repressed desires, fears, and memories, emerges as a pivotal force shaping our behavior and emotional experiences. By bringing the hidden aspects of our psyche into consciousness, psychoanalysis not only enhances self-awareness but also opens the door to emotional healing and personal growth. Defense mechanisms, serving as the mind's protectors against psychological distress, highlight the complexity of our coping strategies, offering clues to the unresolved conflicts and anxieties that drive them.

Transference and countertransference, the dynamic interplay of projections and reactions within the therapeutic relationship, further illuminate the profound impact of past relationships on our present interactions. These phenomena underscore the therapeutic process's relational aspect, offering a unique lens through which to view and address psychological issues.

The application of psychoanalytic concepts extends beyond the realm of therapy, proving to be equally valuable in leadership and executive coaching contexts. Understanding the unconscious motivations, defense mechanisms, and relational dynamics can significantly enhance leadership effectiveness, promoting healthier workplace environments and more authentic leadership styles.

This chapter has underscored the enduring relevance of psychoanalytic theory in contemporary psychology, affirming its significance in deepening our understanding of human behavior. By embracing the insights offered by psychoanalysis, we can navigate the complexities of the human mind with greater empathy, insight, and effectiveness, fostering a deeper connection to ourselves and those around us. Psychoanalytic concepts not only enrich our professional practices but also enrich our personal lives, offering a path to profound transformation and understanding.

As we conclude this exploration of psychoanalytic concepts, it's clear that their relevance extends far beyond the confines of the therapist's office, reaching into the realms of leadership and executive coaching, among others. The insights derived from understanding the unconscious, navigating defense mechanisms, and interpreting the dynamics of transference and countertransference have profound implications across a spectrum of professional and personal contexts.

In clinical psychotherapy, these concepts are foundational tools for facilitating insight, emotional healing, and personal growth, allowing therapists and clients to work through the layers of the unconscious to address the root causes of psychological distress. But the utility of psychoanalytic theory is not limited to therapy alone. In leadership and executive coaching, the same principles provide a framework for understanding complex interpersonal dynamics, enhancing emotional intelligence, and fostering authentic leadership styles that can lead to more cohesive and productive teams.

The application of psychoanalytic concepts in diverse settings underscores the universality of the human psyche's challenges and the potential for growth and understanding that psychoanalytic theory offers. Leaders, coaches, therapists, and individuals alike can benefit from the deep insights into human behavior that psychoanalysis provides, navigating personal and professional relationships with greater empathy and effectiveness. This chapter invites readers to continue exploring and applying psychoanalytic concepts in their work and lives. By integrating these insights into our understanding of human behavior, we can unlock new levels of personal growth, enhance our professional practices, and contribute to healthier, more understanding interpersonal dynamics. The journey into the depths of the psyche is both challenging and rewarding, offering endless opportunities for discovery and transformation. Psychoanalytic theory, with its rich conceptual framework and practical applications, remains a vital resource for anyone seeking to deepen their understanding of the human mind and improve the quality of human interaction across various settings.

Chapter 3: Psychoanalytic Understanding of Personality

Chapter 3 delves into the rich psychoanalytic perspective on personality, unveiling the intricate layers and dynamics that compose the human psyche. This exploration is pivotal for understanding how the mind's structure, personality development stages, and the nuanced interplay of neuroses and character traits coalesce to form the unique tapestry of individual personality. Through the lens of psychoanalytic theory, we embark on a journey to decipher the underlying processes that shape our identities, influence our behaviors, and govern our emotional lives.

The psychoanalytic view offers a profound understanding of personality by dissecting the mind's architecture into the conscious, preconscious, and unconscious realms. Each layer contributes to the complexity of personality, housing desires, fears, memories, and unresolved conflicts that subtly influence our conscious experience and interactions with the world. By examining the structure of the mind, we gain insights into the unseen forces that drive our behaviors and shape our emotional responses.

Personality development, as conceptualized in psychoanalytic theory, unfolds through a series of stages, each marked by specific conflicts and potential resolutions that have lasting effects on an individual's character. From the early struggles of the oral and anal stages to the complexities of the phallic stage and beyond, these developmental milestones highlight the critical role of early experiences in shaping personality. Understanding these stages provides a framework for deciphering the origins of our deepest desires, fears, and relational patterns.

This chapter will explore the concepts of neuroses and character traits, which emerge from the interplay between innate dispositions and environmental influences throughout development. Neuroses, manifesting as anxiety, depression, or other psychological disturbances, often reflect unresolved conflicts and repressed material from earlier stages of development. Character traits, on the other hand, represent the more stable aspects of our personalities, including our habitual ways of thinking, feeling, and behaving. Together, these elements offer a window into the complexities of human nature, revealing how past experiences and unconscious processes converge to shape the individuals we become.

As we navigate the psychoanalytic understanding of personality, we uncover the depth and breadth of human psychological diversity. This chapter invites readers to reflect on the origins of their own personalities, encouraging a deeper self-awareness and appreciation for the nuanced interplay of factors that contribute to our unique identities. Through this exploration, psychoanalytic theory not only enriches our understanding of personality but also opens avenues for personal growth, healing, and transformation.

The psychoanalytic understanding of personality, with its emphasis on the structure of the mind, stages of personality development, and the intricacies of neuroses and character traits, significantly enriches our comprehension of human behavior across a spectrum of settings, from clinical environments to the domains of leadership and coaching. By unraveling the complex tapestry of the unconscious, developmental conflicts, and enduring personality patterns, psychoanalytic theory offers nuanced insights that are invaluable for therapeutic interventions, personal development, organizational dynamics, and beyond.

In clinical settings, this deep dive into the psychoanalytic perspective enables therapists to identify and address the root causes of psychological distress. Understanding the origin of neuroses in unresolved developmental conflicts or repressed desires allows for more targeted and effective therapeutic approaches, facilitating not just symptomatic relief but lasting psychological change. This approach fosters a holistic healing process, where individuals can reconcile with their past, understand their present behaviors, and move towards a more integrated and authentic self.

Beyond the therapy room, the psychoanalytic conception of personality sheds light on the dynamics of leadership and coaching. Leaders and coaches equipped with an understanding of their own unconscious motivations, developmental histories, and character traits can navigate interpersonal relationships with greater empathy and insight. This awareness is crucial for managing transference and countertransference dynamics in professional relationships, enabling leaders and coaches to foster environments of trust, growth, and productivity.

The psychoanalytic framework assists leaders in recognizing the underlying psychological drivers behind team behaviors and organizational culture. By applying these insights, leaders can address not only surface-level challenges but also the deeper, often unconscious issues that influence team dynamics and organizational performance. This leads to more effective leadership strategies that consider the psychological well-being and development of team members, ultimately contributing to a more cohesive and resilient organization.

In coaching, the psychoanalytic perspective enhances the coach's ability to facilitate personal and professional growth. Understanding the client's personality structure and developmental history allows coaches to tailor their approach, addressing not just career goals but also deeper personal aspirations and conflicts. This fosters a coaching relationship that supports profound transformation, empowering individuals to overcome limitations and achieve their full potential.

The application of psychoanalytic concepts to understand human behavior in both clinical and non-clinical settings underscores the theory's versatility and depth. It offers a comprehensive framework for exploring the complexities of the human psyche, enhancing our ability to support healing, growth, and effective leadership. Through this lens, we gain a richer understanding of the psychological underpinnings of behavior, opening pathways to more empathetic, insightful, and transformative practices in therapy, leadership, and coaching.

Structure of the Mind

In Freudian psychoanalytic theory, the structure of the mind is conceptualized as comprising three major components: the id, ego, and superego. These elements interact in complex ways to shape human behavior and psychological processes. Understanding the roles and functions of the id, ego, and superego is essential for grasping the dynamics of the human psyche as envisioned by Freud.

The Id represents the most primitive part of the mind, functioning as the source of instinctual drives and desires. It operates based on the pleasure principle, seeking immediate gratification for its urges, regardless of societal norms or consequences. The id is entirely unconscious and houses basic life instincts (Eros, which includes the sexual instincts) and death instincts (Thanatos). For example, the id might drive an individual to seek out pleasurable experiences without considering their appropriateness or the potential repercussions.

The Ego develops from the id during infancy, serving as the executive component of personality that deals with the demands of reality. It operates according to the reality principle, mediating between the unrealistic demands of the id and the external world. The ego employs rational thought and problem-solving to navigate the complexities of life, striving to satisfy the id's desires in socially acceptable ways. It's the ego's job to balance the desires of the id with the moral guidelines of the superego, often requiring compromise and negotiation. The ego is partly conscious and partly unconscious.

The Superego emerges during childhood as the child internalizes the moral standards and values of their parents and society. It functions as the moral compass of the personality, enforcing rules, and prohibiting unacceptable behaviors. The superego strives for perfection, working to suppress the urges of the id and pushing the ego to consider moral ideals in its decision-making. It consists of two components: the conscience, which punishes the ego through feelings of guilt for violating its standards, and the ideal self, which rewards the ego with feelings of pride and self-worth when its standards are met.

The dynamic interplay between the id, ego, and superego shapes an individual's personality, behavior, and psychological experiences. The ego's continual effort to balance the instinctual demands of the id, the moralistic demands of the superego, and the realities of the external world is central to the Freudian explanation of human psychology. This model highlights the conflict and tension inherent in the human condition, proposing that psychological well-being depends on the ability of the ego to effectively manage these competing demands. Through this lens, psychoanalytic theory provides a framework for understanding the depth and complexity of human motivation, conflict, and behavior.

The dynamic interplay between the id, ego, and superego, as conceptualized in Freudian psychoanalytic theory, is thus fundamental to understanding human behavior, decision-making, and psychological health. This interaction is characterized by a constant negotiation between the instinctual desires of the id, the moral and ethical standards of the superego, and the mediating influence of the ego, which strives to reconcile these often-conflicting demands with the realities of the external world.

The id, driven by the pleasure principle, seeks immediate gratification for its instinctual desires and drives, which include both life-preserving instincts such as hunger and thirst, and primitive sexual and aggressive impulses. It operates unconsciously, without regard for logic, ethics, or social appropriateness. The id's demands are relentless and uncompromising, pushing for satisfaction regardless of potential consequences or societal norms.

The superego, on the other hand, represents the internalized ideals and moral standards acquired from parents, caregivers, and society. It functions as the critical and moralizing component of the personality, constantly monitoring and judging the ego's decisions and behaviors against these internalized standards. The superego operates on the morality principle, striving for perfection and moral superiority, often at the expense of practicality and pleasure. It can induce feelings of guilt, shame, or inferiority when its standards are not met, serving as a powerful deterrent to the id's impulses.

Caught in the middle of this tension is the ego, which functions according to the reality principle. The ego's role is to navigate the demands of both the id and the superego, along with the constraints of the external world, to find realistic and socially acceptable outlets for the id's desires while upholding the superego's moral standards. The ego employs defense mechanisms as strategies to manage the anxiety and conflict arising from this balancing act, modifying the id's impulses in ways that are less disruptive or channeling them into acceptable forms of expression.

The interplay between these three components significantly influences an individual's behavior and decision-making. For instance, a person may feel a strong impulse to engage in a socially or morally questionable activity (id), experience guilt or moral conflict over this impulse (superego), and ultimately decide against the action or find a compromise that aligns with their ethical beliefs and social norms (ego). The ability of the ego to effectively mediate these internal conflicts is crucial for psychological health. An overly dominant id may lead to impulsive, reckless behavior, while an overly strict superego can result in excessive guilt, anxiety, or self-repression. A well-balanced ego, capable of managing the demands of both the id and the superego, is essential for achieving psychological well-being and navigating the complexities of human social life.

The dynamic interplay between the id, ego, and superego shapes the intricate landscape of human psychology. Understanding this interplay provides valuable insights into the complexities of human behavior, the inner conflicts that influence decision-making, and the pathways to achieving psychological balance and health.

The balance and conflict among the id, ego, and superego play a pivotal role in shaping an individual's personality and behaviors, illustrating the complexity of human psychology as envisioned by Freudian psychoanalytic theory. This dynamic interplay determines not only how individuals respond to internal desires and external demands but also influences their emotional health, coping strategies, and interpersonal relationships.

Personality, in this psychoanalytic framework, emerges as a reflection of how effectively the ego mediates between the primal urges of the id and the moralistic demands of the superego. An individual's characteristic patterns of thinking, feeling, and behaving are significantly influenced by how these psychic forces interact and the strategies the ego employs to manage the tension and conflict between them.

When the id exerts a strong influence on the personality, individuals may display impulsivity, a strong pursuit of pleasure, and difficulty adhering to societal norms and expectations. This dominance of the id suggests an ego that struggles to regulate primal desires effectively, leading to behaviors that can be socially disruptive or self-destructive. Such individuals might gravitate towards immediate gratification without considering the long-term consequences, reflecting a personality style marked by hedonism and a lack of restraint.

Conversely, when the superego dominates, individuals may exhibit a rigid adherence to moral standards, excessive self-criticism, and a propensity for guilt and shame over natural desires and impulses. This scenario indicates an ego overwhelmed by the superego's demands, resulting in personalities characterized by perfectionism, a punitive inner voice, and potentially inhibited social and emotional expression. The superego's control can stifle creativity and spontaneity, leading to behaviors driven by a need for approval and an avoidance of disapproval.

A well-balanced ego mediates effectively between the demands of the id and the superego, facilitating adaptive coping strategies and healthy psychological functioning. Individuals with a strong ego can navigate their desires and moral values in ways that are both personally satisfying and socially acceptable. This balance fosters resilience, flexibility, and a capacity for complex emotional and social engagement. Personalities shaped by a well-functioning ego are marked by emotional stability, empathy, and a mature, realistic approach to life's challenges.

The interplay among the id, ego, and superego also influences how individuals cope with stress, resolve internal conflicts, and form relationships. For example, someone with a dominant id may seek out thrill-seeking or escapist behaviors under stress, while someone with a dominant superego might respond to stress with self-criticism and withdrawal. In contrast, an individual with a well-balanced ego might employ more adaptive strategies, such as seeking social support or problem-solving.

The balance and conflict among the id, ego, and superego are central to the development of personality and behaviors. This psychoanalytic perspective offers insights into the underlying mechanisms that shape individual differences, highlighting the importance of achieving a harmonious balance for optimal psychological health and interpersonal functioning. Understanding these dynamics can inform therapeutic interventions, personal growth efforts, and our appreciation of the diverse tapestry of human personality.

Personality Development Stages

Freud's theory of psychosexual development posits that personality formation is a process that unfolds across five distinct stages from infancy through adulthood. Each stage is characterized by the erogenous zone that is the focus of the libido's energy, with specific conflicts and tasks that must be navigated.

The manner in which these conflicts are resolved plays a crucial role in shaping an individual's personality and behaviors.

1. Oral Stage (0-18 months): The first stage of psychosexual development is centered on the mouth as the primary erogenous zone. During this stage, the infant's primary interactions with the world involve sucking and swallowing. Freud believed that experiences during the oral stage, such as weaning, influence the individual's future relationship with gratification and aggression. Fixations at this stage might lead to oral personality traits in adulthood, such as dependency, passivity, or an inclination toward oral activities like smoking or overeating.

2. Anal Stage (18 months - 3 years): The focus shifts to the anus during the anal stage, with the primary conflict revolving around toilet training. The child learns to control bowel movements, which Freud saw as a key battle between the child's desires and societal expectations. How parents handle toilet training can impact the child's personality: overly strict training might lead to an anal-retentive personality characterized by obsessiveness and rigidity, while lenient training might result in an anal-expulsive personality, marked by messiness and recklessness.

3. Phallic Stage (3-6 years): The phallic stage centers on the genital organs. Freud introduced the concepts of the Oedipus complex in boys and the Electra complex in girls, where the child experiences unconscious desires for the opposite-sex parent and jealousy toward the same-sex parent. Resolution of these complexes leads to identification with the same-sex parent, a critical step in the development of gender identity and moral conscience. Fixation at this stage can result in phallic personality traits, such as vanity, recklessness, and difficulty with authority.

4. Latency Stage (6 years - puberty): The libido's energy is suppressed during the latency stage, and sexual interests are put into the background. This period is characterized by a

focus on learning, social interactions, and developing skills and interests. Freud saw this stage as a phase of relative stability, where the sexual and aggressive drives are channeled into productive activities such as schoolwork and friendships.

5. Genital Stage (puberty onward): The final stage of psychosexual development is the genital stage, which begins with puberty. The sexual desires re-emerge and become directed toward heterosexual relationships. The successful resolution of earlier conflicts leads to the capacity for love and a healthy sexual relationship. The genital stage marks the arrival of mature adult sexuality, where individuals seek to form balanced, loving relationships and contribute to society.

Freud's theory of psychosexual development underscores the significance of early childhood experiences in shaping personality. The resolution of conflicts and the manner in which individuals navigate each stage have lasting effects on their psychological makeup, influencing their behaviors, relationships, and overall emotional well-being. While some aspects of Freud's theory have been critiqued and revised over time, the concept of stages of development has remained influential in understanding the complex process of personality formation.

Freud's theory of psychosexual development posits that individuals can experience fixations and regressions as outcomes of unresolved conflicts during any of the psychosexual stages. These phenomena have significant implications for adult personality and behavior, reflecting the enduring influence of early childhood experiences on psychological development.

Fixations occur when an individual's development becomes "stuck" at one of the psychosexual stages, due to either excessive gratification or frustration of the stage-specific needs and desires. This unresolved conflict leads to an overemphasis on the characteristics associated with that stage later in life. For instance:

- An oral fixation might develop if issues during the oral stage (0-18 months) are not adequately resolved, possibly due to weaning too early or too late. This can result in traits such as dependency, passivity, or a propensity for oral activities (e.g., smoking, overeating) in adulthood.

- An anal fixation can arise from conflicts during the anal stage (18 months - 3 years), often related to toilet training experiences. Excessive strictness or leniency can lead to anal-retentive characteristics, such as obsessiveness and perfectionism, or anal-expulsive traits, like messiness and recklessness.

- A phallic fixation may emerge from unresolved Oedipal or Electra complexes during the phallic stage (3-6 years), potentially leading to vanity, narcissism, and difficulties in relationships due to an unresolved competition for the opposite-sex parent's affection.

Regressions represent a retreat to an earlier psychosexual stage in response to stress, anxiety, or other psychological pressures in later life. This defensive mechanism serves as a temporary escape to a time when the individual felt safer or more satisfied. For example:

- During periods of high stress or illness, an individual might regress to the oral stage, exhibiting behaviors such as nail-biting or binge eating, seeking comfort in activities reminiscent of the oral gratification experienced in infancy.

- In the face of authority challenges or control issues, someone might regress to the anal stage, displaying stubbornness or meticulousness as a means of exerting control, echoing the anal stage's themes of power and autonomy.

Both fixations and regressions can significantly impact adult personality and behavior, influencing how individuals respond to stress, form relationships, and manage desires and impulses. These concepts underscore the importance of early experiences in shaping lasting patterns of behavior and emotional responses. In psychotherapy, understanding an individual's potential fixations or tendencies toward regression can provide valuable insights into their psychological challenges, guiding therapeutic interventions aimed at resolving these deep-seated conflicts. This psychoanalytic perspective offers a framework for comprehending the complexity of human behavior, emphasizing the powerful role of early developmental experiences in the formation of adult personality.

The early childhood development stages outlined in Freud's psychosexual theory exert a profound influence on adult relationships, including the dynamics of leadership and coaching. The experiences and conflicts encountered during these formative years can shape an individual's approach to interpersonal interactions, their style of leadership, and their effectiveness as a coach or mentor.

During the oral stage, individuals learn about trust and dependency through their primary caregivers' responsiveness to their needs. This stage lays the groundwork for how individuals form attachments and manage dependency in adult relationships. Leaders and coaches who experienced either over-gratification or frustration during this stage might exhibit tendencies toward either excessive independence or a need for constant reassurance and support from their teams.

The anal stage, focused on control and autonomy, influences one's approach to power, authority, and conformity. Adults who faced challenges during this stage might display leadership styles that are either overly controlling and rigid, reflecting an anal-retentive personality, or disorganized and laissez-faire, echoing an anal-expulsive tendency. Understanding these patterns can help leaders and coaches recognize their predispositions toward control and autonomy, allowing them to adopt more balanced approaches in managing teams and guiding clients.

The phallic stage introduces concepts of competition, jealousy, and identification, which are crucial in the development of self-esteem and gender identity. These early dynamics can influence how individuals navigate rivalry and authority in the workplace. Leaders might struggle with authority either by overly asserting it or by shying away from it, depending on their resolution of the Oedipal or Electra complex. Coaches aware of these dynamics can better understand the underlying issues affecting their clients' professional relationships and leadership challenges.

The latency stage, a period of socialization and skill development, plays a critical role in shaping one's ability to work within teams, form friendships, and pursue goals. Adults who successfully navigated this stage tend to exhibit effective collaboration skills and a balanced approach to competition and cooperation. In leadership and coaching, these skills translate into the ability to foster teamwork, mentor others, and contribute positively to organizational culture.

The genital stage, marking the maturation of sexual interests and the establishment of mature relationships, influences one's capacity for intimacy, creativity, and generativity. Leaders and coaches who have achieved a healthy balance in this stage are likely to demonstrate empathy, ethical conduct, and a capacity for genuine connection, contributing to their effectiveness in guiding and supporting others.

The influence of early childhood development stages on adult relationships, leadership, and coaching dynamics is significant. By reflecting on these developmental experiences, leaders and coaches can gain insights into their interpersonal behaviors and motivations, enabling them to navigate their roles with greater awareness and adaptability. This understanding not only enhances personal growth but also enriches the quality of professional relationships and leadership practices.

Neuroses and Character Traits

Neuroses are psychological disorders characterized by anxiety and abnormal behavior that arise from unresolved conflicts between the id, ego, and superego, as conceptualized in Freudian psychoanalytic theory. These conflicts typically stem from the failure to adequately resolve developmental challenges during the psychosexual stages, leading to persistent internal tensions that the ego struggles to manage. Unlike psychoses, which involve a break from reality, neuroses represent a spectrum of anxiety-driven responses and behaviors that, while distressing, allow the individual to remain in touch with reality.

The nature of neurotic symptoms can vary widely, including manifestations such as phobias, obsessions, compulsions, anxiety disorders, and depressive states. These symptoms are understood as maladaptive attempts by the ego to manage the overwhelming anxiety produced by the unresolved conflicts between the instinctual demands of the id, the moralistic demands of the superego, and the limitations imposed by reality. For example, an individual with obsessive-compulsive neurosis may engage in compulsive rituals as a way to alleviate the anxiety stemming from unconscious conflicts related to control and cleanliness.

Neuroses highlight the importance of the ego's regulatory function and its capacity to employ defense mechanisms in an attempt to protect the individual from psychological distress. However, when these mechanisms are overused or become rigid, they can contribute to the development and maintenance of neurotic symptoms. The persistence of these symptoms often reflects the deep-rooted nature of the original conflicts and the individual's difficulty in finding more adaptive ways to resolve them.

The concept of neuroses is pivotal in psychoanalytic therapy, where the goal is to uncover and work through the underlying unconscious conflicts driving the neurotic symptoms. By bringing these conflicts into consciousness and helping the individual develop healthier coping mechanisms, therapy aims to reduce neurotic anxiety and improve psychological functioning.

In addition to their significance in clinical settings, the understanding of neuroses also offers insights into everyday behaviors and personality dynamics. Recognizing the neurotic patterns in oneself or others can provide valuable perspectives on the psychological factors that influence human behavior, contributing to greater empathy and self-awareness.

Common neurotic patterns, as identified within psychoanalytic theory, manifest in various forms, each reflecting underlying unresolved conflicts and psychological distress. These patterns include anxiety disorders, obsessive-compulsive disorder (OCD), and hysteria, which exhibit distinct behaviors and symptoms but are all rooted in the neurotic attempt to manage overwhelming anxiety.

Anxiety Disorders: Characterized by excessive worry, fear, and anxiety that are disproportionate to the actual threat or danger present. These disorders can manifest in several specific forms, including generalized anxiety disorder (GAD), panic disorder, and social anxiety disorder. Individuals with GAD may experience persistent, uncontrollable worry about a wide range of topics, leading to physical symptoms such as restlessness, muscle tension, and sleep disturbances. Panic disorder is marked by sudden, intense episodes of fear or discomfort, known as panic attacks, accompanied by physical symptoms like heart palpitations, dizziness, and shortness of breath. Social anxiety disorder involves an intense fear of being judged or negatively evaluated in social situations, leading to avoidance of social interactions and significant distress in social contexts.

Obsessive-Compulsive Disorder (OCD): OCD is characterized by recurrent, intrusive thoughts (obsessions) and repetitive behaviors or mental acts (compulsions) that the individual feels driven to perform in response to the obsessions. The compulsions are intended to neutralize or reduce anxiety or prevent a feared event or situation, even though they are usually not realistically connected to what they are designed to neutralize or are clearly excessive. For example, an individual with OCD might have a persistent fear of contamination, leading to compulsive handwashing rituals.

Hysteria (now more commonly referred to as Conversion Disorder or Histrionic Personality Disorder): Historically termed hysteria, this pattern involves the conversion of psychological distress into physical symptoms or the exhibition of attention-seeking behaviors and emotional expression. Conversion disorder is characterized by neurological symptoms (such as paralysis, blindness, or seizures) that are inconsistent with medical diagnosis and are believed to result from psychological conflict. Histrionic Personality Disorder is marked by a pattern of excessive emotionality and attention-seeking, including discomfort with not being the center of attention, inappropriate seductiveness, and rapidly shifting emotions.

These common neurotic patterns reflect the diverse ways in which individuals may attempt to cope with internal conflicts and anxieties. While the specific symptoms and behaviors vary, they all signify an underlying struggle to manage emotional turmoil stemming from unresolved psychosexual conflicts. Psychoanalytic therapy aims to address these underlying issues, offering individuals a path towards understanding and resolving the psychological sources of their neurotic patterns, ultimately leading to healthier coping mechanisms and improved overall functioning.

From a psychoanalytic perspective, character traits are understood as enduring patterns of behavior, thought, and emotion that are shaped by an individual's psychosexual development and the management of instinctual drives. These traits emerge as a result of the complex interplay between the individual's innate dispositions (id) and the experiences encountered during the early stages of development, including the resolutions of conflicts between the id, ego, and superego.

Character traits are deeply ingrained in the personality and influence how individuals perceive the world, interact with others, and cope with internal and external stresses. They are formed as individuals navigate the critical phases of psychosexual development—oral, anal, phallic, latency, and genital stages— each of which presents specific challenges and conflicts that must be resolved. The manner in which these conflicts are managed, along with the successes and failures experienced in each stage, contributes to the development of characteristic ways of thinking, feeling, and behaving.

For example, an individual who received either excessive gratification or experienced significant frustration during the oral stage might develop character traits associated with dependency or aggression. Similarly, the anal stage, centered around issues of control and autonomy related to toilet training, can lead to the development of traits such as obstinacy, meticulousness, or generosity, depending on how the conflicts of this stage are resolved.

The phallic stage, with its focus on identifying with parental figures and resolving the Oedipus or Electra complex, can influence the development of traits related to authority, self-esteem, and sexual identity. The way an individual navigates these early challenges significantly impacts their later personality and character traits.

Psychoanalytic theory posits that character traits are not merely superficial behaviors but reflect deeper psychological processes. They serve both adaptive and defensive functions, helping individuals navigate their social environments while also protecting the ego from anxiety and conflict. For instance, a trait such as assertiveness might reflect an adaptive resolution of oedipal conflicts, while extreme passivity might indicate a defensive response to fears of aggression or competition.

Understanding character traits from a psychoanalytic perspective requires exploring the underlying unconscious motivations and conflicts that give rise to these enduring patterns. This exploration can offer valuable insights into the psychological mechanisms driving an individual's behavior and can be a focal point in psychotherapy, where the goal is to bring unconscious material into consciousness, facilitating personal growth and healthier ways of relating to the self and others.

Character traits, as conceptualized in psychoanalytic theory, are the manifestation of the intricate psychological processes shaped by early experiences, conflicts, and resolutions. They encapsulate the dynamic interplay between instinctual drives and the demands of reality, embodying the individual's unique psychological history and adaptive strategies.

The influence of neuroses and character traits on leadership effectiveness, interpersonal relationships, and the potential for growth or change through coaching is profound and multifaceted. Understanding these psychoanalytic concepts provides valuable insights into the complexities of leadership behavior and the dynamics of coaching relationships, highlighting the psychological underpinnings that can either facilitate or hinder personal and professional development.

Neuroses can significantly affect a leader's effectiveness by shaping their responses to stress, decision-making processes, and ways of relating to team members. For example, a leader with an anxiety disorder may struggle to make decisive choices, particularly under pressure, due to overwhelming fear of negative outcomes. Similarly, leaders exhibiting obsessive-compulsive traits might focus excessively on details, potentially losing sight of the bigger picture and stifling creativity and flexibility within their teams. These neurotic patterns can lead to a work environment characterized by stress, indecision, and inefficiency.

Conversely, certain character traits can enhance leadership effectiveness by promoting resilience, adaptability, and empathetic understanding. Leaders who have developed a strong ego through successful navigation of psychosexual stages may demonstrate balanced assertiveness, the ability to manage conflict constructively, and a capacity for genuine connection with others. These traits foster a positive organizational culture, encourage teamwork, and facilitate effective leadership.

Neuroses and character traits deeply influence the quality of interpersonal relationships within professional contexts. Leaders with unresolved neurotic conflicts may project their insecurities onto colleagues, perceive threats where none exist, or engage in avoidance behaviors, undermining trust and communication. For instance, a leader with a phallic-stage fixation might exhibit competitive or domineering behavior, challenging team cohesion and collaboration.

In contrast, positive character traits such as integrity, fairness, and concern for others' well-being can strengthen relational bonds, build trust, and enhance mutual respect. Leaders who demonstrate these qualities are more likely to inspire loyalty, motivate their teams, and cultivate an environment where open communication and constructive feedback are valued.

Coaching offers a unique opportunity for leaders to explore and address the impact of their neuroses and character traits on their professional and personal lives. A coaching relationship provides a reflective space where leaders can gain awareness of their unconscious motivations, behavioral patterns, and the ways in which these dynamics influence their leadership style and interpersonal relationships. Effective coaching can help leaders recognize and work through neurotic patterns that hinder their effectiveness, guiding them towards healthier coping mechanisms and more adaptive behaviors. Additionally, coaching can support leaders in leveraging their positive character traits, further developing their leadership capabilities, and aligning their actions with their values and goals.

Through the process of coaching, leaders can embark on a journey of personal growth, enhancing their emotional intelligence, improving their relational skills, and increasing their capacity for empathy and understanding. This personal development has a ripple effect, positively impacting team dynamics, organizational culture, and ultimately, leadership effectiveness.

The psychoanalytic concepts of neuroses and character traits offer critical insights into leadership and coaching dynamics. By understanding and addressing these psychological dimensions, leaders can enhance their effectiveness, foster healthier interpersonal relationships, and maximize their potential for growth and change.

Application in Psychoanalytic Therapy

Psychoanalytic therapy, grounded in Freudian theory, aims to uncover and resolve unconscious conflicts that are believed to underlie psychological distress and maladaptive behaviors. This therapeutic approach focuses on bringing to consciousness the repressed material that influences an individual's thoughts, feelings, and actions, thereby allowing for insight, healing, and change. Two of the foundational techniques employed in psychoanalytic therapy to achieve these goals are dream analysis and free association.

Freud considered dreams the "royal road to the unconscious," providing a direct pathway to the hidden desires, thoughts, and conflicts buried deep within the psyche. In dream analysis, the therapist and client work together to explore the content of dreams, both their manifest content (the literal storyline or imagery of the dream) and latent content (the hidden psychological meanings). By interpreting the symbolism in dreams, individuals can gain insight into unresolved issues, repressed desires, and internal conflicts. This process not only fosters a deeper understanding of oneself but also offers clues to the origins of current psychological problems, facilitating their resolution.

The Free Association technique involves the client speaking freely about whatever thoughts, memories, or images come to mind, without censorship or selection. The therapist listens attentively, noting patterns, resistances, and emotional responses that emerge during this process. Free association allows for the spontaneous expression of thoughts and feelings that are usually kept at bay by conscious defenses. By following these threads of thought, clients and therapists can trace back to the unconscious conflicts and repressed material, bringing them into awareness. This uncovering of the unconscious content provides valuable insights that can help address the root causes of the client's distress.

Both dream analysis and free association are predicated on the therapeutic relationship and the safe, non-judgmental space it provides for exploration and discovery. Through these techniques, psychoanalytic therapy delves into the depths of the unconscious, seeking to understand and resolve the complex web of psychological factors that contribute to an individual's current struggles. The ultimate goal is to achieve a greater degree of psychological freedom, allowing for more adaptive coping strategies, healthier relationships, and an enhanced capacity for joy and fulfillment in life.

Psychoanalytic therapy plays a critical role in addressing neuroses and modifying character traits, facilitating healthier personality development and functioning. This therapeutic approach, rooted in the understanding of unconscious processes, developmental conflicts, and the dynamic interplay between the id, ego, and superego, offers a pathway to profound psychological change.

Neuroses, which manifest as anxiety, phobias, obsessions, and other psychological disturbances, often arise from unresolved conflicts and repressed desires dating back to early psychosexual development. Psychoanalytic therapy seeks to uncover the unconscious roots of these neurotic symptoms by exploring the client's past experiences, dreams, and free associations. This process helps to identify the specific conflicts and developmental stages where fixations may have occurred, contributing to the client's current struggles.

By bringing these unconscious conflicts into consciousness, psychoanalytic therapy allows individuals to work through their unresolved issues, rather than continuing to be driven by them unconsciously. As clients gain insight into the origins of their neuroses, they can begin to understand their symptoms in the context of their life story, reducing their power and alleviating distress. Furthermore, therapy provides a supportive environment in which clients can experiment with new ways of thinking and behaving, gradually adopting healthier coping mechanisms and responses.

Character traits, those enduring patterns of thought, emotion, and behavior, are also shaped by early experiences and the resolution of psychosexual conflicts. Psychoanalytic therapy addresses maladaptive character traits by examining their roots in the client's developmental history and unconscious conflicts. This exploration can reveal how certain traits may have served as defenses against anxiety or as ways to manage difficult relationships and situations.

As therapy progresses, clients are encouraged to reflect on how these traits affect their current functioning and relationships. The therapeutic relationship itself provides a corrective emotional experience, where clients can safely explore alternative ways of relating and responding. Through this process, individuals can develop greater flexibility in their behaviors and attitudes, gradually integrating aspects of their personality that were previously cut off or underdeveloped.

The ultimate goal of psychoanalytic therapy is to foster a more integrated and balanced personality, where the individual has greater access to their thoughts and feelings and can navigate their relationships and life challenges more effectively. This is achieved through the resolution of unconscious conflicts, the development of insight, and the modification of maladaptive character traits.

By addressing the root causes of psychological distress and fostering a deeper understanding of oneself, psychoanalytic therapy promotes healing and growth. Clients emerge from the process with a stronger sense of self, improved emotional regulation, and a greater capacity for intimacy and creativity. In this way, psychoanalytic therapy contributes not only to the resolution of specific psychological symptoms but also to the overall enrichment of the individual's life, enhancing their ability to engage with the world in a more authentic and fulfilling way.

Relevance to Leadership and Executive Coaching

Applying psychoanalytic concepts of personality to understand leadership involves delving into the unconscious motivations, developmental histories, and the dynamic interplay of the id, ego, and superego that underpin complex leader behaviors and interpersonal dynamics. This psychoanalytic lens offers profound insights into the nuanced and often unconscious factors that influence leadership styles, decision-making processes, and the quality of leader-follower relationships.

1. Unconscious Motivations: Leaders, like all individuals, are driven by a complex mix of conscious and unconscious motivations. Understanding these motivations requires exploring the leader's early psychosexual development and the resolution of conflicts inherent to each stage. For instance, a leader with a strong need for control and perfection may be unconsciously motivated by anxieties rooted in the anal stage of development, where issues of control and autonomy are paramount. Similarly, a leader who consistently seeks validation and admiration from their followers might be influenced by unresolved oedipal dynamics from the phallic stage, reflecting a deep-seated need for approval and recognition.

2. Defense Mechanisms: Leaders also employ various defense mechanisms to manage internal conflicts and protect their self-esteem. For example, a leader who frequently uses rationalization may justify questionable decisions or failures by attributing them to external factors, thereby avoiding confrontation with their own shortcomings. Projection is another defense mechanism where a leader might attribute their own unacceptable feelings or thoughts to their followers, leading to misunderstandings and conflict within the team. Recognizing these defense mechanisms can illuminate the psychological underpinnings of certain leader behaviors and attitudes, offering pathways to more adaptive coping strategies and interpersonal interactions.

3. Id, Ego, and Superego Dynamics: The balance between the id, ego, and superego within a leader plays a crucial role in shaping their leadership style and effectiveness. A leader dominated by id impulses might exhibit impulsivity and aggression, prioritizing personal desires over the team's needs or organizational goals. In contrast, a leader with an overly dominant superego may be excessively critical and rigid,

imposing unrealistic standards on themselves and their followers. Ideally, a leader's ego effectively mediates between these forces, balancing personal desires, moral values, and the realities of the leadership context to make decisions that are both ethical and pragmatic.

4. Interpersonal Dynamics: The psychoanalytic concept of transference and countertransference also sheds light on the complex interpersonal dynamics between leaders and followers. Followers may unconsciously transfer feelings related to past authority figures onto the leader, which can color their perceptions and reactions in ways that are unrelated to the leader's actual behavior. Similarly, leaders may experience countertransference reactions to their followers, which can influence their leadership approach and the quality of their interactions. Awareness of these dynamics can help leaders and followers navigate their relationship more effectively, fostering greater understanding and collaboration.

Psychoanalytic concepts provide valuable tools for understanding the deep-seated influences on leader behavior, motivations, and interpersonal dynamics. By exploring the unconscious motivations, defense mechanisms, and the interplay of the id, ego, and superego, leaders can gain insights into their own behavior and its impact on others. This understanding can facilitate personal growth, improve leadership effectiveness, and enhance the overall functioning of the team or organization.

Insights from psychoanalytic personality theory offer a rich and nuanced framework for executive coaching, providing deep understanding and strategies for enhancing self-awareness, emotional regulation, and conflict resolution. By integrating psychoanalytic concepts, executive coaches can help leaders explore the unconscious motivations, conflicts, and defense mechanisms that influence their behavior and leadership style, leading to more effective and emotionally intelligent leadership.

Psychoanalytic theory emphasizes the importance of understanding the unconscious aspects of the psyche, including repressed desires and unresolved conflicts from early psychosexual development stages. In coaching, this insight encourages leaders to delve into their unconscious motivations and recognize how these hidden forces shape their perceptions, decisions, and actions. For example, a leader might discover that their need for control and perfection stems from anxiety related to early childhood experiences during the anal stage. By becoming aware of these underlying motivations, leaders can work towards modifying their behaviors in ways that are more aligned with their conscious values and goals, enhancing their leadership effectiveness.

The psychoanalytic concept of defense mechanisms provides a framework for understanding how individuals manage emotional distress and protect their self-esteem. In the context of executive coaching, exploring these mechanisms can help leaders identify maladaptive ways they might be coping with stress or emotional challenges, such as by using denial, projection, or rationalization. Coaches can guide leaders in recognizing these patterns and developing healthier strategies for emotional regulation, such as mindfulness, seeking constructive feedback, and expressing emotions in appropriate ways. Improved emotional regulation allows leaders to respond to workplace challenges with greater composure and resilience, fostering a positive organizational climate.

Psychoanalytic insights into transference and countertransference can significantly enhance leaders' abilities to navigate interpersonal conflicts. Understanding that conflicts may be influenced by unconscious projections—where feelings from past relationships are displaced onto present interactions—can help leaders and their followers recognize the deeper emotional undercurrents at play. Executive coaches can use these concepts to help leaders develop strategies for addressing and resolving conflicts that consider both the surface-level issues and the underlying emotional dynamics. This approach promotes more empathetic and effective communication, leading to resolutions that acknowledge and address the needs and concerns of all parties involved.

Recognizing the role of the ego in mediating between the id's instinctual drives and the superego's moral standards can aid leaders in finding balanced solutions to conflicts, negotiating the often-competing demands of personal desires, ethical considerations, and organizational goals.

The application of psychoanalytic personality theory in executive coaching provides leaders with profound insights into their psychological makeup, offering tools for personal growth and enhanced leadership capabilities. By focusing on self-awareness, emotional regulation, and conflict resolution, leaders can cultivate a leadership style that is not only effective but also authentic and responsive to the needs of their teams and organizations. This psychoanalytically informed approach enriches the coaching process, leading to more meaningful and lasting changes in leadership behavior.

Case Study 1: Transformation Through Uncovering Unconscious Motivations

John, a senior executive in a multinational corporation, struggled with delegation and trust, often micromanaging his team to the point of exhaustion. Despite his successes, his leadership style led to high turnover rates within his team and a tense work environment. Through executive coaching grounded in psychoanalytic theory, John began to explore the roots of his compulsive need for control.

The coaching process involved deep reflection on John's early life experiences, particularly his relationship with his parents, who were highly critical and controlling. This exploration revealed that John's leadership style was significantly influenced by a deep-seated fear of failure and a strong desire to meet his parents' high expectations, even in adulthood. These unconscious motivations drove him to exert excessive control over his work environment as a means to avoid the perceived threat of failure and criticism.

Through understanding these underlying dynamics, John worked with his coach to develop strategies for building trust in his team and gradually relinquishing control. This process involved not only cognitive-behavioral techniques but also a reevaluation of his self-worth independent of external achievements. Over time, John experienced a profound transformation in his leadership behavior, becoming more trusting and supportive. This shift led to improved team morale, increased productivity, and a more positive organizational culture, demonstrating the profound impact of addressing unconscious motivations in leadership development.

Case Study 2: Enhancing Emotional Intelligence Through Insight into Defense Mechanisms

Sara, a tech startup founder, was known for her visionary ideas but had difficulty managing her emotions under stress. Her reactions ranged from intense anger to withdrawal, affecting her relationships with co-founders and employees. Recognizing the need for change, Sara engaged in executive coaching with a psychoanalytic approach to enhance her emotional intelligence.

The coaching sessions focused on understanding Sara's use of defense mechanisms, particularly projection and regression, as ways to cope with stress and conflict. By reflecting on specific incidents where her emotional responses were disproportionate, Sara and her coach uncovered a pattern of projecting her insecurities onto others and regressing to childlike behaviors when feeling threatened.

This exploration traced back to Sara's childhood experiences of feeling powerless and criticized, leading her to develop these defense mechanisms as protective strategies. With these insights, Sara worked on recognizing the early signs of her defensive responses and employing healthier emotional regulation strategies, such as seeking feedback and expressing her needs directly.

As Sara became more adept at managing her emotions and understanding the origins of her reactions, she noticed a significant improvement in her interpersonal relationships and leadership effectiveness. Her ability to remain calm and communicative, even in challenging situations, inspired confidence and respect in her team, fostering a collaborative and innovative work environment. This case illustrates the transformative power of psychoanalytic insights in enhancing leadership through greater emotional intelligence and self-awareness.

Conclusion

This chapter has explored the depths of psychoanalytic theory to illuminate the complex landscape of personality, unraveling how unconscious processes, developmental stages, and the dynamic interplay between the id, ego, and superego shape individual behaviors, motivations, and interpersonal dynamics. Through the exploration of neuroses, character traits, and the pivotal stages of psychosexual development, we have seen how early experiences and unresolved conflicts contribute to the mosaic of human personality.

The application of psychoanalytic concepts to the understanding of personality offers invaluable insights into the nuanced and often hidden aspects of human behavior. For leaders and clients in coaching contexts, this psychoanalytic lens provides a powerful tool for self-exploration and growth, enabling a deeper comprehension of the unconscious motivations and defense mechanisms that influence decision-making, relationship-building, and leadership style.

In leadership development, a psychoanalytic understanding of personality can illuminate the root causes of various leadership challenges, from difficulties in delegation and trust to struggles with emotional regulation under stress. By uncovering and addressing these underlying issues, leaders can undergo profound transformations, enhancing their effectiveness, fostering healthier team dynamics, and contributing to a more positive organizational culture.

Similarly, in coaching contexts, psychoanalytic insights into personality can guide clients toward greater self-awareness and emotional intelligence. By exploring the origins of their behaviors and attitudes, clients can develop a richer understanding of themselves, leading to more adaptive coping strategies, improved interpersonal relationships, and a greater capacity for personal and professional growth.

The value of a psychoanalytic understanding of personality lies in its ability to provide a comprehensive and deeply nuanced view of individuals. This perspective not only enriches our comprehension of human behavior but also offers practical pathways for addressing psychological challenges, facilitating personal development, and enhancing leadership and coaching practices. Through the psychoanalytic exploration of personality, individuals can achieve a greater sense of self-awareness, emotional well-being, and fulfillment in their personal and professional lives.

As we conclude this exploration into the depths of psychoanalytic theory and its application to personality, it becomes evident that the insights gleaned from this perspective hold immense potential for catalyzing personal and professional growth, enhancing leadership capabilities, and fostering more effective coaching relationships. The journey into the unconscious, with its intricate web of desires, conflicts, and motivations, offers a unique lens through which to understand the underpinnings of our actions and interactions. This deep dive not only illuminates the complexities of human behavior but also provides a roadmap for transformative change.

The application of psychoanalytic concepts encourages individuals to embark on a profound journey of self-discovery, revealing the unconscious factors that shape their thoughts, feelings, and behaviors. This process of introspection and insight fosters a heightened sense of self-awareness, which is instrumental in personal development. As individuals gain a deeper understanding of themselves, they are better positioned to navigate their internal landscapes, leading to more adaptive coping mechanisms, emotional resilience, and a richer, more nuanced approach to interpersonal relationships.

In leadership, the psychoanalytic perspective offers invaluable tools for understanding the psychological dynamics that influence leadership styles and effectiveness. Leaders who engage with these concepts can achieve a greater alignment between their unconscious motivations and their conscious actions, resulting in leadership that is both authentic and responsive to the needs of their teams. This alignment enhances the leader's ability to inspire trust, motivate performance, and cultivate a positive organizational culture, ultimately driving success and fulfillment for both the leader and their team.

The integration of psychoanalytic theory into coaching practices enriches the coach-client relationship, enabling coaches to address not only the explicit goals of their clients but also the deeper, often unconscious barriers to achieving those goals. This approach allows for interventions that are tailored to the unique psychological makeup of each client, facilitating lasting change and empowering clients to reach their full potential. The final section of this chapter underscores the transformative power of psychoanalytic concepts in personal and professional contexts. By bridging the gap between the depths of the unconscious and the surface of conscious awareness, psychoanalytic theory opens up new pathways for growth, leadership development, and coaching effectiveness. Through this exploration, individuals, leaders, and coaches alike can unlock new levels of understanding, empathy, and impact, fostering environments where growth and development flourish.

Part II: Psychoanalysis in the Context of Leadership

This section of our book opens a compelling dialogue on leadership through the psychoanalytic perspective, offering a profound lens to examine the intricate, often unconscious psychological dynamics that underpin leadership behavior and the leader-follower relationship. Our exploration is anchored in the conviction that leadership transcends mere behavioral acts or skills—it is deeply intertwined with the leader's psychological fabric, encompassing unconscious drives, fears, and desires.

Our objective is to dissect leadership as a psychological phenomenon, delving into the unconscious factors that mold the leader-follower dynamic, and scrutinizing the complex interplay of authority, power, and dependency within leadership contexts. We embark on this journey with a view to redefine leadership through a psychoanalytic lens—beginning with its definition as an expression of the leader's inner psychological world.

Leadership, when viewed through a psychoanalytic lens, emerges not just as a set of external behaviors or skills, but as a reflection of the leader's deep-seated psychological makeup. This section explores how a leader's decision-making, communication style, and conflict resolution approach are influenced by layers of unconscious processes.

We delve into the linkage between psychoanalytic theories of personality and diverse leadership styles, illustrating how leaders' early life experiences and underlying unconscious motivations sculpt their leadership approach. This exploration sheds light on the profound impact of the unconscious on leadership effectiveness.

The dynamics between leaders and followers often transcend conscious interactions, deeply rooted in the psychoanalytic phenomena of transference and projection. Followers may unconsciously displace feelings and expectations from past authority figures onto leaders, while leaders might project their own unacknowledged desires and fears onto their followers.

We introduce the concept of the "unconscious contract," an unspoken agreement laden with expectations and behaviors influenced by these unseen dynamics. This section unveils how identification and idealization processes, underpinned by psychological mechanisms, play out in the leader-follower relationship, impacting organizational dynamics. The essence of authority in leadership, examined through a psychoanalytic prism, reveals its psychological underpinnings. This section explores how leaders are perceived as authoritative figures and delves into the unconscious factors that contribute to the acceptance or rejection of their authority.

We examine the intricate role of power in leadership, focusing on the negotiation of power between leaders and followers and the unconscious dynamics that influence these exchanges. Additionally, the exploration of dependency needs highlights how both leaders and followers navigate desires for approval, guidance, and security, influencing their interactions and the potential for both constructive and destructive outcomes.

Utilizing Jung's concept of the shadow, this section ventures into the darker, often overlooked aspects of leadership. It examines how the unacknowledged parts of a leader's personality—the shadow—can influence leadership behavior and organizational culture. The discussion extends to how leaders might project their shadow onto followers or the organization, leading to challenges such as toxic leadership behaviors and organizational dysfunction.

This concluding section offers strategies for leaders to enhance their self-awareness and integrate insights from their unconscious into more effective leadership practices. It provides guidance on developing healthier leader-follower dynamics and navigating the complex terrain of power and dependency with a psychoanalytic understanding.

In the intricate tapestry of leadership, the styles and approaches leaders adopt are not solely the outcome of deliberate strategies or conscious decision-making. Beneath the surface of these observable behaviors lie the profound influences of the leader's unconscious processes—hidden currents that shape leadership in ways not immediately apparent. Recognizing and understanding these underlying forces is crucial for enhancing leadership effectiveness and fostering personal growth. This section also sets out to explore the multifaceted relationship between various leadership styles and the unconscious, aiming to reveal how deep-seated unconscious factors sculpt these styles and impact leadership effectiveness. Through a psychoanalytic lens, we embark on a journey to uncover the hidden dimensions of leadership, providing insights into the psychological foundations that underpin leadership behaviors and the dynamic between leaders and their followers.

By delving into the psychoanalytic perspective, this chapter illuminates the significant role that unconscious motivations, conflicts, and desires play in defining leadership styles. From the influence of early childhood experiences and ego development to the deployment of defense mechanisms, we explore how these unconscious elements manifest in distinct leadership approaches. Our exploration spans the spectrum of common leadership styles—transformational, transactional, autocratic, democratic, and laissez-faire—examining them through the insightful lens of psychoanalytic theory.

As we navigate this complex terrain, we aim to shed light on the profound impact of unconscious processes on leadership effectiveness. We delve into how unconscious biases can subtly steer a leader's decision-making, how emotional intelligence is intertwined with the management of unconscious emotions, and how the use of defense mechanisms can both protect and hinder a leader's effectiveness. Through case studies of historical and contemporary leaders, along with personal reflections from leaders who have engaged with psychoanalytic therapy or coaching, we offer concrete examples of how understanding the unconscious can transform leadership practice.

This section also provides strategies for leaders to enhance self-awareness and integrate insights from their unconscious into their leadership approach. By reflecting on unconscious motivations and employing psychoanalytic therapy, coaching, and reflective practices, leaders can embark on a transformative journey toward more effective and authentic leadership.

We underscore the invaluable contribution of psychoanalytic insights to our understanding of leadership behavior and the personal and professional development of leaders. By continuing to explore the unconscious, leaders and coaches can unlock new depths of leadership excellence, navigating the challenges and rewards of this profound journey with commitment and insight. This exploration not only enriches the leader's personal growth but also promises to elevate the quality of leadership and organizational culture, making the journey into the unconscious a rewarding endeavor for those dedicated to achieving the pinnacle of leadership excellence.

Chapter 4: The Psychoanalytic Perspective on Leadership

In the vast and multifaceted world of leadership, the psychoanalytic perspective emerges as a profoundly insightful lens, offering a depth of understanding that transcends conventional analyses. This unique approach delves into the complex tapestry of the human psyche, illuminating the deeper, often unconscious, psychological dynamics that significantly influence leadership behavior and the intricacies of the leader-follower relationship. By drawing on psychoanalytic theory, this chapter aims to unravel the subtle forces beneath the surface of observable leadership actions and decisions, exploring how unconscious motives, fears, desires, and conflicts shape the way leaders navigate their roles and interact with their followers.

The psychoanalytic perspective on leadership invites us to consider leadership not merely as a set of skills or behaviors but as a manifestation of the leader's inner psychological world. It posits that the roots of leadership styles, decision-making processes, and relational dynamics lie deep within the unconscious mind, influenced by past experiences, emotional residues, and unresolved conflicts. This approach emphasizes the significance of understanding these hidden psychological underpinnings to fully grasp the complexities of leadership and to foster more effective, empathetic, and adaptive leadership practices.

In embarking on this exploration, the chapter sets out to examine the leader-follower dynamic through a psychoanalytic lens, shedding light on how unconscious transference and countertransference processes play out within this relationship, influencing perceptions, expectations, and interactions on both sides. It delves into the psychological constructs of authority, power, and dependency, unraveling how these elements are experienced and negotiated within the leadership context, often driven by unconscious motivations and fears.

Through the psychoanalytic perspective, we gain invaluable insights into the psychological phenomenon of leadership, offering a richer, more nuanced understanding of what drives leaders, how they influence and are influenced by their followers, and how deep-seated psychological patterns impact organizational culture and effectiveness. This exploration not only enriches our theoretical knowledge of leadership but also provides practical pathways for leaders seeking to understand themselves and their followers better, ultimately leading to more profound personal growth and enhanced leadership effectiveness.

The primary objective of this chapter is to explore leadership as a deeply psychological phenomenon, offering a lens through which we can better understand the complexities and nuances of leadership beyond the surface level. By delving into the psychoanalytic perspective, we aim to uncover the unconscious factors that significantly influence leadership behavior and the intricate dynamics between leaders and their followers. This exploration is not only about recognizing the existence of these unconscious elements but also about understanding how they manifest in the day-to-day reality of leadership and organizational life.

A key focus of the chapter is to examine the leader-follower dynamic, a relationship that, while visibly shaped by external actions and verbal communications, is profoundly influenced by underlying, unconscious processes. These processes include transference and countertransference dynamics, where both leaders and followers project onto each other feelings, desires, and fears rooted in past experiences, significantly impacting their interactions and the overall leadership dynamic.

The chapter seeks to unravel the complex interplay of authority, power, and dependency within leadership contexts. Authority is not merely a position or title; it's a psychological state influenced by the leader's and followers' unconscious perceptions and reactions. Similarly, power dynamics within leadership are deeply embedded in the psychological underpinnings of both the leader's and the followers' actions and attitudes. Dependency, often overlooked in discussions of leadership, plays a crucial role in shaping the leader-follower relationship, with both parties harboring unconscious dependency needs that can either facilitate or hinder effective leadership and collaboration.

By achieving these objectives, the chapter aims to provide readers with a deeper, more nuanced understanding of leadership as a psychological phenomenon. This understanding allows for a more empathetic and insightful approach to leadership, encouraging leaders to reflect on their own unconscious motivations and how these might affect their leadership style, decision-making, and relationships with followers. Ultimately, this exploration of the psychoanalytic perspective on leadership seeks to enrich our comprehension of leadership and offer avenues for personal and professional growth, improved leadership capabilities, and the development of healthier, more productive leader-follower dynamics.

Leadership as a Psychological Phenomenon

Defining leadership through a psychoanalytic lens invites us to venture beyond conventional interpretations that focus primarily on observable behaviors, skills, or traits. Instead, it positions leadership as a profound expression of the leader's psychological makeup, intricately woven from the fabric of their innermost unconscious drives, fears, and desires. This perspective illuminates leadership as a deeply personal journey, one that is as much about navigating the complexities of the human psyche as it is about guiding others or achieving organizational goals.

From this vantage point, leadership is understood not merely in terms of what leaders do or the strategies they employ but as a reflection of who they are at their core—their values, conflicts, and emotional landscapes. The psychoanalytic lens peels back the layers of the leader's persona, revealing how early life experiences, unresolved psychological conflicts, and the dynamic interplay between the id, ego, and superego shape their approach to leadership. It acknowledges that leaders, like all individuals, are driven by a mix of conscious intentions and unconscious motivations that can significantly influence their behavior and decision-making processes.

Leadership, therefore, becomes a manifestation of the leader's ongoing engagement with their unconscious. This includes how they cope with anxiety, manage internal conflicts, and fulfill their instinctual desires within the socially acceptable bounds of their role. For instance, a leader's tendency to assert control or seek consensus may stem from deep-seated needs for security or approval, rooted in early developmental experiences.

By defining leadership as an expression of the leader's psychological makeup, we open the door to a richer understanding of leadership dynamics. This approach encourages a more introspective and reflective form of leadership practice, where leaders are prompted to explore the origins of their motivations, fears, and desires. Such exploration can lead to greater self-awareness, emotional regulation, and empathy, ultimately enhancing the leader's effectiveness and fostering more meaningful connections with followers.

Viewing leadership through a psychoanalytic lens does not diminish the importance of skills, behaviors, or competencies. Instead, it enriches our understanding of these elements by situating them within the broader context of the leader's psychological world, offering insights into the complex human dimensions of leadership. This holistic view underscores the importance of psychological growth and self-discovery in the pursuit of effective leadership, highlighting the intertwined nature of personal development and leadership excellence.

The influence of unconscious processes on a leader's decision-making, communication style, and approach to conflict is profound and multifaceted. Rooted in the depths of the leader's psyche, these processes are the silent drivers behind many aspects of leadership behavior, often operating outside the leader's conscious awareness. By delving into the psychoanalytic understanding of these unconscious dynamics, we can gain valuable insights into the complexities of leadership.

Decision-Making

A leader's decision-making process is significantly shaped by unconscious motivations and desires. Unresolved conflicts from early psychosexual development stages, for instance, can manifest as a predisposition towards risk-taking or aversion to change. Leaders might unconsciously gravitate toward decisions that reaffirm their sense of identity or alleviate underlying anxieties, rather than those based purely on rational analysis or organizational needs. This dynamic can be particularly pronounced in high-stress situations where the unconscious mind exerts greater influence, leading to decisions that may reflect personal unresolved issues rather than objective judgment.

Communication Style

The way leaders communicate with their teams and peers is also deeply influenced by unconscious processes. For example, a leader who experienced rejection or criticism in early life may develop a communication style characterized by defensiveness or aggression, as a way to protect themselves from perceived threats to their self-esteem. Conversely, leaders with a strong need for approval, rooted in their unconscious desire to please authority figures from their past, may adopt a more appeasing or overly conciliatory communication style. These patterns, while unintentional, can significantly impact the leader's ability to connect with and effectively lead their team.

Approach to Conflict

Leaders' responses to conflict often reveal the influence of unconscious processes. Defense mechanisms such as projection, where leaders attribute their own unacceptable feelings or thoughts to others, can escalate conflicts and hinder resolution. Similarly, leaders may unconsciously regress to earlier modes of behavior under stress, displaying reactions that are disproportionate to the actual conflict at hand. The leader's approach to conflict may also be shaped by their fundamental beliefs about authority and power, which are formed in early childhood and operate unconsciously, influencing how they navigate disagreements and assert their leadership in challenging situations.

Understanding the influence of these unconscious processes requires leaders to engage in introspection and self-exploration, often with the help of coaching or psychotherapy. By bringing these unconscious dynamics to light, leaders can develop a more nuanced understanding of their own behavior and its impact on their leadership. This awareness enables them to make more informed choices, communicate more effectively, and handle conflict with greater empathy and insight. Ultimately, acknowledging and addressing the role of unconscious processes in leadership not only enhances individual leadership effectiveness but also contributes to building healthier, more resilient organizational cultures.

Psychoanalytic theories of personality provide a compelling framework for understanding the diverse array of leadership styles observed in organizational settings. These theories suggest that a leader's approach to their role is deeply influenced by their early life experiences, unconscious motivations, and the complex interplay of their id, ego, and superego. By examining leadership styles through the lens of psychoanalytic personality theory, we can uncover how the psychological makeup of a leader shapes their behavior, decision-making, and overall leadership effectiveness.

1. Transformational Leadership and the Quest for Significance

Transformational leaders, known for inspiring and motivating followers to exceed their own interests for the sake of the organization, may be driven by an unconscious desire for significance and validation, possibly stemming from early experiences of feeling undervalued or a lack of attention. Such leaders might channel their need for affirmation into positive endeavors, striving to achieve recognition through the success and development of their followers and organization.

2. Transactional Leadership and the Control Dynamics

Transactional leaders, who focus on clear exchanges between the leader and followers to achieve routine organizational goals, may exhibit an unconscious need for control and order. This need could originate from experiences during the anal stage of development, where issues of control and autonomy are prominent. Leaders with a transactional approach might unconsciously seek to recreate an environment where clear rules and structured interactions provide a sense of security and predictability.

3. Autocratic Leadership and Authority Issues

Autocratic leaders, who make decisions unilaterally and maintain strict control over followers, may be influenced by unresolved authority issues from their childhood. An unconscious struggle with authority figures from the past can manifest as a need to assert dominance and control in the workplace, compensating for feelings of powerlessness or insecurity experienced during early developmental stages.

4. Democratic Leadership and the Desire for Connectedness

Democratic leaders, who prioritize participation and consensus in decision-making, may be driven by an unconscious desire for connectedness and approval. This leadership style may reflect an adaptive response to early relational dynamics, where the leader learned to value collaboration and validation from peers or authority figures. Such leaders may unconsciously seek to recreate a harmonious, inclusive environment that mirrors their idealized early experiences of being valued and heard.

5. Laissez-Faire Leadership and Avoidance of Conflict

Laissez-faire leaders, characterized by a hands-off approach and reluctance to make decisions, may be influenced by a deep-seated avoidance of conflict and responsibility. This style could stem from unconscious fears of criticism or failure, rooted in early experiences where taking initiative was met with negative outcomes. Leaders adopting this style may unconsciously seek to protect themselves from the anxiety associated with decision-making and assertiveness.

Understanding the link between psychoanalytic theories of personality and leadership styles allows for a deeper exploration of the psychological underpinnings of leadership behavior. It highlights how unconscious motivations shaped by early life experiences can influence a leader's approach to their role, impacting their effectiveness and the dynamics within their teams. Recognizing and addressing these unconscious factors can facilitate personal growth and development for leaders, enabling them to adopt more adaptive and effective leadership styles.

The Leader-Follower Dynamic: Unconscious Factors at Play

Transference and projection are psychoanalytic concepts that play a significant role in the dynamics of leadership, deeply influencing the interactions between leaders and their followers. These unconscious processes can shape perceptions, behaviors, and the overall climate within organizations, offering insight into the complex psychological undercurrents of leadership.

Transference occurs when followers unconsciously transfer feelings, expectations, and desires originally associated with significant authority figures from their past (such as parents or previous leaders) onto their current leaders. This process can significantly affect how followers perceive and react to their leaders, often coloring these interactions with emotions and expectations that are not directly related to the leaders' actual behaviors or intentions. For example, a follower who experienced authoritarian parenting might perceive their leader's assertiveness as oppressive or threatening, regardless of the leader's actual approach or intent. Conversely, a follower who lacked supportive figures in their past might idealize their leader, attributing them with qualities of nurturance or protection that exceed reality.

Projection involves leaders unconsciously projecting their own fears, desires, and unresolved conflicts onto their followers. This can manifest in various ways, such as a leader who fears incompetence seeing their own perceived inadequacies in their team members, leading to undue criticism or micromanagement. Similarly, a leader who desires affirmation might project their need for approval onto their followers, expecting constant reassurance or agreement, which can stifle open communication and innovation. Projection can distort a leader's perception of their followers' capabilities and motivations, leading to misinterpretations and conflicts that are rooted more in the leader's internal struggles than in the followers' actual behaviors.

Both transference and projection can have profound implications for the leader-follower relationship, influencing leadership effectiveness, team dynamics, and organizational outcomes. These processes can create misunderstandings, perpetuate conflicts, and hinder the development of healthy, productive working relationships. However, when leaders and followers become aware of these unconscious dynamics, they can begin to address and mitigate their impacts.

Awareness allows for the exploration and reinterpretation of these transferred feelings and projected desires, facilitating more authentic and constructive interactions between leaders and followers. Leaders who understand and acknowledge the potential for transference and projection can develop more empathetic and responsive leadership styles, fostering an environment where followers feel understood and valued for their genuine contributions. Similarly, followers who recognize their own tendencies to transfer feelings onto their leaders can take steps to differentiate past experiences from current realities, leading to more objective and rewarding engagements with leadership.

Transference and projection are powerful psychoanalytic processes that influence the fabric of leadership and follower dynamics. By understanding and addressing these unconscious underpinnings, both leaders and followers can work towards more effective, fulfilling relationships that enhance personal growth and organizational success.

Identification and idealization are psychological processes that play critical roles in the dynamics between leaders and their followers, significantly influencing organizational behavior and culture. These processes stem from deep-seated psychological needs and can profoundly affect how followers perceive and interact with leaders, as well as how leaders are motivated to behave in their roles.

Identification occurs when followers adopt aspects of the leader's attitudes, behaviors, or characteristics as their own. This process is driven by the followers' unconscious desire to be associated with someone they perceive as successful, powerful, or admirable. From a psychoanalytic perspective, identification is a fundamental mechanism of personality development, allowing individuals to expand their sense of self by integrating qualities of others whom they admire or respect. In organizational contexts, followers might identify with leaders who embody the values, skills, or attributes they aspire to develop. This identification can foster a sense of belonging and loyalty within the team, motivating followers to align their efforts with the leader's vision and goals. However, excessive identification may lead to a loss of individuality among followers, stifling diversity of thought and creativity.

Idealization involves followers attributing exaggeratedly positive qualities to leaders, often viewing them as infallible or superhuman. This process is rooted in the followers' unconscious need for security and stability, looking up to the leader as a protective figure who can provide guidance and reassurance. Idealization can be linked to early childhood experiences where parents or caregivers were perceived as all-knowing and all-powerful. In the workplace, followers may idealize leaders as a way to cope with uncertainty, complexity, or anxiety. While idealization can temporarily boost a leader's authority and influence, it can also create unrealistic expectations, setting leaders up for failure in the eyes of their followers. Moreover, it can hinder critical feedback and open communication, as followers may be reluctant to challenge or question the idealized leader.

Both identification and idealization have significant implications for organizational dynamics. Identification can promote a strong, cohesive organizational culture with shared values and goals, enhancing teamwork and collective effort. However, it requires careful management to ensure that it does not suppress individuality and critical thinking. Idealization, on the other hand, may initially unify followers behind a charismatic leader, but over time it can lead to disillusionment and disengagement if the leader fails to live up to the idealized image.

Leaders who are aware of these dynamics can take steps to foster a healthy level of identification among their followers, emphasizing shared values while encouraging diversity of thought and expression. They can also manage idealization by being transparent about their limitations, sharing vulnerabilities, and promoting a culture of realism and constructive feedback. Understanding the psychological mechanisms behind identification and idealization, and their impact on organizational dynamics, provides valuable insights for leaders aiming to develop effective, authentic, and resilient leadership practices. By navigating these processes thoughtfully, leaders can cultivate a balanced organizational culture that values both unity and individuality, driving success and fulfillment for both leaders and their followers.

The concept of the "unconscious contract" refers to the unspoken, unconscious agreements that exist between leaders and followers, significantly shaping expectations, behaviors, and the dynamics of their relationship. This psychological contract operates beneath the surface of conscious awareness, driven by the implicit needs, desires, and fears of both parties. Rooted in early developmental experiences and the internalization of societal norms, these contracts dictate a set of mutual expectations that are not formally articulated but are deeply felt and adhered to by both leaders and followers.

The unconscious contract is forged from the complex interplay of transference and projection, where leaders and followers bring their past experiences, particularly those involving authority figures, into the present relationship. Followers might, for example, unconsciously expect leaders to provide the same protection and guidance they sought from parental figures, while leaders may unconsciously seek the admiration and compliance they associate with their own idealized self or authority figures from their past. These expectations often go unvoiced but exert a powerful influence on how leaders and followers interact, the roles they assume, and the way power is exercised and accepted within the relationship.

The dynamics of the unconscious contract can profoundly impact organizational life, influencing leadership effectiveness, team cohesion, and the overall cultural atmosphere. When the terms of this contract align well with conscious goals and organizational values, they can foster a sense of security, loyalty, and shared purpose among team members. However, discrepancies between the unconscious contract and the conscious expectations or goals of the organization can lead to confusion, frustration, and unmet needs, potentially undermining leadership effectiveness and organizational performance.

Understanding and addressing the unconscious contract requires leaders to engage in deep self-reflection and to cultivate an awareness of their own unconscious motivations and those of their followers. This process can be facilitated by psychoanalytic coaching or therapy, which provides the tools to uncover and reinterpret the unconscious agreements shaping the leader-follower dynamic. By bringing these contracts into conscious awareness, leaders and followers can renegotiate their terms, creating a more explicit and mutually satisfying agreement that aligns with individual and organizational goals.

The unconscious contract is a foundational element of the psychoanalytic perspective on leadership, offering a nuanced understanding of the deep-seated psychological forces that underpin leader-follower relationships. By exploring and renegotiating these unconscious agreements, leaders can foster healthier, more productive relationships with their followers, enhancing organizational effectiveness and creating a culture of openness, trust, and mutual respect.

Authority, Power, and Dependency

The psychological basis of authority in leadership is deeply embedded in the intricate web of individual and collective unconscious processes. Understanding the dynamics that influence how leaders are perceived and accepted as authoritative figures requires delving into the realms of early developmental experiences, projection, idealization, transference, and the leader's own self-concept.

Early interactions with parental and other authority figures significantly shape an individual's perceptions and attitudes towards authority. These foundational experiences influence whether a leader is readily accepted or met with resistance. Leaders who evoke positive associations with supportive and fair authority figures from one's past are more likely to be embraced, whereas those who unconsciously mirror negative aspects of past authority figures might provoke rejection.

Projection and idealization further complicate the landscape of authority. Followers often project their own desires and fears onto leaders, imbuing them with qualities they admire or aspire to. This process can elevate a leader's status, but it also sets the stage for potential disillusionment if the leader fails to meet these idealized expectations.

Transference dynamics, where followers transfer unresolved emotional conflicts from past relationships onto their leaders, also play a pivotal role. Leaders adept at navigating these dynamics, providing empathetic and understanding responses, are more likely to solidify their authority.

The collective unconscious, with its archetypical images of authority, offers another layer of psychological influence. Leaders who embody these archetypes can tap into deep, shared psychic structures, resonating with followers on a symbolic level and enhancing their perceived authority. Lastly, a leader's self-concept, including unconscious beliefs about their worthiness and capability to lead, significantly impacts their authority. Leaders struggling with internal doubts may inadvertently undermine their authority, while those with a secure and integrated sense of self are more likely to project the confidence and competence necessary for effective leadership.

The establishment and maintenance of authority in leadership are contingent upon a complex interplay of psychological factors that extend far beyond conscious strategies and behaviors. Leaders who are mindful of these undercurrents and adept at managing them can foster a more authentic and effective leadership presence, enhancing their relationships with followers and promoting a healthy organizational culture.

From a psychoanalytic perspective, power in leadership is not just a matter of organizational structure or position; it's deeply intertwined with the unconscious dynamics between leaders and followers. These dynamics influence how power is perceived, negotiated, and enacted within the leadership context. Understanding the role of power requires delving into the complex interplay of desires, fears, and unresolved conflicts that both leaders and followers bring to the relationship.

The negotiation of power between leaders and followers often mirrors early familial and social experiences where power dynamics first took shape. For instance, a leader's approach to wielding power may be influenced by their experiences with authority figures in childhood, affecting how they view control, autonomy, and dependency. Similarly, followers' reactions to power can reflect their own historical relationships with authority, including how they learned to assert themselves, comply with, or resist power.

Unconscious dynamics play a crucial role in these negotiations. Projection, where leaders and followers unconsciously attribute their own feelings or desires to the other, can significantly affect power dynamics. A leader who feels insecure about their authority may project confidence outwardly while unconsciously seeking validation from their followers, creating a dynamic where power is constantly being reassessed and negotiated.

Transference and countertransference further complicate power dynamics. Followers may transfer feelings associated with past authority figures onto the leader, influencing their expectations and responses. Leaders might experience countertransference, reacting to followers based on their own unresolved issues with authority. These transference reactions can lead to misinterpretations and conflicts that obscure the true nature of the power dynamic at play.

The psychoanalytic concept of the shadow, the unconscious aspects of the personality that the individual is unaware of, also affects power negotiations. Leaders unaware of their shadow aspects may unknowingly project these onto followers, creating a dissonance in how power is exercised and perceived. Recognizing and integrating these shadow aspects can lead to a more authentic and balanced exercise of power.

Ultimately, power in leadership, viewed through a psychoanalytic lens, is a fluid and dynamic force, shaped by deep-seated unconscious processes. Leaders and followers engage in a continuous dance of negotiation, influenced by their psychological histories, desires, and fears. By becoming more aware of these unconscious dynamics, leaders can navigate power relationships more effectively, fostering healthier interactions and organizational cultures. This awareness allows for power to be used not as a means of domination but as a tool for collective growth and achievement, aligning with the deeper needs and aspirations of both leaders and followers.

In the intricate dynamics of leadership, both leaders and followers harbor dependency needs that significantly shape their interactions. These needs, often rooted in the desire for approval, guidance, and security, stem from deep psychological processes and can have a profound impact on leadership contexts. Understanding the nuances of these dependency needs is crucial for navigating the complex relationships within organizations and can lead to either constructive or destructive outcomes depending on how they are managed.

Leaders, though often perceived as figures of authority and self-sufficiency, may seek validation and support from their followers to bolster their confidence and legitimacy. This quest for approval, if left unchecked, can lead to an over-reliance on follower affirmation, potentially compromising the leader's ability to make unpopular but necessary decisions. Similarly, leaders might look to their followers for guidance and reassurance, especially in moments of uncertainty, reflecting an underlying dependency that belies the traditional notion of leadership autonomy. The need for security, manifested as a desire for loyalty and predictability from followers, can drive leaders to create overly rigid structures that stifle innovation and creativity.

Followers, on the other hand, often look to leaders to fulfill their own dependency needs. They may seek approval to validate their worth within the organization, viewing the leader's acknowledgment as a measure of their professional value. The desire for guidance from leaders is also a common dependency need, with followers relying on leaders to navigate the complexities of their roles and the broader organizational landscape. Security needs among followers frequently manifest as a yearning for stability and protection, with leaders viewed as shields against the volatility of the external environment.

These dependency needs, while natural, can lead to constructive outcomes when managed with awareness and empathy. Leaders who recognize and address their own and their followers' dependency needs can foster a culture of mutual respect and support, encouraging open communication, shared decision-making, and a sense of collective purpose. This approach can enhance team cohesion, drive engagement, and bolster overall organizational resilience.

However, when these needs are not acknowledged or are managed poorly, they can lead to destructive outcomes. Leaders overly dependent on follower approval may avoid necessary confrontations, weakening their position and undermining organizational objectives. Followers excessively reliant on leaders for approval, guidance, or security may become passive, overly compliant, or resistant to change, impeding personal growth and organizational innovation.

The interplay of dependency needs between leaders and followers is a critical aspect of leadership dynamics, with the potential to significantly influence organizational culture and effectiveness. By recognizing and thoughtfully managing these needs, leaders can navigate the delicate balance between providing support and fostering independence, leading to healthier, more productive leader-follower relationships and positive organizational outcomes.

The Shadow Side of Leadership

The concept of the shadow, introduced by Carl Jung, offers a profound insight into the darker, often unacknowledged aspects of leadership. This concept refers to the parts of ourselves that we deny or reject, considering them incompatible with our conscious identity. In the context of leadership, the shadow encompasses those traits, impulses, and emotions that leaders prefer not to acknowledge or display, such as vulnerability, aggression, or fear of inadequacy. These shadow aspects, though hidden, exert a powerful influence on leadership behavior and, by extension, on organizational culture.

Leaders who remain unaware of their shadow sides may inadvertently project these aspects onto others, misattributing their own insecurities, desires, or shortcomings to their team members or colleagues. Such projection can lead to misunderstandings, conflict, and a culture of blame rather than one of accountability and growth. For example, a leader who internally struggles with feelings of incompetence may overemphasize the importance of flawless performance, creating an environment where failure is feared and mistakes are hidden rather than used as learning opportunities.

The shadow can manifest in leadership styles that are overly authoritarian or, conversely, excessively permissive, as leaders unconsciously compensate for the traits they are unwilling to confront within themselves. This can lead to imbalances in power dynamics, with leaders either dominating their followers to avoid feeling vulnerable or avoiding confrontation to escape the discomfort of asserting authority.

The influence of the shadow on organizational culture cannot be overstated. When leaders operate from an unexamined place, allowing their shadow aspects to drive their behavior, it can lead to a culture that mirrors these unconscious dynamics. Such a culture may be marked by fear, secrecy, and competition rather than transparency, collaboration, and trust.

Recognizing and integrating the shadow is a crucial task for effective leadership. Leaders who engage in this process of self-exploration can gain a deeper understanding of themselves, acknowledging and accepting the full range of their personality, including those aspects they previously rejected. This acceptance allows leaders to manage their impulses more consciously and interact with their team in more authentic and constructive ways. It encourages a leadership approach that values self-awareness and personal growth, fostering a culture where openness, vulnerability, and mutual respect are prized.

By exploring the concept of the shadow in leadership, we uncover the profound impact that unrecognized or unacknowledged parts of the leader's personality can have on their behavior and the broader organizational culture. Embracing the shadow offers a path toward more genuine and effective leadership, where the full complexity of human experience is acknowledged and integrated into how leaders lead and how organizations operate.

The projection of the shadow in leadership contexts involves leaders unconsciously casting the undesirable or unacknowledged parts of their own personality onto their followers or the organization as a whole. This psychological mechanism, rooted in the leaders' attempt to deal with their own inner conflicts and insecurities, can have far-reaching and often detrimental effects on organizational culture and effectiveness. When leaders project their shadow, they may attribute their own fears, weaknesses, or negative traits to their team members without realizing that these perceptions are more reflective of their internal struggles than of the realities of those around them.

This dynamic can manifest in various toxic leadership behaviors. For instance, a leader who has not come to terms with their own tendencies toward aggression or authoritarianism might perceive their team as overly passive or in need of strict control. As a result, they may adopt an unnecessarily harsh or domineering leadership style, stifling open communication and innovation. Similarly, leaders who deny their own vulnerabilities might project a facade of invulnerability, expecting unrealistic levels of resilience and perfection from their team. Such expectations can create a work environment where mistakes are hidden rather than addressed, and where team members feel undervalued and overworked.

Projection of the shadow can also lead to organizational dysfunction. When leaders are not aware of their shadow aspects, they may unknowingly cultivate a culture that mirrors these hidden elements. For example, if a leader harbors unconscious biases or prejudices, these attitudes can become embedded in the organizational culture, affecting hiring practices, team dynamics, and decision-making processes. Moreover, when leaders project their insecurities onto the organization, it can result in a culture of fear and mistrust, where followers are more concerned with avoiding criticism or punishment than with contributing to the organization's success.

Recognizing and addressing the projection of the shadow requires leaders to engage in deep self-reflection and to seek feedback from others to gain insight into their unconscious biases and behaviors. By becoming more aware of the aspects of themselves they have rejected or ignored, leaders can begin to integrate these elements into their conscious identity, reducing the need to project them onto others. This process not only mitigates the negative outcomes associated with shadow projection but also fosters a more authentic and inclusive leadership style.

The projection of the shadow by leaders onto their followers or the organization can lead to a range of negative outcomes, from toxic leadership behaviors to organizational dysfunction. By acknowledging and integrating their shadow aspects, leaders can create a healthier, more positive work environment that encourages growth, innovation, and mutual respect. This transformation not only benefits the organization but also contributes to the personal growth and development of the leader.

Overcoming Challenges through Psychoanalytic Insights

Awareness and integration of unconscious motivations into leadership practices require a deliberate and reflective approach, enabling leaders to navigate the complexities of their roles with greater insight and authenticity. Achieving this level of self-awareness involves a multifaceted strategy that encompasses introspection, feedback, and the application of psychological insights into daily leadership behaviors.

The journey towards greater self-awareness often begins with introspection, a process where leaders dedicate time and space to reflect on their feelings, reactions, and the deeper motivations behind their actions. This introspective practice can be enhanced through journaling, meditation, or simply setting aside quiet time for self-reflection. The goal is to peel back the layers of immediate conscious thought and to probe the underlying beliefs, fears, and desires that drive behavior. Leaders might explore questions about the origins of their leadership style, their responses to stress and conflict, and their interactions with team members, looking for patterns that suggest deeper unconscious influences.

Seeking feedback from others is another crucial strategy for uncovering unconscious motivations. Colleagues, mentors, and coaches can offer invaluable outside perspectives on a leader's behavior, providing insights that the leader might not be able to see on their own. This feedback can highlight discrepancies between the leader's self-perception and how others experience their leadership, pointing to unconscious biases, assumptions, or emotional triggers that influence leadership practices.

Engagement with psychological concepts and theories, particularly those from psychoanalytic and Jungian traditions, offers leaders a framework for understanding the complexity of human behavior, including their own. By studying these theories, leaders can gain vocabulary and concepts to make sense of their introspections and the feedback they receive, recognizing the role of the shadow, projection, and transference in their leadership dynamics.

Integrating these insights into more effective, conscious leadership practices involves a willingness to confront uncomfortable truths about oneself and to embrace vulnerability. Leaders who acknowledge their weaknesses and blind spots can work to mitigate their impact, perhaps by adjusting their leadership style, seeking out complementary skills in their team members, or implementing structures that compensate for their limitations.

Developing practices that encourage ongoing self-awareness and reflection is also key. Leaders might establish regular check-ins with themselves and their teams to assess the health of their relationships, the effectiveness of their leadership approach, and the alignment between their intentions and their actions. They might also commit to continuous learning, engaging with literature, workshops, and seminars that challenge their thinking and encourage personal growth.

The awareness and integration of unconscious motivations into leadership practices is a dynamic and ongoing process. It demands courage, curiosity, and a commitment to growth, both personal and professional. Leaders who embark on this journey can expect to not only enhance their effectiveness but also to foster a culture of openness, resilience, and mutual respect within their organizations.

Developing healthier leader-follower dynamics involves a nuanced understanding of the unconscious dynamics that underpin these relationships. Leaders who are adept at recognizing and addressing these underlying forces can create an environment characterized by trust, mutual respect, and collaborative engagement. This process requires leaders to embark on a journey of self-discovery, to cultivate open communication, and to implement practices that acknowledge and respect the psychological needs of their followers.

A critical first step for leaders is to engage in self-reflection and personal development work aimed at uncovering their own unconscious motivations, biases, and the shadow aspects of their personality. This may involve seeking psychoanalytic coaching or therapy, participating in leadership development programs that focus on emotional intelligence, or engaging in reflective practices such as journaling or mindfulness. By becoming more aware of their own inner landscape, leaders can prevent their unconscious biases and fears from negatively impacting their interactions with followers.

Encouraging open communication is another vital aspect of fostering healthier dynamics. Leaders can create safe spaces for followers to express their thoughts, feelings, and concerns without fear of retribution. This includes actively listening to feedback, being receptive to different perspectives, and acknowledging the validity of followers' experiences. Such an approach helps to mitigate the effects of projection and transference, as both leaders and followers feel seen and understood.

Leaders can also address unconscious dynamics by being transparent about their decision-making processes, sharing their vulnerabilities, and admitting to mistakes. This level of openness humanizes the leader, reduces the potential for idealization and unrealistic expectations, and promotes a culture of accountability and learning. It signals to followers that it is safe to take risks, be creative, and learn from failures. Implementing structured feedback mechanisms can provide regular opportunities for leaders and followers to address and recalibrate their relationship. This could take the form of 360-degree feedback, regular one-on-one meetings, or team reflection sessions. Such structures ensure that unconscious dynamics are regularly brought to light, discussed, and addressed, preventing them from undermining the leader-follower relationship.

Leaders can foster healthier dynamics by actively working to understand and meet the psychological needs of their followers, such as the need for autonomy, mastery, and relatedness. This involves assigning tasks that align with followers' strengths and interests, providing opportunities for skill development, and fostering a sense of belonging within the team. By addressing these needs, leaders can reduce dependency, enhance motivation, and support the personal and professional growth of their followers.

Developing healthier leader-follower dynamics requires leaders to acknowledge and address the unconscious dynamics at play. Through self-awareness, open communication, vulnerability, structured feedback, and a focus on meeting psychological needs, leaders can create a more positive, productive, and fulfilling work environment for themselves and their followers. This approach not only enhances individual and team performance but also contributes to the overall health and success of the organization.

Understanding the psychoanalytic underpinnings of power and dependency offers leaders a profound insight into the intricate dynamics that shape their relationships with followers. This deepened awareness can illuminate the often-unconscious forces driving behaviors related to authority, influence, and reliance within teams and organizations. By acknowledging and addressing these underlying factors, leaders can navigate power and dependency dynamics more constructively, fostering an environment that balances autonomy and support, encourages growth, and enhances organizational effectiveness.

Recognizing the origins of one's own relationship with power is a crucial first step. Leaders can benefit from reflecting on how their early life experiences with authority figures have shaped their perceptions of power and control. This introspection can reveal how past dynamics might influence current leadership styles, potentially leading to overassertion of authority or, conversely, avoidance of power. By understanding these patterns, leaders can work towards a more balanced approach that neither dominates nor abdicates responsibility, but rather empowers and collaborates with followers.

Similarly, exploring the roots of dependency needs within the leader-follower relationship can shed light on expectations for guidance, approval, and support. Leaders should consider how their own needs for validation and assurance might manifest in their interactions with followers, possibly creating dynamics of over-reliance or undue independence. Conversely, understanding followers' dependency needs can help leaders provide the right level of support and challenge, encouraging followers to develop their skills and confidence while remaining available as a source of guidance and stability.

Open dialogue about power and dependency can also play a pivotal role in managing these dynamics constructively. Leaders can initiate conversations that explore mutual expectations, boundaries, and the balance between support and autonomy. This transparency can demystify the power dynamics at play, reducing anxieties and misconceptions while promoting a shared understanding of how to engage productively with these forces.

Incorporating practices that regularly examine and adjust the balance of power and dependency within the team is another effective strategy. This might include regular check-ins, feedback sessions, and opportunities for followers to lead projects or initiatives. Such practices encourage a culture of mutual respect and shared leadership, where power is viewed as a tool for collective achievement rather than personal aggrandizement.

Leaders can benefit from ongoing personal and professional development focused on understanding the psychological aspects of leadership. Engaging with psychoanalytic theory, seeking mentorship, or participating in leadership coaching can provide valuable insights into managing power and dependency more effectively. These learning opportunities can equip leaders with the tools to recognize and address the unconscious dynamics influencing their leadership, ultimately leading to more fulfilling and productive leader-follower relationships.

Navigating power and dependency dynamics in leadership requires a nuanced understanding of the psychoanalytic factors at play. By engaging in self-reflection, fostering open dialogue, implementing adaptive practices, and pursuing continuous learning, leaders can manage these dynamics in ways that support the growth and development of both themselves and their followers, contributing to the overall health and success of the organization.

Conclusion

Exploring leadership through a psychoanalytic lens unveils the profound impact of unconscious processes on the dynamics between leaders and their followers. This perspective enriches our understanding of leadership beyond the observable behaviors and skills, delving into the depths of the human psyche to reveal the underlying motivations, fears, and desires that shape leadership styles and interactions. The insights gained from this exploration highlight the intricate interplay of early developmental influences, unconscious motivations, and the shadow aspects of personality in determining how leaders wield power, relate to followers, and navigate the complexities of organizational life.

A key insight from the psychoanalytic perspective is the recognition that leadership is not merely a role or a set of responsibilities but a reflection of the leader's entire psychological makeup. This realization underscores the importance of self-awareness and introspection for leaders, encouraging them to confront and integrate their unconscious biases, unresolved conflicts, and shadow selves to foster more authentic and effective leadership practices.

The exploration of transference and projection within the leader-follower relationship reveals how past experiences and unconscious expectations can color perceptions and interactions, often leading to miscommunications and conflicts. By becoming aware of these dynamics, leaders and followers can work towards more genuine connections, where empathy and understanding pave the way for healthier and more productive relationships.

Understanding the psychoanalytic underpinnings of power and dependency challenges conventional notions of authority, highlighting the psychological needs that drive both leaders and followers to seek control, approval, and guidance. This awareness can help leaders manage these dynamics more constructively, balancing the need for leadership with the importance of fostering independence and growth among followers.

The value of exploring the unconscious aspects of leadership lies in the potential for profound personal and organizational transformation. Leaders who engage with their unconscious motivations and address the psychological dynamics at play can enhance their emotional intelligence, improve their decision-making, and cultivate a culture of openness, trust, and mutual respect. This approach not only benefits the individual leader and their followers but also contributes to the overall health, resilience, and effectiveness of the organization.

The psychoanalytic perspective on leadership offers invaluable insights into the deep-seated psychological forces that shape leadership behavior and the leader-follower dynamic. By acknowledging and exploring these unconscious aspects, leaders can embark on a journey of growth and development that enhances their leadership capabilities and fosters more meaningful and productive relationships within their organizations. This exploration is a testament to the complexity of leadership and the enduring impact of the unseen forces that drive human behavior in organizational contexts.

The journey through the psychoanalytic perspective on leadership uncovers a rich tapestry of insights that have the potential to profoundly influence leadership practices and organizational cultures. By delving into the depths of the unconscious, leaders are offered a unique opportunity to understand the complex interplay of emotions, motivations, and conflicts that underlie their actions and relationships. This exploration holds the promise of fostering more nuanced and effective leadership practices, characterized by a deeper self-awareness and a more empathetic approach to managing teams and navigating organizational challenges.

Psychoanalytic theory, with its focus on the unseen forces that shape human behavior, provides leaders with the tools to recognize and address the unconscious dynamics at play within themselves and their organizations. This awareness can lead to a transformation in leadership styles, from those based on power and control to practices that prioritize connection, understanding, and mutual growth. Leaders who embrace this perspective can develop a more authentic leadership presence, one that resonates with followers on a deeper level and inspires trust, loyalty, and engagement.

The insights gained from psychoanalytic theory have the potential to cultivate healthier organizational cultures. By acknowledging and integrating the shadow aspects of leadership, organizations can move away from cultures of fear and secrecy towards environments that value transparency, inclusivity, and psychological safety. This shift not only enhances the well-being and satisfaction of employees but also drives innovation, adaptability, and resilience in the face of change.

The application of psychoanalytic concepts to leadership and organizational development encourages a holistic approach to managing human capital. Recognizing that the challenges and opportunities organizations face are not merely strategic or operational but deeply psychological, leaders can adopt strategies that address the root causes of dysfunction and disengagement. This approach fosters a culture where individuals feel understood and valued, where diversity of thought is celebrated, and where the full potential of the human spirit is harnessed towards collective achievement.

The potential for psychoanalytic theory to contribute to more nuanced, effective leadership practices and healthier organizational cultures is immense. By exploring the unconscious aspects of leadership, leaders can embark on a journey of transformation that not only enhances their own effectiveness but also nurtures an organizational environment that is vibrant, sustainable, and aligned with the deepest human values. This exploration is not just a pathway to better leadership but a call to redefine what it means to lead and to thrive in the complex world of organizational life.

Chapter 5: Leadership Styles and the Unconscious

Chapter 5 explores the intriguing intersection of leadership styles and the unconscious, presenting a premise that extends far beyond conventional understandings of leadership as merely the sum of conscious strategies and decisions. At the heart of this exploration lies the recognition that the essence of leadership is intricately woven with the leader's unconscious processes—those hidden currents of desires, fears, and motivations that silently steer the ship of leadership. This chapter argues for the critical importance of unveiling and understanding these unconscious influences as they play a decisive role in shaping leadership behaviors, decisions, and the overall dynamics within teams and organizations.

The unconscious mind, with its complex tapestry of past experiences, unresolved conflicts, and deep-seated emotional imprints, exerts a profound influence on the way leaders perceive their role, interact with followers, and navigate the challenges of leadership. These underlying processes can color a leader's approach, often in ways that remain invisible to the conscious mind, yet powerfully impact leadership effectiveness and the quality of interpersonal relationships within the organizational sphere.

Understanding these unconscious influences is not merely an academic exercise; it holds tangible benefits for enhancing leadership effectiveness and fostering personal growth. By bringing these hidden dimensions to light, leaders can gain insights into the origins of their leadership style, identify potential blind spots, and uncover the emotional drivers behind their actions. This journey of self-discovery opens up new pathways for personal and professional development, enabling leaders to refine their approach, build more authentic connections with their followers, and create a leadership legacy that resonates with depth and integrity.

This chapter aims to equip leaders with the knowledge and tools to explore the unconscious aspects of their leadership styles. Through a psychoanalytic lens, we will examine how early life experiences, psychological conflicts, and the dynamic interplay between different aspects of the psyche contribute to the formation of leadership styles. We will also explore practical strategies for integrating these insights into more conscious and adaptive leadership practices. The ultimate goal is to foster leadership that is not only effective but also deeply aligned with the leader's authentic self and responsive to the needs and aspirations of their followers.

In embarking on this exploration, we invite leaders to consider the profound ways in which the unseen forces of the unconscious shape the art and science of leadership. By engaging with these deeper dimensions, leaders can unlock new levels of insight, empathy, and effectiveness, enriching their leadership journey and contributing to the creation of healthier, more vibrant organizational cultures.

As we venture deeper into the exploration of leadership styles through a psychoanalytic lens, we embark on a journey that transcends traditional boundaries of leadership theory. This exploration is rooted in the premise that the tapestry of leadership is woven not only with the threads of conscious intention and strategic decision-making but also with the intricate, often invisible fibers of the unconscious mind. Through this psychoanalytic lens, we aim to uncover the profound ways in which unconscious factors—those hidden elements of our psyche shaped by early experiences, unresolved conflicts, and deep-seated desires—mold and influence various leadership styles and their effectiveness.

This journey into the psychoanalytic dimensions of leadership invites us to examine the rich spectrum of leadership styles—ranging from the transformational to the transactional, from the autocratic to the democratic, and beyond—through an entirely new perspective. We seek to understand how these styles are not merely the result of learned behaviors or adopted strategies but are deeply influenced by the leader's psychological makeup. For instance, a leader's gravitation towards a transformational style may be rooted in an unconscious desire to heal unresolved personal conflicts through positive influence on others, while a preference for autocratic leadership might reflect an unconscious need for control stemming from early experiences of powerlessness or insecurity.

By delving into the psychological underpinnings of leadership styles, we uncover the role of the unconscious in shaping not only how leaders lead but also how they perceive their role, relate to followers, and respond to challenges. This exploration considers how unconscious motivations, such as the desire for approval, the fear of failure, or the need for security, can drive leaders to adopt certain styles over others, impacting their effectiveness and the overall dynamics within their teams and organizations.

The impact of these unconscious factors on leadership effectiveness cannot be overstated. Leaders who remain unaware of the unconscious influences on their behavior may find themselves repeating unhelpful patterns, misinterpreting challenges, or struggling to connect authentically with their followers. Conversely, leaders who engage in self-reflection and seek to understand the unconscious dimensions of their leadership style are better equipped to adapt their approach, address their followers' needs more effectively, and navigate the complexities of organizational life with greater insight and empathy.

This chapter sets the stage for a deep dive into the psychoanalytic exploration of leadership styles, inviting leaders to reflect on the unseen forces that shape their approach to leadership. By engaging with this perspective, leaders can embark on a path of personal and professional growth, enhancing their leadership effectiveness and fostering healthier, more dynamic organizational cultures. The exploration promises not only to illuminate the hidden dimensions of leadership styles but also to offer practical insights for integrating these understandings into more conscious, adaptive, and effective leadership practices.

Analyzing Leadership Styles through a Psychoanalytic Lens

Analyzing leadership styles through a psychoanalytic lens invites a profound exploration beyond the conventional descriptors, probing into the psychological foundations that underpin these familiar modes of leadership. Each style, from transformational to laissez-faire, encapsulates not just a set of behaviors but also mirrors the leader's inner world, their unconscious motivations, and their developmental history.

- Transformational Leadership is characterized by the leader's ability to inspire and motivate followers to achieve more than they originally intended, often transcending their own self-interests for the sake of the organization or a higher cause. Transformational leaders are visionaries who foster an environment of trust, encourage innovation, and are adept at recognizing followers' needs and developing them towards higher levels of performance.

- Transactional Leadership, in contrast, is based on a clear exchange between the leader and the followers. This style emphasizes the role of supervision, organization, and group performance, relying on a system of rewards and punishments to motivate followers. Transactional leadership focuses on achieving set goals and tasks through a structured framework and clear directives.

- Autocratic Leadership is defined by individual control over all decisions with little input from team members. Autocratic leaders typically make choices based on their judgments and ideas, often without consulting followers. This style can be effective in situations that require quick decision-making and where there is little need for team input.

- Democratic Leadership, or participative leadership, contrasts sharply with autocratic leadership, as it involves the inclusion of team members in the decision-making process. Democratic leaders encourage collaboration and share decision-making responsibilities with their followers, fostering a sense of ownership and investment among team members.

- Laissez-Faire Leadership takes a hands-off approach, allowing followers to set their own schedules and deadlines, and to solve problems on their own. This style of leadership can be beneficial in environments where followers are highly skilled, motivated, and capable of working independently. However, it may lead to a lack of direction and oversight if not applied judiciously.

Through the psychoanalytic lens, these leadership styles are not merely strategic choices but reflections of deeper psychological processes. For instance, a transformational leader's capacity to inspire might stem from an unconscious desire to heal or to be revered, while the control exerted by an autocratic leader might relate to underlying anxieties about chaos or dependency. Similarly, the collaborative nature of democratic leadership could reflect an unconscious need for approval or fear of isolation, and the laissez-faire leader's hands-off approach might be linked to unconscious conflicts around authority and power.

By exploring these styles through psychoanalytic theory, we gain insights into how leaders' unconscious motivations and past experiences shape their approach to leadership. This deeper understanding not only illuminates the complexities of leadership behavior but also opens pathways for growth and development, both for leaders and the organizations they guide.

The psychoanalytic perspective offers a rich and nuanced framework for understanding leadership styles, drawing attention to the profound influence of early childhood experiences, ego development, and the use of defense mechanisms. These concepts, foundational to psychoanalytic theory, provide insight into the unconscious motivations and psychological structures that underpin a leader's behavior and interactions with others.

According to psychoanalytic theory, the experiences and relationships we navigate in early childhood play a significant role in shaping our personalities, including our approach to leadership. For instance, a leader who experienced authoritative parenting might gravitate towards an autocratic leadership style, finding comfort and familiarity in exerting control. Conversely, those who grew up in more collaborative family environments might lean towards a democratic or transformational style, valuing consensus and empowerment. These early experiences influence not just our preferences for certain leadership styles but also how we relate to authority and autonomy, our tolerance for ambiguity, and our approach to conflict and collaboration.

The ego, in psychoanalytic theory, acts as the mediator between the id's primal desires, the superego's moral constraints, and the external world's realities. A leader's ego development thus significantly affects their leadership style. Leaders with a well-developed ego can balance their own needs with those of their followers and the organization, likely adopting a more adaptive and flexible leadership style. They are better equipped to handle stress, manage conflicts, and navigate the complexities of organizational life without resorting to rigid or defensive behaviors. In contrast, leaders with less developed egos might struggle with these challenges, potentially leading to leadership styles that are more reactive, less empathetic, and overly dependent on defense mechanisms.

Leaders, like all individuals, employ defense mechanisms to protect themselves from psychological discomfort. These unconscious strategies can significantly influence leadership behavior. For example, a leader using denial might refuse to acknowledge emerging problems within their team, while one relying on projection might attribute their own shortcomings to their followers. Understanding the role of defense mechanisms in leadership allows for a deeper analysis of leadership styles. It reveals how these unconscious processes can distort a leader's perception of reality, affect their decision-making, and impact their relationships with followers.

By integrating these psychoanalytic concepts into the analysis of leadership styles, we uncover the complex interplay between a leader's unconscious world and their outward behavior. This approach not only enriches our understanding of different leadership styles but also opens up avenues for personal growth and development. Leaders who become aware of the unconscious influences on their leadership approach can engage in self-reflection and growth work, potentially transforming their leadership style into one that is more conscious, adaptive, and effective. This psychoanalytic exploration thus offers a powerful tool for enhancing leadership effectiveness and fostering healthier organizational cultures.

The interplay between unconscious factors and leadership styles is a complex and profound domain, where unresolved conflicts, unconscious desires, and fears significantly shape how leaders navigate their roles. This nuanced interconnection offers a deeper understanding of why leaders act the way they do, beyond mere personality traits or learned behaviors. By delving into these unconscious undercurrents, we can see how they manifest in various leadership styles, influencing everything from decision-making processes to interpersonal dynamics.

Unresolved conflicts from a leader's past, particularly those rooted in early childhood experiences, can have a lasting impact on their approach to leadership. For example, a leader who experienced significant authority clashes in their formative years might adopt an autocratic style as a means of asserting control, or conversely, might lean towards a laissez-faire approach to avoid replicating the authoritarian figures from their past. These conflicts can drive a leader's need to validate their authority, influence their tolerance for dissent, and shape their response to challenges.

Similarly, unconscious desires—such as the longing for acceptance, recognition, or the need to fulfill unmet childhood aspirations—can color a leader's style. A transformational leader's drive to inspire and uplift their team, for instance, might stem from an unconscious desire to be the benevolent figure they lacked in their own upbringing. On the other hand, a transactional leader's focus on rewards and punishments could reflect a deeper, perhaps unacknowledged, craving for structure and predictability that was absent in their early environment.

Fears and insecurities, often lurking beneath the surface of conscious awareness, can also influence leadership behavior. A leader's fear of failure might result in a tendency to micromanage, reflecting a deeper anxiety about losing control or being perceived as inadequate. Alternatively, the fear of vulnerability might lead a leader to adopt a more distant, reserved leadership style, as a protective measure against potential criticism or rejection.

These unconscious factors can lead to leadership styles that are highly effective in certain contexts but may also result in rigidity, miscommunication, or conflict in others. Leaders who engage in self-reflection and seek to understand the roots of their leadership approach can gain valuable insights into their behavior and motivations. This process of self-exploration, often facilitated by psychoanalytic coaching or therapy, can empower leaders to modify or adapt their leadership style in ways that are more conscious, flexible, and responsive to the needs of their followers and the demands of their organizational context.

Understanding the role of the unconscious in shaping leadership styles not only enriches our comprehension of leadership as a psychological phenomenon but also highlights the potential for growth and change. Leaders who acknowledge and work through their unresolved conflicts, desires, and fears can transform their approach to leadership, fostering healthier, more productive relationships with their followers and contributing to a more dynamic and resilient organizational culture. This exploration of the unconscious factors at play in leadership styles offers a pathway to more authentic and effective leadership, grounded in a deep awareness of the self and others.

The Impact of Unconscious Processes on Leadership Effectiveness

The impact of unconscious processes on leadership effectiveness becomes particularly evident in the realm of decision-making, where unconscious biases can subtly, yet significantly, influence a leader's judgments and actions. These biases, ingrained patterns of thought that operate below the level of conscious awareness, can skew perception and lead to decisions that are not only less effective but also potentially unethical.

Unconscious biases are shaped by a myriad of factors including cultural norms, personal experiences, and social conditioning. They can manifest in various forms, such as confirmation bias, where leaders favor information that confirms their preexisting beliefs, or in-group bias, where they prefer individuals who are perceived as being part of their own group. These biases can lead to a narrow perspective, limiting the leader's ability to assess situations objectively and consider a diverse range of viewpoints and solutions.

In the context of decision-making, unconscious biases can result in the overlooking of qualified candidates for promotions, the unequal distribution of resources, or the failure to recognize and mitigate potential risks. For example, a leader with an unconscious bias towards overconfidence may underestimate challenges, leading to overly optimistic assessments and ill-advised decisions. Similarly, biases related to stereotypes can influence a leader's expectations and evaluations of team members, affecting morale, productivity, and the overall workplace climate.

The repercussions of decisions influenced by unconscious biases extend beyond immediate outcomes; they can erode trust, hamper collaboration, and perpetuate a culture of inequity and exclusion within the organization. Such an environment not only undermines leadership effectiveness but can also stifle innovation, reduce employee engagement, and damage the organization's reputation.

Addressing the impact of unconscious biases on decision-making requires leaders to engage in introspection and continuous learning. This process involves recognizing the existence of biases, understanding how they influence perception and behavior, and actively seeking to mitigate their effects. Strategies such as seeking diverse perspectives, implementing structured decision-making processes, and utilizing data-driven criteria can help reduce the influence of biases. Furthermore, training and development programs focused on unconscious bias can raise awareness and equip leaders with the tools to make more informed, ethical, and effective decisions.

Exploring how unconscious biases influence decision-making underscores the importance of self-awareness and critical reflection in leadership. By acknowledging and addressing these unconscious processes, leaders can enhance their effectiveness, fostering a culture of fairness, ethical behavior, and inclusivity that drives organizational success and aligns with the highest standards of leadership excellence.

At the heart of emotional intelligence lies the leader's ability to engage with their own inner emotional landscape, much of which operates below the threshold of conscious awareness. Unconscious emotions, shaped by past experiences and deep-seated beliefs, can significantly influence a leader's reactions and decisions. For example, unresolved fear or anxiety might manifest as overcautiousness or indecision, while unacknowledged anger might lead to undue harshness or impulsive actions. Leaders who develop the capacity to recognize and manage these underlying emotions can mitigate their negative impact, leading instead with a balanced and thoughtful approach.

- Emotional intelligence, a critical component of effective leadership, encompasses the ability to recognize, understand, manage, and use emotions in constructive ways. This skill set is particularly significant when considering the influence of unconscious processes on leadership behavior. A leader's capacity to navigate their own unconscious emotions and to attune to the emotions of others underpins their ability to lead with empathy, make informed decisions, and foster a positive organizational culture.

- Emotional intelligence enables leaders to create a vision that resonates on an emotional level with their followers, inspiring commitment and action. By aligning their leadership with the emotional drives and values of their team, leaders can mobilize collective energy and focus it towards achieving meaningful and impactful outcomes.

- Emotional intelligence involves the ability to perceive and respond to the emotions of others, a skill that requires sensitivity to the complex web of unconscious feelings that influence team dynamics. Leaders adept in emotional intelligence can discern the unspoken anxieties, motivations, and needs of their followers, allowing them to address concerns, motivate effectively, and resolve conflicts in ways that acknowledge and validate these underlying emotional currents. This empathetic engagement not only enhances leader-follower relationships but also contributes to a work environment characterized by trust, cooperation, and psychological safety.

The impact of a leader's emotional intelligence on leadership effectiveness is profound. Leaders who are emotionally intelligent are better equipped to navigate the challenges of organizational life, from managing stress and adversity to inspiring and rallying their teams towards shared goals. Their ability to connect on an emotional level, to communicate with authenticity, and to lead with compassion fosters an organizational culture that values emotional well-being, encourages open dialogue, and supports personal and professional growth.

The role of emotional intelligence in leadership, especially in the context of managing unconscious emotions, is indispensable for effective leadership. By cultivating emotional intelligence, leaders can enhance their awareness of their own and others' emotional undercurrents, leading to more informed, empathetic, and effective leadership practices. This emotional acumen not only elevates the leader's effectiveness but also enriches the organizational culture, paving the way for a more engaged, motivated, and cohesive workforce.

Defense mechanisms, unconscious strategies employed to protect oneself from psychological discomfort, play a significant role in shaping leadership styles and effectiveness. While these mechanisms serve an essential protective function, their influence on leadership can be profound, often steering leaders away from confronting uncomfortable truths or dealing with organizational challenges effectively.

Denial, one such mechanism, involves refusing to acknowledge reality or facts that cause emotional pain. In leadership, denial might manifest as ignoring critical feedback, overlooking emerging problems, or underestimating the complexity of challenges. This can lead to a disconnect between the leader's perception and the organization's actual needs, potentially resulting in missed opportunities for growth or unaddressed issues that escalate into crises.

Projection involves attributing one's own unacceptable thoughts, feelings, or motivations to others. Leaders using projection might misinterpret the actions or intentions of their team members, seeing their own insecurities or faults in those they lead. This can create a culture of blame and mistrust, where followers feel unfairly judged or misunderstood, hampering open communication and collaboration.

Rationalization offers another example, where leaders justify irrational or unacceptable behavior with logical but false reasoning. This mechanism can lead leaders to excuse their own or their organization's failures by shifting blame to external circumstances or minimizing the significance of setbacks. While this may temporarily shield the leader from feeling failure or regret, it also impedes learning from mistakes and fostering a culture of accountability and resilience.

The use of these defense mechanisms can significantly affect a leader's style and effectiveness. Leaders who frequently resort to denial may appear disconnected or overly optimistic, failing to engage with the reality faced by their organization. Those who project may adopt an authoritarian or paranoid leadership style, driven by the need to control perceived threats that are more reflective of their inner turmoil than of their team's behavior. Leaders prone to rationalization might foster a culture of justification where excuses replace action, stifling innovation and growth.

Recognizing and addressing the use of defense mechanisms requires a high degree of self-awareness and emotional intelligence. Leaders can benefit from reflective practices, seeking feedback, and engaging in professional development or therapy to uncover and understand the psychological roots of their defensive behaviors. By becoming more aware of these unconscious processes, leaders can learn to respond to challenges more openly and authentically, adopting leadership styles that are more adaptive, responsive, and aligned with the needs of their followers and the organization.

While defense mechanisms serve to protect leaders from psychological discomfort, their impact on leadership style and effectiveness underscores the importance of self-awareness and growth. Leaders who engage in this self-exploratory work can transform their approach to leadership, moving from defensiveness to openness, fostering healthier organizational cultures, and achieving more sustainable and effective leadership outcomes.

Case Studies of Leaders and Their Unconscious Influences

Exploring the unconscious motivations and conflicts of historical leaders through psychoanalytic lenses provides profound insights into how these internal dynamics have shaped their leadership styles and decisions. While direct psychoanalytic analysis without personal interaction has its limitations, examining available historical records, biographies, and behaviors can offer speculative yet illuminating perspectives on the psychological underpinnings of their leadership.

Winston Churchill

Churchill's leadership during World War II exemplifies resilience, determination, and the capacity to inspire in times of crisis. Psychoanalytically speaking, Churchill's famed "Never surrender" ethos and his ability to rally the British people might be traced back to his childhood experiences of neglect and a desire to prove himself. Growing up in an aristocratic family where his parents were often absent, Churchill might have developed a deep-seated need for recognition and approval. This unconscious motivation could have driven his relentless pursuit of success and his determination to stand firm against Nazism, reflecting a personal battle against perceived abandonment and inadequacy.

Abraham Lincoln

Lincoln's leadership during the American Civil War and his commitment to the abolition of slavery demonstrate profound empathy, moral conviction, and a willingness to engage with deep societal divisions. Psychoanalytic theory might suggest that Lincoln's early experiences of loss and hardship—having lost his mother and sister in childhood—contributed to a heightened capacity for empathy and an unconscious identification with the suffering of others. His leadership style, characterized by compassion, patience, and a deep sense of justice, could thus be seen as reflective of an unconscious attempt to heal divisions and alleviate suffering, mirroring his internal struggles with grief and loss.

Steve Jobs

The co-founder of Apple Inc., Jobs transformed the technology industry with his visionary leadership and innovative products. Psychoanalytically, Jobs's notorious perfectionism and drive for innovation could be partly attributed to an unconscious quest for identity and self-worth, stemming from his adoption at birth. His intense focus on design and user experience, coupled with a leadership style that was both charismatic and demanding, might reflect an unconscious effort to create a legacy that would affirm his significance and address deep-seated fears of abandonment and rejection.

These case studies, while speculative, illustrate how psychoanalytic theory can provide valuable insights into the unconscious motivations and conflicts that shape leadership styles and decisions. Understanding these dynamics not only enriches our perspective on historical leaders but also highlights the universal influence of unconscious processes on leadership. By examining the lives and leadership of these figures through a psychoanalytic lens, we gain a deeper appreciation for the complex interplay between personal history, psychological development, and leadership effectiveness.

Given the constraints on discussing specific contemporary figures without their explicit consent and the necessary depth of personal insight, we can focus on hypothetical yet realistic scenarios that illustrate how unconscious factors can influence contemporary leadership behavior and organizational outcomes. These anonymized case studies, while fictional, are grounded in common leadership dynamics I have observed across various fields, offering insights into the psychoanalytic underpinnings of leadership in today's context.

Case Study 1: The Tech Innovator

A charismatic leader at the helm of a cutting-edge technology startup is renowned for pushing the boundaries of innovation. However, their drive for perfection and control leads to high employee turnover and a culture of fear. Psychoanalytically, this leader's behavior may stem from an unconscious fear of failure, possibly linked to early experiences of high parental expectations. Their relentless pursuit of perfection and control could be a defense mechanism against the deep-seated fear of not living up to those expectations, manifesting in their leadership style as a need to micromanage and demand unrealistic standards of performance from their team.

Case Study 2: The Non-Profit Visionary

The founder of a non-profit organization dedicated to social justice exhibits a deep commitment to their cause but struggles with delegation and trust. Despite the organization's growth, they remain heavily involved in all decisions, leading to bottlenecks and burnout. Psychoanalytically, this leader's inability to delegate may reflect an unconscious attachment to their organization as a source of personal identity and worth, rooted in a childhood need to be seen as valuable. This attachment might drive their need to be involved in every aspect of the organization, as relinquishing control threatens their sense of self and purpose.

Case Study 3: The Corporate Executive

An executive in a multinational corporation is known for their strategic acumen but has difficulty forming close working relationships with their peers and subordinates. While highly respected for their professional capabilities, they are often described as distant and unapproachable. From a psychoanalytic perspective, this leader's aloofness could be a defense mechanism against vulnerability, stemming from an unconscious fear of intimacy that may trace back to early relational traumas. Their professional success and strategic focus might serve as a way to compensate for these fears, ensuring they are valued for their intellect and achievements rather than their emotional connections.

These case studies illustrate the profound impact of unconscious factors on leadership behavior and organizational outcomes. By understanding these underlying dynamics, leaders can embark on a journey of personal growth and development, seeking to integrate these unconscious aspects into their conscious leadership practice. This process not only enhances their effectiveness as leaders but also contributes to creating healthier, more resilient organizational cultures. Recognizing and addressing the influence of unconscious factors requires a commitment to self-awareness, reflection, and, often, professional support to navigate the complex interplay between personal history and leadership behavior.

Navigating the Unconscious for Leadership Development

Navigating the unconscious for leadership development requires a commitment to cultivating self-awareness and engaging in deep reflection on one's motivations, behaviors, and the underlying psychological forces that drive them. This journey into the inner self can unlock profound insights and foster personal growth, ultimately enhancing leadership effectiveness. Here are some strategies that leaders can employ to increase self-awareness and reflect on their unconscious motivations:

- Engage in Psychoanalytic Therapy: Psychoanalytic therapy offers a structured approach to exploring the unconscious mind, providing leaders with a safe space to delve into their past experiences, unresolved conflicts, and hidden motivations. Through this therapeutic process, leaders can uncover the root causes of their behaviors and attitudes, gaining insights that can lead to more conscious and intentional leadership practices.

- Seek Professional Coaching: Leadership coaching, especially when informed by psychoanalytic principles, can help leaders understand the psychological underpinnings of their leadership style. Coaches can guide leaders in reflecting on their emotional responses, interpersonal dynamics, and decision-making processes, helping them identify patterns that may be rooted in unconscious motivations. This reflective process can facilitate personal development and enhance leadership capabilities.

- Adopt Reflective Practices: Regularly engaging in reflective practices such as journaling, meditation, or mindfulness can significantly increase self-awareness. By setting aside time for introspection, leaders can become more attuned to their inner thoughts and feelings, including those that operate below the level of conscious awareness. Journaling about daily leadership experiences and emotional reactions can provide valuable insights into unconscious motivations and behaviors.

- Seek Feedback from Others: Gathering feedback from peers, mentors, and team members can offer a mirror to a leader's behavior and how it is perceived by others. This external perspective can highlight discrepancies between the leader's self-perception and the impact of their actions, prompting reflection on the unconscious biases or assumptions that may influence their leadership style.

- Participate in Leadership Development Programs: Many leadership development programs incorporate elements of self-awareness and reflection, often drawing on psychological theories to help leaders understand the deeper aspects of their behavior. Participating in these programs can provide leaders with the tools and frameworks to explore their unconscious motivations and learn how to integrate these insights into their leadership approach.

- Cultivate Emotional Intelligence: Developing emotional intelligence skills, such as empathy, self-regulation, and social awareness, can enhance a leader's ability to recognize and manage their own emotions and those of others. This awareness can lead to a deeper understanding of the unconscious emotional drivers behind leadership behaviors and improve interpersonal relationships within the organization.

By embracing these strategies, leaders can embark on a transformative journey of self-discovery that not only enriches their personal lives but also amplifies their effectiveness as leaders. Navigating the unconscious for leadership development is not a quick fix but a continuous process of growth that requires curiosity, openness, and a willingness to confront uncomfortable truths. The rewards, however, are immeasurable, leading to more authentic, empathetic, and effective leadership.

Integrating insights from an exploration of the unconscious into leadership practice represents a profound journey towards greater authenticity and effectiveness. This process involves not just the recognition of unconscious motivations and patterns but actively applying these insights to reshape leadership behaviors and interpersonal dynamics. Here's how leaders can embark on this transformative journey:

1. Acknowledgment and Acceptance: The first step in integrating unconscious insights into leadership practice is acknowledging the existence of these hidden drivers. This means accepting that past experiences, unresolved conflicts, and deep-seated fears or desires can influence current leadership behaviors. Acceptance doesn't imply resignation but rather an openness to understanding these aspects as integral parts of one's leadership identity.

2. Reflection and Analysis: With acknowledgment comes the need for deep reflection and analysis. Leaders can benefit from regularly setting aside time to reflect on their actions, decisions, and interactions, asking themselves why they responded in certain ways and how their unconscious might have influenced these responses. This reflective practice can be supported by journaling, meditation, or discussions with a coach or therapist, providing a structured approach to uncovering and understanding unconscious motivations.

3. Seeking Feedback: Integrating insights from the unconscious into leadership practice also involves seeking and being open to feedback from others. Peers, mentors, and team members can offer valuable perspectives on a leader's behavior, some of which the leader might be unaware of. This feedback can serve as a mirror, reflecting back the leader's unconscious patterns and how they manifest in the workplace.

4. Adaptive Leadership Styles: Armed with deeper self-knowledge, leaders can begin to adapt their leadership styles to be more aligned with their authentic selves and the needs of their followers. This might involve consciously choosing to respond rather than react in stressful situations, employing empathy more intentionally, or adjusting communication styles to foster openness and trust within the team.

5. Fostering Emotional Intelligence: Emotional intelligence is a critical skill in integrating unconscious insights into leadership practice. By developing greater emotional awareness and regulation, leaders can better manage their own emotions and those of their followers. This enhanced emotional intelligence allows leaders to create a more positive and productive organizational culture, where emotions are acknowledged as valuable sources of information and guidance.

6. Implementing Change: Integrating unconscious insights often leads to change, both within the leader and in their approach to leadership. Leaders may find themselves altering their goals, redefining success, or changing how they engage with their team. Implementing these changes requires courage, commitment, and the willingness to experiment and learn from the outcomes.

7. Continuous Learning and Growth: Finally, integrating insights from the unconscious into leadership practice is an ongoing process of learning and growth. Leaders should remain open to new insights, continually engage in self-reflection, and seek opportunities for personal and professional development. This commitment to growth ensures that the integration of unconscious insights remains a dynamic and enriching part of the leader's journey.

By embracing these steps, leaders can transform their leadership style to one that is more effective, authentic, and responsive to the complexities of human behavior and organizational life. Integrating unconscious insights not only enhances leadership effectiveness but also contributes to a deeper sense of fulfillment and purpose in the leader's role.

Executive coaching plays a pivotal role in helping leaders explore and address the unconscious influences that shape their leadership style, decision-making processes, and interpersonal dynamics. Through a collaborative and confidential relationship, executive coaches provide a safe space for leaders to delve into the deeper aspects of their psyche, uncovering and understanding the unconscious motivations, fears, and desires that drive their behavior. The exploration of these unconscious influences is facilitated by a variety of coaching techniques tailored to the individual leader's needs and context.

One key technique involves reflective questioning, where coaches pose thoughtful, open-ended questions that encourage leaders to consider their actions and reactions from new perspectives. This process stimulates self-awareness, prompting leaders to reflect on the origins of their beliefs and behaviors and how these may be connected to unconscious patterns established in earlier life experiences.

Another effective technique is the use of feedback as a mirror. Coaches often gather 360-degree feedback from colleagues, direct reports, and others who work closely with the leader. This feedback provides valuable insights into how the leader's behavior is perceived by others, offering clues to unconscious biases or assumptions that may be influencing their leadership style.

Coaches also employ visualization and role-playing exercises to help leaders imagine different outcomes or approaches to challenging situations. These exercises can reveal unconscious fears or conflicts that hinder effective leadership, allowing leaders to experiment with new behaviors in a supportive environment.

Mindfulness and emotional regulation techniques are also central to executive coaching. By teaching leaders how to become more present and aware of their thoughts and feelings, coaches help them recognize the influence of unconscious emotions on their behavior. This awareness enables leaders to manage their emotions more effectively, enhancing their ability to respond rather than react in stressful situations.

Executive coaching often incorporates goal setting and action planning, with a focus on integrating insights into practical leadership improvements. Coaches work with leaders to identify specific areas for development and to create actionable strategies for change. This process includes addressing unconscious influences and translating new self-awareness into behaviors that enhance leadership effectiveness and authenticity.

The role of executive coaching in exploring and addressing unconscious influences is not just about remediation; it's about unlocking a leader's full potential. By bringing unconscious patterns to light, leaders can gain a deeper understanding of themselves and their impact on others. This enhanced self-knowledge empowers leaders to lead with greater empathy, clarity, and purpose, ultimately contributing to more effective leadership and healthier organizational cultures. Executive coaching, with its focus on individual growth and transformation, is an invaluable tool in this journey toward more conscious and impactful leadership.

Conclusion

This chapter has illuminated the profound impact of unconscious processes on leadership styles and effectiveness, revealing the intricate ways in which hidden motivations, unresolved conflicts, and deep-seated fears shape the behaviors and decisions of leaders. Through the lens of psychoanalytic theory, we've explored how early childhood experiences, ego development, and defense mechanisms contribute to the formation of leadership styles, influencing how leaders relate to their followers and navigate the complexities of organizational life.

The exploration of unconscious influences on leadership underscores the importance of self-awareness and reflection for leaders. It highlights the necessity of acknowledging and integrating these unconscious elements to foster leadership practices that are not only more effective but also more authentic and aligned with the leaders' true selves and the needs of their organizations.

Psychoanalytic insights offer valuable pathways for the personal and professional development of leaders. By engaging with the deeper aspects of their psyche, leaders can uncover the root causes of their behaviors and attitudes, opening up opportunities for growth and transformation. This deeper understanding enables leaders to adapt their styles in ways that enhance their effectiveness, improve their relationships with followers, and contribute to a positive organizational culture.

The role of executive coaching has been emphasized as a crucial tool in helping leaders navigate their unconscious influences. Coaches, using techniques such as reflective questioning, feedback analysis, and emotional regulation, facilitate leaders' journeys toward greater self-knowledge and improved leadership capabilities. This process not only benefits the leaders themselves but also has a ripple effect, enhancing the well-being and performance of their teams and the organization as a whole.

The exploration of unconscious processes in leadership through psychoanalytic theory provides a rich and nuanced understanding of leadership behavior. It underscores the value of delving into the unconscious mind to unearth insights that can lead to more nuanced, effective, and authentic leadership practices. By embracing these insights, leaders can embark on a transformative journey of personal and professional development, unlocking their full potential and fostering healthier, more dynamic organizational environments.

The exploration of the unconscious represents a profound and often challenging journey for leaders and coaches alike, yet it is undeniably rewarding for those committed to achieving excellence in leadership. Delving into the depths of the unconscious mind opens up a world of insights into our deepest motivations, fears, and desires, shedding light on the unseen forces that shape our leadership styles and effectiveness. This journey, while requiring courage and vulnerability, offers unparalleled opportunities for personal and professional growth.

Leaders and coaches are encouraged to view the exploration of the unconscious not as a daunting task but as a vital component of leadership development. The process of uncovering unconscious influences provides a pathway to more authentic, empathetic, and responsive leadership. It enables leaders to connect more deeply with themselves and their followers, fostering relationships based on mutual understanding and respect. By integrating these insights into their leadership practice, leaders can transform their approach, moving from reactive patterns to more intentional and strategic behaviors that align with their core values and the needs of their organization.

The journey into the unconscious is indeed challenging, requiring a willingness to confront uncomfortable truths and to question long-held beliefs and behaviors. However, the rewards of this exploration are immeasurable. Leaders who embark on this journey can expect to enhance their emotional intelligence, improve their decision-making, and cultivate a leadership presence that inspires trust and confidence. Moreover, by embracing the complexities of human psychology, leaders can contribute to creating organizational cultures that value growth, learning, and psychological safety.

Coaches play a crucial role in guiding leaders through this exploration, offering support, insight, and expertise to navigate the complexities of the unconscious mind. They provide a safe and confidential space for leaders to reflect, learn, and grow, facilitating the integration of psychoanalytic insights into practical and effective leadership strategies.

The examination of the unconscious is an essential aspect of leadership development, offering deep insights that can lead to profound personal and professional transformation. Leaders and coaches are encouraged to continue this exploration, embracing the challenges and rewards that come with delving into the depths of the unconscious mind. For those committed to achieving excellence in leadership, the journey into the unconscious is not just beneficial—it is indispensable. By engaging with this process, leaders can unlock their full potential, leading with greater authenticity, empathy, and effectiveness, and making a lasting impact on their organizations and the people they lead.

Part III: Applying Psychoanalytic Theory to Executive Coaching

Part III of this exploration delves into the application of psychoanalytic theory to executive coaching, offering a comprehensive framework for understanding and enhancing the coaching process. This segment begins with Chapter 6, which lays the groundwork by introducing the Foundations of Psychoanalytic Coaching. This chapter is designed to bridge the rich insights of psychoanalytic theory with the practical demands of executive coaching, providing a solid foundation for coaches and leaders alike to navigate the complex terrain of leadership development.

Psychoanalytic theory, with its deep roots in understanding the human psyche, offers a unique lens through which executive coaching can be viewed and practiced. It illuminates the unconscious processes, motivations, and conflicts that influence behavior and interpersonal dynamics, thereby offering a profound depth of understanding and intervention for executive coaches. Chapter 6 sets the stage for applying these insights, showing how the unconscious mind plays a pivotal role in shaping leadership styles, decision-making, and organizational culture.

The chapter aims to equip coaches with the knowledge and tools to integrate psychoanalytic concepts into their coaching practice. This includes understanding the significance of early childhood experiences, transference and countertransference dynamics, defense mechanisms, and the shadow self in the context of leadership development. By grounding their practice in psychoanalytic theory, coaches can more effectively guide leaders through the process of self-discovery and transformation, helping them to unlock their full potential and navigate the challenges of leadership with greater insight and flexibility.

We address the practical aspects of psychoanalytic coaching, such as establishing a therapeutic alliance, creating a safe and confidential space for exploration, and using reflective questioning techniques to probe deeper into the leader's psyche. It also discusses the ethical considerations and boundaries that are essential to maintaining a professional and effective coaching relationship.

Building on the foundational concepts introduced in Chapter 6, Chapter 7 delves deeper into the Techniques and Tools for Psychoanalytic Coaching, equipping coaches with specific strategies to facilitate leaders' exploration and integration of unconscious processes. This chapter is designed to translate the theoretical underpinnings of psychoanalytic theory into practical applications within the coaching context, enabling coaches to guide leaders through the complex landscape of their inner worlds.

The chapter begins by exploring the various techniques that are central to psychoanalytic coaching, emphasizing the importance of active listening, empathetic engagement, and the nuanced interpretation of verbal and non-verbal cues. Coaches learn how to create a reflective space where leaders can safely confront and explore their unconscious motivations, fears, and desires. Techniques such as dream analysis, free association, and the exploration of significant life events are discussed, highlighting their relevance in uncovering the unconscious influences on leadership behavior.

Chapter 7 introduces tools designed to facilitate the psychoanalytic coaching process. These include the use of metaphor and storytelling, which can help leaders articulate and make sense of their internal experiences, and reflective exercises that encourage leaders to engage with their shadow selves and defense mechanisms. The chapter also covers the use of journaling as a tool for self-reflection, enabling leaders to document and reflect on their thoughts, feelings, and behaviors as they navigate their coaching journey.

A significant focus of this chapter is on navigating the dynamics of transference and countertransference within the coaching relationship. Coaches are provided with strategies to recognize and manage these complex interactions, ensuring that they can maintain an effective coaching alliance while facilitating deep psychological exploration. The chapter emphasizes the importance of self-awareness and ongoing supervision for coaches, ensuring that they remain attuned to their own unconscious processes and how these might influence the coaching relationship.

In Chapter 7 we also address the challenges and ethical considerations inherent in psychoanalytic coaching, offering guidance on how to navigate sensitive issues and maintain professional boundaries. Coaches are encouraged to adopt a stance of curiosity and openness, fostering a non-judgmental environment that supports leaders in their journey towards self-discovery and personal growth. Techniques and Tools for Psychoanalytic Coaching provides a comprehensive overview of the practical aspects of applying psychoanalytic theory to executive coaching. By equipping coaches with a robust set of techniques and tools, this chapter aims to enhance the effectiveness of psychoanalytic coaching, enabling leaders to achieve greater self-understanding, overcome unconscious barriers to their leadership effectiveness, and embark on a path of transformative personal and professional development.

Completing the exploration within Part III, Chapter 8: Addressing Leadership Challenges Psychoanalytically, ventures into the practical application of psychoanalytic principles to confront and navigate the myriad challenges leaders face in the modern organizational landscape. This chapter synthesizes the foundational knowledge and techniques discussed in previous chapters, illustrating how these can be applied to specific leadership issues, thereby offering a roadmap for transformative solutions that address the root causes of these challenges.

Chapter 8 provides an in-depth examination of common leadership challenges, including decision-making under pressure, conflict resolution, fostering team cohesion, managing change, and enhancing emotional intelligence. It then demonstrates how a psychoanalytic approach can unearth the unconscious dynamics underlying these issues, such as unresolved conflicts, projection, and the influence of the leader's shadow. By bringing these unconscious factors to light, leaders can gain a deeper understanding of the psychological forces at play, enabling them to address challenges more effectively and authentically.

The chapter emphasizes the value of psychoanalytic coaching in helping leaders navigate these challenges. Through case studies and real-life examples, it showcases how coaches can guide leaders to recognize their unconscious motivations, navigate their internal conflicts, and transform their leadership practices. This process not only aids in resolving immediate challenges but also contributes to the leader's ongoing personal and professional development, fostering a leadership style that is more reflective, resilient, and responsive to the complexities of organizational life.

We explore the impact of addressing leadership challenges psychoanalytically on organizational culture. It illustrates how leaders who engage with their unconscious motivations and conflicts can inspire a culture of openness, introspection, and growth. Such a culture not only supports the resolution of individual and team challenges but also enhances the organization's overall adaptability, innovation, and effectiveness.

Chapter 8 underscores the transformative potential of integrating psychoanalytic insights into leadership development. It encourages leaders and coaches to embrace the complexity of the human psyche, leveraging the depth and richness of psychoanalytic theory to foster leadership that is not only effective in navigating challenges but also profound in its capacity to catalyze personal growth and organizational change. Through this psychoanalytic lens, leaders are equipped to turn challenges into opportunities for development, leading to more nuanced, empathetic, and impactful leadership.

Chapter 6: Foundations of Psychoanalytic Coaching

Chapter 6 delves into the Foundations of Psychoanalytic Coaching, a transformative approach that marries the depth of psychoanalytic theory with the dynamic field of executive coaching. At the heart of psychoanalytic coaching lies the goal of facilitating profound personal and professional development by delving into and interpreting the unconscious processes that underlie human behavior and thought. This approach seeks to illuminate the hidden motivations, unresolved conflicts, and deep-seated fears and desires that influence a leader's actions, decisions, and interactions within the organizational context.

Psychoanalytic coaching is predicated on the belief that by bringing the unconscious into conscious awareness, individuals can achieve greater insight into their behaviors and motivations, leading to more authentic and effective leadership. It operates on the principle that our past experiences, particularly those from early childhood, shape our personality, our approach to relationships, and our leadership style in ways that we are often not consciously aware of. These unconscious influences can manifest in various aspects of leadership, from decision-making and conflict resolution to interpersonal dynamics and organizational culture.

The process of psychoanalytic coaching involves a deep, reflective exploration of the self, guided by a trained coach who uses psychoanalytic concepts and techniques to facilitate this journey. The coach and leader engage in a collaborative relationship, where the leader is encouraged to reflect on their experiences, emotions, and behaviors. Through this reflective process, leaders can begin to recognize the patterns that have been unconsciously guiding their actions and to understand the origins of these patterns in their past experiences.

This chapter will introduce the key concepts and theories that form the basis of psychoanalytic coaching, including the structure of the psyche, defense mechanisms, transference and countertransference, and the role of the unconscious in shaping behavior. It will also explore the goals of psychoanalytic coaching, which extend beyond immediate problem-solving to encompass a more comprehensive understanding of the self and its impact on leadership.

By engaging with psychoanalytic coaching, leaders are offered a unique opportunity to confront and integrate aspects of themselves that have remained in the shadows, thereby unlocking new levels of self-awareness, emotional intelligence, and leadership effectiveness. This chapter sets the stage for a deeper exploration of the techniques and tools of psychoanalytic coaching, preparing the reader to apply these insights to the challenges and opportunities of leadership development. Through this exploration, psychoanalytic coaching emerges as a powerful avenue for achieving profound personal growth and transformative leadership.

Chapter 6 delves into the foundational elements of psychoanalytic coaching, focusing on the intricacies of the coaching relationship and the techniques that enable deep psychological exploration and development. Central to this exploration are three core concepts: the coach's role as a reflective container, the interpretation of unconscious communication, and the nuanced dynamics of transference and countertransference. Each of these elements plays a crucial role in facilitating the leader's personal and professional growth by unlocking insights into the unconscious processes that influence behavior and decision-making.

The concept of the coach as a reflective container is pivotal in psychoanalytic coaching. In this role, the coach provides a safe, supportive, and non-judgmental space where leaders can explore their thoughts, feelings, and experiences without fear of criticism or rejection. This environment allows leaders to express and reflect upon their innermost thoughts and emotions, including those that are unconscious or difficult to articulate. The coach acts as a mirror, reflecting the leader's communications in a way that facilitates deeper self-awareness and understanding. This reflective process is essential for unpacking the complex layers of the leader's psyche and for fostering transformative insights.

A fundamental aspect of psychoanalytic coaching is the coach's ability to interpret unconscious communication. Leaders often convey thoughts and feelings indirectly through their words, actions, and non-verbal cues, revealing underlying motivations and conflicts of which they may not be consciously aware. Skilled psychoanalytic coaches can decode these signals, helping leaders to recognize and understand the unconscious dynamics that influence their leadership style. This interpretation involves a delicate balance of listening, questioning, and feedback, requiring the coach to be attuned to the subtleties of the leader's communication and to respond in a way that encourages further exploration and insight.

Transference and countertransference are complex dynamics that arise in the psychoanalytic coaching relationship, mirroring patterns from past relationships. Transference occurs when leaders project feelings and attitudes from significant past relationships onto the coach, potentially viewing the coach through the lens of these previous experiences. Countertransference, on the other hand, involves the coach's own emotional responses to the leader's transference, influenced by the coach's personal history and unconscious processes. Navigating these dynamics is crucial for maintaining an effective coaching relationship. Coaches must remain aware of and manage their own reactions to ensure that they can continue to provide the reflective support necessary for the leader's development.

This chapter aims to unpack these foundational elements, offering insights into how psychoanalytic coaching can facilitate a deep dive into the leader's unconscious mind. By exploring the role of the coach as a reflective container, the interpretation of unconscious communication, and the dynamics of transference and countertransference, leaders are guided towards a profound understanding of themselves and their impact on others. This process not only enhances leadership effectiveness but also promotes personal growth and self-awareness, laying the groundwork for lasting transformation.

The Role of the Coach as a Reflective Container

The concept of containment, rooted in psychoanalytic theory, refers to the process by which one individual receives and understands another's emotional communication, thereby allowing the latter to process and make sense of their emotions, thoughts, and unconscious material. In the context of psychoanalytic coaching, the coach serves as a reflective container, a crucial role that involves absorbing, holding, and reflecting back the coachee's emotional experiences in a way that promotes understanding and insight.

Containment is predicated on the coach's ability to be emotionally attuned to the coachee, to listen deeply not just to the content of what is being said but to the emotions and unconscious dynamics underlying the communication. This requires a high level of empathy, patience, and the capacity to tolerate one's own emotional responses without becoming overwhelmed or defensively shutting down. The coach, by remaining present and engaged, offers a secure psychological space where the coachee can explore their innermost thoughts and feelings, including those that may have been repressed or not fully understood.

As a reflective container, the coach does not merely passively receive the coachee's emotional material but actively processes it and offers it back in a more digestible form. This might involve clarifying the coachee's experiences, highlighting patterns of thought or behavior, or gently challenging the coachee's assumptions and defenses. The aim is to help the coachee gain insight into their emotional and psychological processes, fostering a deeper understanding of themselves and their interactions with others.

The process of containment and reflection enables coachees to work through complex emotions and unconscious material that might otherwise remain unexamined and continue to influence their behavior in unproductive ways. By bringing these aspects into conscious awareness, coachees can begin to address underlying issues, resolve internal conflicts, and make more informed choices in their personal and professional lives.

For coaches, serving as a reflective container requires a delicate balance of involvement and detachment. Coaches must be emotionally engaged enough to be empathetic and attuned to the coachee's needs, yet sufficiently detached to maintain objectivity and avoid becoming entangled in the coachee's emotional dynamics. This balance allows coaches to provide the necessary support and guidance while enabling coachees to take responsibility for their own growth and development.

The concept of the reflective container is central to psychoanalytic coaching, providing a framework for understanding and facilitating the coachee's emotional and psychological development. Through this process, coaches can help coachees navigate the depths of their unconscious, unlocking new levels of insight and self-awareness that are essential for effective leadership and personal fulfillment.

Creating a safe and holding environment in coaching is fundamental to fostering a space where coachees feel secure enough to explore their vulnerabilities, deep-seated issues, and unconscious conflicts. This environment is characterized by trust, empathy, and non-judgment, essential for facilitating profound personal and professional development. To achieve such an atmosphere, coaches can employ several strategies:

1. Establish Trust and Rapport: Building a strong foundation of trust and rapport is the first step in creating a safe coaching environment. This involves demonstrating reliability, consistency, and confidentiality from the outset. Coaches can foster trust by being transparent about the coaching process, setting clear boundaries, and respecting the coachee's experiences and perspectives. Personal warmth, active

listening, and genuine interest in the coachee's well-being further contribute to this foundational trust.

2. Empathetic Listening: Empathetic listening goes beyond hearing the words spoken; it involves understanding the emotions and underlying thoughts that the coachee communicates. By reflecting back what they hear and validating the coachee's feelings, coaches can demonstrate empathy and acceptance, encouraging coachees to open up and share more deeply. This level of attunement signals to coachees that their inner experiences are seen and valued, reinforcing the safety of the coaching environment.

3. Non-Judgmental Stance: Maintaining a non-judgmental stance is crucial for encouraging openness and vulnerability. Coaches should cultivate an attitude of curiosity rather than evaluation, where all aspects of the coachee's experience are welcome for exploration. This approach helps coachees feel accepted and understood, reducing the fear of judgment or criticism that can inhibit self-disclosure.

4. Encourage Self-Compassion: Coaches can promote an atmosphere of self-compassion, guiding coachees to treat themselves with kindness and understanding, especially when confronting difficult or painful aspects of their psyche. By modeling self-compassion and highlighting its importance, coaches can help coachees develop a more forgiving and gentle approach to their own imperfections and struggles.

5. Provide Reassurance and Support: As coachees delve into sensitive areas, they may experience heightened vulnerability or emotional discomfort. Coaches can offer reassurance and support, affirming the coachee's courage in facing these challenges and emphasizing the growth and insight that can emerge from such exploration. This supportive presence helps coachees feel held and encouraged, even in the midst of difficult introspection.

6. Gradual Deepening: Coaches should recognize the pace at which each coachee is comfortable diving into deeper issues and adjust their approach accordingly. Gradual deepening allows coachees to build resilience and readiness to explore more complex layers of their psyche over time. Coaches can facilitate this process by gently introducing more probing questions or reflections as the coaching relationship evolves, always attuned to the coachee's readiness and response.

Creating a safe and holding environment is an ongoing process, requiring coaches to be responsive to the coachee's needs and emotional states throughout the coaching journey. By implementing these strategies, coaches can establish a supportive space where coachees feel empowered to engage in meaningful self-exploration and tackle the unconscious conflicts that impact their leadership and personal growth. This environment is not only conducive to addressing deep-seated issues but also pivotal in enabling the transformative potential of psychoanalytic coaching.

The coach's emotional regulation is a cornerstone of effective psychoanalytic coaching, playing a critical role in maintaining a reflective stance that is essential for a productive coaching relationship. The capacity of coaches to manage their own emotional responses ensures that the coaching space remains focused on the coachee's needs and development, rather than being influenced by the coach's personal reactions or issues. This ability to regulate emotions is not only vital for creating a safe and supportive environment but also for modeling emotional intelligence and resilience for the coachee.

Emotional regulation in coaching involves several key aspects. Firstly, it requires self-awareness, as coaches must be attuned to their emotional states and understand how these might be triggered during coaching sessions. This awareness allows coaches to recognize when their responses are more about their own feelings or experiences than about the coachee's issues. By identifying these moments, coaches can choose how to best manage their emotions, ensuring that their interventions are thoughtful and aligned with the coachee's needs.

Emotional regulation is essential for dealing with the complex dynamics of transference and countertransference that can arise in psychoanalytic coaching. Coaches might find themselves on the receiving end of strong emotions or projections from the coachee, which can evoke personal feelings or memories. The ability to regulate these emotional responses enables coaches to remain objective and maintain a reflective stance, facilitating a deeper exploration of the coachee's unconscious processes without being derailed by their own emotional reactions.

Maintaining a reflective stance through emotional regulation also exemplifies for the coachee a healthy approach to managing emotions. This modeling can be particularly impactful, teaching coachees, often implicitly, how to recognize, understand, and regulate their emotions more effectively. It reinforces the idea that emotions, even difficult ones, can be navigated constructively, leading to greater emotional intelligence and resilience.

The coach's emotional regulation contributes to a coaching relationship where trust, openness, and exploration can flourish. It allows coaches to challenge coachees in a supportive manner, provide feedback that is both honest and empathetic, and navigate the coaching process with flexibility and insight. This approach not only enhances the immediate coaching relationship but also contributes to the coachee's long-term development, as they learn to approach their leadership challenges and personal growth with a similar level of emotional awareness and regulation. The coach's ability to manage their emotional responses and maintain a reflective stance is fundamental to the success of psychoanalytic coaching. It underpins the creation of a productive coaching relationship, supports the coachee's exploration of deep-seated issues, and models effective strategies for emotional intelligence and resilience. Through careful emotional regulation, coaches can facilitate transformative experiences that enable coachees to achieve greater self-understanding, personal growth, and leadership effectiveness.

Understanding and Interpreting Unconscious Communication

In the coaching context, unconscious communication can manifest in a myriad of subtle yet revealing ways, offering windows into the coachee's deeper thoughts, feelings, and conflicts. These manifestations provide invaluable clues for the psychoanalytic coach, who is trained to attune to and interpret these signals. Understanding these forms of unconscious communication enables coaches to explore beneath the surface of what is explicitly stated, facilitating a deeper dive into the coachee's psyche.

- Verbal Slips: Often referred to as Freudian slips, verbal slips occur when coachees say something other than what they intended, potentially revealing underlying thoughts or desires. These slips can be particularly revealing, as they may express wishes, fears, or feelings that the coachee is not fully aware of. Coaches attentive to these slips can gently explore their significance, guiding coachees to uncover and confront hidden aspects of their experiences.

- Body Language: Non-verbal cues, such as gestures, postures, and facial expressions, are powerful forms of unconscious communication. They can convey emotions and attitudes that coachees may not be verbally expressing, such as anxiety, defensiveness, or openness to change. By observing these physical expressions, coaches can gain insights into the coachee's emotional state and internal conflicts, even when their words may suggest otherwise.

- Emotional Reactions: The intensity and nature of emotional reactions during coaching sessions can also signal unconscious processes at work. Sudden shifts in mood, disproportionate emotional responses to certain topics, or the avoidance of emotional expression altogether can indicate areas of sensitivity or unresolved issues. These emotional reactions offer clues to the coach about areas that may require further exploration.

- Use of Metaphors: The metaphors and analogies coachees use to describe their experiences, challenges, or relationships can reveal much about their internal world. Metaphors often encapsulate complex emotions and situations in a way that direct language cannot, providing insights into how coachees perceive themselves and their environments. Coaches can explore these metaphors to help coachees articulate and understand their unconscious beliefs and feelings.

Recognizing and interpreting these forms of unconscious communication require a coach to be deeply attuned to the coachee, employing a high degree of empathy and perceptiveness. This attentiveness allows the coach to identify patterns, contradictions, and themes in the coachee's communication, which can then be explored to facilitate self-awareness and insight.

By paying close attention to verbal slips, body language, emotional reactions, and the use of metaphors, psychoanalytic coaches can navigate the depths of the coachee's unconscious, bringing to light the underlying dynamics that influence their thoughts, behaviors, and leadership style. This exploration is central to psychoanalytic coaching, enabling coachees to achieve a deeper understanding of themselves and to develop more authentic and effective ways of leading.

Interpreting unconscious communication in the coaching context requires a nuanced understanding of psychoanalytic theories and the application of specific techniques that can unlock the deeper meanings behind a coachee's words, behaviors, and emotional expressions. Techniques such as dream analysis, free association, and symbolic interpretation serve as bridges to the unconscious, facilitating insights into the coachee's inner world and promoting transformative personal development.

Dream analysis is a classic psychoanalytic technique that involves exploring the content and emotions of dreams to uncover underlying thoughts and feelings. In coaching, when coachees share dreams related to their professional lives or personal challenges, the coach can guide them through an examination of the dream's imagery and narratives. This process can reveal unconscious fears, desires, and conflicts, offering valuable insights that might not be accessible through conventional dialogue.

Free association is another technique drawn from psychoanalysis, encouraging coachees to express whatever thoughts come to mind without censorship or judgment. This stream-of-consciousness approach can lead to unexpected connections and revelations, as the seemingly random thoughts and images that emerge often have underlying associations that reflect the coachee's unconscious preoccupations. Coaches skilled in facilitating free association can help coachees navigate these thoughts, identifying patterns and themes that shed light on their unconscious motivations and barriers.

Symbolic interpretation involves the analysis of metaphors, symbols, and analogies used by coachees to describe their experiences and feelings. These symbolic expressions can convey complex emotional states and internal conflicts in a condensed form, revealing aspects of the coachee's psyche that are difficult to articulate directly. By unpacking these symbols and exploring their meanings, coaches can help coachees gain a deeper understanding of their unconscious drivers and how these influence their behavior and decision-making.

The application of these interpretation techniques requires sensitivity and skill on the part of the coach. It is essential to maintain an atmosphere of trust and safety, ensuring that coachees feel supported and understood as they explore the vulnerable territories of their unconscious mind. Coaches must also be attuned to the coachee's readiness to engage with this level of depth, pacing the exploration in a way that respects the coachee's boundaries and psychological resilience.

Coaches should approach the interpretation of unconscious communication with humility and openness, acknowledging the speculative nature of this work and the coachee's autonomy in making meaning of their experiences. The goal is not to provide definitive answers but to facilitate a process of inquiry and reflection that empowers coachees to discover their own truths and pathways to growth.

Techniques for interpreting unconscious communication, such as dream analysis, free association, and symbolic interpretation, are invaluable tools in psychoanalytic coaching. They enable coaches to guide coachees through the exploration of their unconscious mind, uncovering insights that can lead to profound personal and professional development. By drawing upon these psychoanalytic techniques, coaches can deepen their practice, offering coachees a unique and transformative coaching experience that fosters greater self-awareness, authenticity, and effectiveness in their roles.

Understanding unconscious communication significantly enhances the coaching process by offering deep insights into the coachee's internal conflicts, desires, and defense mechanisms. This deeper understanding can transform the coaching relationship, making it a powerful conduit for personal and professional development. Here are examples illustrating how the interpretation of unconscious communication can be applied in coaching to facilitate profound growth and insight.

Case Example 1: Uncovering Hidden Conflicts Through Verbal Slips

A coachee frequently makes verbal slips, referring to their team as "children" rather than "team members." Upon exploring these slips, the coach gently probes the coachee's feelings towards their leadership role. It's revealed that the coachee unconsciously views themselves in a parental role, feeling overly responsible for solving all problems and protecting the team from any form of criticism or failure. This insight leads to a discussion about healthy boundaries, delegation, and empowering team members, addressing the coachee's hidden conflict between wanting to foster independence and fearing loss of control.

Case Example 2: Understanding Defense Mechanisms through Emotional Reactions

A coachee exhibits strong emotional reactions when discussing feedback about needing to improve their communication skills. They quickly become defensive, rationalizing their communication style and blaming others for misunderstandings. By recognizing this pattern as a defense mechanism, the coach invites the coachee to explore the emotions underlying their defensiveness. This exploration reveals a deep-seated fear of being perceived as inadequate, stemming from early career experiences. Acknowledging this fear allows the coachee to approach feedback more openly, seeing it as an opportunity for growth rather than a threat.

Case Example 3: Decoding Desires through Symbolic Interpretation

A coachee often uses the metaphor of "hitting a wall" when describing attempts to innovate within their organization. The coach explores the imagery and feelings associated with this metaphor, revealing feelings of isolation and a desire for more collaborative and supportive organizational culture. This metaphor becomes a starting point for discussing strategies to build alliances and foster a culture of innovation and support, directly addressing the coachee's underlying desire for connection and teamwork.

Case Example 4: Free Association Revealing Unconscious Desires

During a session focused on career progression, the coach employs free association, asking the coachee to share immediate thoughts related to their future goals. The coachee unexpectedly mentions a long-forgotten hobby, which sparks a conversation about creativity and fulfillment. This detour uncovers an unconscious desire to integrate more creative expression into their work, leading to actionable steps to align the coachee's career trajectory with these newly acknowledged values and desires.

Case Example 5: Body Language Indicating Unresolved Conflicts

A coachee consistently avoids eye contact and closes their body posture when discussing their leadership role. The coach observes these non-verbal cues and inquiries about the coachee's feelings towards being in a position of authority. This prompts a reflection on past experiences of being micromanaged, revealing an unresolved conflict around autonomy and control. By addressing this conflict, the coachee and coach can work on strategies for the coachee to assert their leadership style confidently while fostering autonomy within their team.

These examples illustrate the power of understanding unconscious communication in the coaching process. By interpreting verbal slips, emotional reactions, symbolic language, and body language, coaches can uncover significant insights into coachees' internal worlds. This understanding facilitates a coaching journey that not only addresses surface-level issues but also engages with the deeper psychological dynamics at play, paving the way for lasting change and development.

The Use of Self in Coaching: Transference and Countertransference Dynamics

Transference, a concept originally developed in psychoanalysis, plays a significant role in the coaching relationship as well. It refers to the process by which coachees unconsciously transfer feelings, attitudes, and desires from significant past relationships onto the coach. This phenomenon is rooted in the human tendency to replicate patterns of interaction and emotional responses that were formed in early relationships, particularly with primary caregivers or influential figures. In the coaching context, transference can manifest in various ways, influencing how coachees perceive and interact with their coach, often without conscious awareness of the transfer of these past emotional experiences.

For example, a coachee might start to see the coach as a parental figure, seeking approval and fearing criticism in a manner that mirrors their relationship with a parent. This might lead the coachee to either strive excessively for the coach's validation or, conversely, to rebel against the coach's guidance, mirroring dynamics from their past. Similarly, if a coachee had experiences with authoritative figures who were dismissive or undermining, they might unconsciously expect similar behaviors from the coach, leading to feelings of defensiveness or resistance even when the coach is supportive and encouraging.

Transference can significantly impact the coaching process, affecting the coachee's openness, receptivity to feedback, and overall engagement in the coaching relationship. It can bring forth a rich tapestry of emotions and reactions that, while not directly related to the current coaching relationship, offer valuable insights into the coachee's inner world. Recognizing and addressing transference can thus be a powerful avenue for personal growth and development within the coaching process.

The coach's role involves observing and interpreting these transference dynamics without becoming entangled in them. By maintaining a reflective and neutral stance, the coach can help the coachee understand and work through these transferred feelings and attitudes. This might involve gently bringing awareness to the ways in which past experiences are influencing the coachee's perceptions of the coaching relationship, facilitating a deeper exploration of these underlying patterns, and supporting the coachee in developing new, healthier ways of relating to others.

The acknowledgment and exploration of transference within the coaching relationship can lead to transformative breakthroughs, as coachees gain insights into their unconscious motivations, fears, and desires. This process can help coachees to disentangle past emotional experiences from present interactions, enabling them to engage more authentically and productively in their relationships both within and outside the coaching context.

Transference in coaching represents both a challenge and an opportunity. By understanding and skillfully navigating these dynamics, coaches can facilitate a process of profound personal discovery and change, helping coachees to overcome limiting patterns and to achieve greater emotional freedom and effectiveness in their personal and professional lives.

Countertransference, a concept integral to psychoanalytic theory, refers to the emotional reactions and responses that coaches (or therapists) have towards their coachees. It encompasses the feelings, attitudes, and fantasies that are unconsciously projected onto the coachee, often stemming from the coach's own past experiences and unresolved conflicts. Understanding and managing countertransference is crucial for coaches, as it not only affects the dynamics of the coaching relationship but also serves as a valuable source of insight into the coachee's inner world and the challenges they face.

Countertransference can manifest in various ways, such as feeling overly responsible for a coachee's success, experiencing irritation or frustration towards a coachee, or finding oneself unusually aligned with or defensive of a coachee's perspective. These reactions, while natural, can cloud the coach's objectivity and hinder the coaching process if not properly recognized and managed. However, when understood and used reflectively, countertransference becomes a powerful tool, offering deep insights into the coachee's emotional state and relational patterns.

The necessity for coaches to recognize and understand their own emotional reactions lies in the fact that these reactions can reveal much about the coachee's psychological dynamics. For example, if a coach finds themselves feeling consistently drained or overwhelmed after sessions with a particular coachee, it might indicate the coachee's unexpressed feelings of exhaustion or their tendency to over-rely on others for emotional support. Similarly, if a coach notices an urge to rescue or fix problems for a coachee, it may reflect the coachee's difficulty in taking responsibility for their actions or their unconscious expectation for others to solve their challenges.

To effectively navigate countertransference, coaches must cultivate a high degree of self-awareness and engage in continuous self-reflection. This involves acknowledging one's own emotional responses and exploring their origins, ideally with the support of supervision or personal psychotherapy. Such practices help coaches to differentiate their own emotional material from that of their coachees, ensuring that their responses are grounded in the coachee's needs rather than their own unconscious projections.

Recognizing countertransference allows coaches to adjust their approach and interventions more accurately to the coachee's underlying issues. By reflecting on their emotional responses, coaches can gain clues about what the coachee might be struggling to express directly, guiding them to probe more deeply into certain areas or to provide the support the coachee needs to explore difficult emotions.

Countertransference is an essential aspect of the coaching process, offering valuable insights into both the coachee's inner world and the coach's own psychological landscape. By recognizing and understanding their emotional reactions to coachees, coaches can enhance their effectiveness, foster deeper connections, and facilitate more meaningful and transformative coaching outcomes. The ability to navigate countertransference with insight and skill reflects a coach's professional maturity and dedication to their own and their coachee's growth and development.

Managing transference and countertransference in coaching is crucial for maintaining a productive and ethical coaching relationship. These dynamics, if not recognized and managed, can obscure the coach's objectivity and impede the coachee's progress. However, when effectively navigated, they can enrich the coaching process, providing deeper insights into the coachee's experiences and facilitating significant growth. Here are strategies for managing these complex dynamics constructively:

- Supervision: Engaging in regular supervision is paramount for coaches to manage transference and countertransference effectively. Supervision provides a reflective space for coaches to explore their feelings, reactions, and the dynamics of their coaching relationships in a confidential setting. A skilled supervisor can help coaches identify instances of transference and countertransference, understand their origins, and develop strategies for addressing them. This external perspective is invaluable for maintaining professional boundaries and ensuring the coaching process remains focused on the coachee's development.

- Personal Therapy for Coaches: Coaches can benefit significantly from undergoing personal therapy, especially if it includes a psychoanalytic component. Therapy offers coaches a personal experience of working through their own psychological issues, including unconscious biases, unresolved conflicts, and emotional triggers. This self-exploration enhances a coach's self-awareness and emotional regulation, making them more attuned to the subtleties of transference and countertransference in their professional work. Personal therapy also models the process of introspection and growth that coaches facilitate for their coachees.

- Ongoing Self-Reflection: Coaches should cultivate a practice of ongoing self-reflection to manage transference and countertransference effectively. This can involve journaling about coaching sessions, reflecting on emotional responses to coachees, and regularly assessing one's own well-being and professional practice. Self-reflection helps coaches to remain grounded in their professional role, to recognize their emotional responses as they arise, and to consider how these might influence the coaching process. By actively engaging in self-reflection, coaches can navigate these dynamics more consciously and use them as sources of insight rather than allowing them to become obstacles.

- Educational Development: Continuously expanding one's knowledge and understanding of psychoanalytic theories and their application to coaching is another strategy for managing transference and countertransference. Participating in workshops, courses, and reading relevant literature can provide coaches with additional tools and frameworks for identifying and working with these dynamics. Education in this area reinforces a coach's ability to recognize the deeper psychological processes at play in coaching relationships and to apply psychoanalytic concepts in a manner that supports coachee growth.

- Establishing Clear Boundaries: Clear professional boundaries are essential for managing transference and countertransference. Coaches should communicate the structure, goals, and limits of the coaching relationship from the outset and revisit these as needed throughout the coaching process. Boundaries help to create a safe and professional environment where transference and countertransference can be explored without compromising the integrity of the coaching relationship.

Effectively managing transference and countertransference requires a multifaceted approach that includes supervision, personal therapy, ongoing self-reflection, educational development, and clear boundary setting. By adopting these strategies, coaches can ensure that these complex dynamics are used constructively, enhancing the coaching process and supporting the coachee's journey toward deeper self-awareness and personal development.

Ethical Considerations in Psychoanalytic Coaching

Maintaining ethical boundaries and confidentiality is paramount in the coaching relationship, particularly when delving into the sensitive terrain of unconscious material. The exploration of this deeply personal and often vulnerable aspect of a coachee's psyche necessitates a foundation of trust and safety, which is established and upheld through the coach's commitment to these ethical principles.

Boundaries delineate the professional nature of the coaching relationship, distinguishing it from other types of relationships and ensuring that interactions remain focused on the coachee's development and well-being. Clear boundaries help prevent misunderstandings, protect both the coach and the coachee from potential harm, and create a structured space where exploration and growth can occur. This is especially crucial when unconscious dynamics such as transference and countertransference are at play, as they can blur the lines between personal and professional realms. Coaches must be vigilant in recognizing and managing these dynamics to maintain the integrity of the coaching engagement.

Confidentiality is equally critical, serving as the bedrock of the coaching relationship. It assures coachees that the intimate details of their thoughts, feelings, and experiences shared during coaching sessions are protected. This assurance fosters an environment where coachees feel safe to disclose and examine aspects of themselves that they may have never verbalized or fully acknowledged. The sensitive nature of unconscious material, which may include repressed emotions, past traumas, or unresolved conflicts, amplifies the need for strict confidentiality. Breaching this trust can cause significant harm to the coachee, potentially derailing their developmental journey and damaging the professional credibility of the coach.

In practice, maintaining boundaries and confidentiality involves several key actions. Coaches should clearly communicate the limits of confidentiality at the outset of the coaching relationship, including any legal or ethical circumstances under which confidentiality might need to be broken. Regularly revisiting and reinforcing these boundaries throughout the coaching process can help to keep the relationship on professional footing, even as deep and potentially challenging material is explored.

Coaches should engage in continuous self-reflection and seek supervision to navigate their own reactions and responses to coachees' disclosures. This reflective practice supports coaches in staying within ethical boundaries while effectively managing their countertransference, ensuring that their guidance remains in the best interest of the coachee.

The ethical imperatives of maintaining boundaries and confidentiality are not just regulatory requirements but fundamental to creating a transformative coaching experience. They allow for a depth of exploration and vulnerability that can lead to profound insights and change, making the journey into the unconscious a powerful catalyst for personal and professional development. By upholding these principles, coaches honor the trust placed in them by their coachees and contribute to the integrity and efficacy of the coaching profession.

Managing intense emotional material in coaching requires a thoughtful, ethical, and sensitive approach to ensure the coachee's safety and respect for their psychological well-being. When coachees share deeply personal or distressing experiences, or when they exhibit strong emotional reactions, coaches must navigate these situations with care, maintaining a supportive environment that fosters healing and growth. Here are guidelines for handling such delicate dynamics:

1. Establish a Safe and Trusting Environment: The foundation for managing intense emotions is a coaching relationship built on trust, safety, and confidentiality. Coachees need to feel secure in sharing their feelings and vulnerabilities. Coaches can foster this environment by consistently demonstrating empathy, understanding, and non-judgment, and by reinforcing the confidentiality of the coaching sessions.

2. Recognize and Validate Emotions: Coaches should acknowledge and validate the coachee's emotions, showing that it's acceptable and safe to express feelings openly. Validation involves actively listening, reflecting back what you've heard, and conveying understanding of the coachee's emotional experience. This acknowledgment can help coachees feel seen and supported, reducing feelings of isolation or shame associated with intense emotions.

3. Maintain Emotional Composure and Professionalism: Coaches must manage their own emotional responses to maintain a calm and steady presence. This composure helps in providing a stabilizing influence for coachees navigating difficult emotions. Coaches should be mindful of their

reactions and use supervision or personal therapy to address any feelings that might impact their ability to support the coachee effectively.

4. Guide Without Leading: When dealing with intense emotional disclosures, it's important for coaches to guide coachees through their feelings without directing or leading the conversation to a predetermined conclusion. Coaches should facilitate exploration and self-discovery, allowing coachees to process their emotions at their own pace and find their own resolutions.

5. Know When to Refer: Coaches must recognize the limits of their expertise and the coaching relationship. If a coachee's emotional needs exceed what coaching can provide, especially if there are signs of psychological distress that require therapeutic intervention, coaches should ethically and sensitively discuss the possibility of referral to a mental health professional. This conversation should be approached with care, emphasizing the coachee's well-being and the benefits of seeking specialized support.

6. Provide Resources and Support: In cases where coachees are dealing with intense emotions, coaches can offer additional resources such as readings, exercises, or workshops that support emotional regulation and resilience-building. However, these resources should complement, not replace, professional mental health support if needed.

7. Follow Up and Check-In: After an intense emotional disclosure or reaction, coaches should follow up with coachees to check in on their well-being. This follow-up demonstrates care and concern for the coachee's welfare and provides an opportunity to discuss any lingering effects of the emotional material explored in previous sessions.

Handling intense emotional material with sensitivity and respect is crucial in coaching. By adhering to these guidelines, coaches can ensure that they provide a supportive space for coachees to explore their emotions and challenges, fostering psychological safety and promoting meaningful personal development.

Conclusion

This chapter has underscored the profound value of integrating psychoanalytic principles into coaching practice, highlighting how this approach can facilitate deeper, more transformative coaching outcomes. By delving into the unconscious aspects of the coachee's psyche, psychoanalytic coaching opens up avenues for significant personal and professional growth that go beyond the surface-level changes typically addressed in more conventional coaching methods.

Key points from the chapter include:

- The Importance of the Unconscious: The chapter began by establishing the critical role of unconscious processes in shaping behaviors, decisions, and interpersonal dynamics. Understanding these processes enables coaches to address the root causes of coachees' challenges, leading to more sustainable and impactful changes.

- Foundational Elements of Psychoanalytic Coaching: The discussion on the foundational elements highlighted the coach's role as a reflective container, the interpretation of unconscious communication, and the management of transference and countertransference dynamics. These elements are essential for creating a safe and supportive space where coachees feel empowered to explore their inner worlds.

- Techniques for Uncovering the Unconscious: Techniques such as dream analysis, free association, and symbolic interpretation were outlined as methods for accessing and interpreting the unconscious material. These approaches allow coaches to guide coachees through the exploration of their deepest thoughts and feelings, unlocking insights that can lead to profound personal insights and change.

- Ethical Considerations: The chapter emphasized the importance of maintaining ethical boundaries and confidentiality, especially when dealing with sensitive and unconscious material. Ethical practice ensures that the coaching relationship remains a safe and trusted space for coachees to engage in deep self-exploration.

- Managing Emotional Material: Guidelines for handling intense emotional reactions and disclosures sensitively and ethically were provided, underscoring the coach's responsibility to manage their own emotional responses and to support coachees in navigating their emotional landscapes.

Integrating psychoanalytic principles into coaching practice enriches the coaching experience, offering coachees a unique opportunity to engage in a level of self-exploration and development that is rarely achieved through other methods. This approach not only addresses immediate coaching goals but also facilitates a deeper understanding of oneself, leading to transformative changes that are both profound and lasting. Psychoanalytic coaching, with its focus on the unconscious, equips coaches with the tools to facilitate truly transformative outcomes, reinforcing the immense value of this approach in fostering personal growth and achieving excellence in leadership and beyond.

The coach's role in facilitating the deep and transformative process of psychoanalytic coaching extends far beyond the application of techniques and theoretical understanding. It encompasses the coach's presence, reflexivity, and ethical commitment, elements that are foundational to creating a meaningful and impactful coaching experience.

The coach's presence—being fully engaged and attuned to the coachee in each moment—serves as a powerful force in the coaching relationship. This quality of presence allows coaches to create a space where coachees feel seen, heard, and understood on a profound level. It involves a level of empathy and connection that reassures coachees, encouraging them to explore and share aspects of their inner world that they may have never articulated or fully understood. The coach's ability to remain present, despite the emotional intensity or complexity of the material being explored, fosters an environment of trust and safety, critical for delving into unconscious processes.

Reflexivity in coaching refers to the coach's ongoing practice of self-examination and critical reflection on their own reactions, biases, and the dynamics of the coaching relationship. This reflective practice is essential for navigating transference and countertransference dynamics effectively and for ensuring that the coach's interventions are guided by the coachee's needs rather than the coach's unconscious motivations. Reflexivity also enables coaches to continually refine their approach, learning from each coaching engagement to become more responsive and attuned to the nuances of psychoanalytic coaching.

An unwavering ethical commitment underpins every aspect of psychoanalytic coaching, guiding the coach in maintaining confidentiality, respecting boundaries, and prioritizing the coachee's well-being above all else. This commitment to ethics ensures that the exploration of unconscious material is conducted with sensitivity and respect, protecting coachees from potential harm. Ethical commitment also involves recognizing the limits of one's competence and the boundaries between coaching and therapy, requiring coaches to make referrals to mental health professionals when appropriate.

The coach's role, therefore, is multifaceted and complex, requiring a balance of skill, sensitivity, and professionalism. Coaches must not only be adept at applying psychoanalytic principles and techniques but also embody the qualities of presence, reflexivity, and ethical commitment. It is through the integration of these elements that coaches can facilitate a psychoanalytic coaching process that is both transformative and healing, supporting coachees in achieving deep personal insight and lasting change. This holistic approach to coaching emphasizes the significance of the coach's role not merely as a facilitator of techniques but as a vital presence that guides coachees through the intricate journey of self-discovery and development.

The journey into psychoanalytic coaching is one of continual learning and self-exploration. For coaches, the commitment to their own development and the deepening of their understanding of psychoanalytic concepts is not just a professional obligation but a cornerstone of their ability to facilitate transformative experiences for their coachees. As such, coaches are encouraged to actively pursue their growth and exploration within this rich and complex field, recognizing that their capacity to guide others is intricately linked to their own level of insight, awareness, and emotional depth.

Engaging with psychoanalytic theory and its applications in coaching offers a pathway to more profound connections with coachees, enabling coaches to navigate the subtleties of the human psyche with greater nuance and effectiveness. Delving deeper into concepts such as transference, countertransference, defense mechanisms, and the dynamics of the unconscious enriches the coach's toolkit, providing them with a broader and more sophisticated range of strategies to support coachees in their developmental journeys.

Continuing education through workshops, courses, and seminars on psychoanalytic coaching and related subjects is vital for staying informed about the latest developments and perspectives in the field. Participation in these learning opportunities not only enhances the coach's theoretical knowledge but also fosters a community of practice, offering valuable networks for support, supervision, and collaboration.

Coaches are encouraged to engage in their own psychoanalytic therapy or personal coaching. Experiencing the psychoanalytic process firsthand deepens the coach's empathy and understanding of the coachee's experience, illuminating the challenges and breakthroughs that accompany deep psychological exploration. This personal work also supports the coach's emotional regulation, self-awareness, and ability to manage the complex dynamics of the coaching relationship.

Supervision plays an indispensable role in a coach's ongoing development, providing a reflective space to explore the intricacies of their coaching practice, including how their unconscious processes might influence their work. Regular supervision ensures that coaches maintain an ethical, reflective, and effective practice, grounded in a deep understanding of psychoanalytic principles.

In cultivating a commitment to ongoing development and exploration, coaches not only enhance their own practice but also contribute to the richness of the coaching profession as a whole. This dedication to growth ensures that coaches can offer the most impactful and transformative experiences to their coachees, supporting them in achieving not just their immediate goals but fostering profound personal and professional development.

The encouragement for coaches to continue their exploration and development within psychoanalytic coaching is a call to deepen their engagement with the complex and rewarding work of facilitating change. Through sustained learning, personal exploration, and professional supervision, coaches can enrich their practice, offering coachees a powerful avenue for self-discovery, growth, and transformation.

Chapter 7: Techniques and Tools for Psychoanalytic Coaching

Chapter 7: Techniques and Tools for Psychoanalytic Coaching delves into the heart of psychoanalytic coaching by focusing on the specific techniques and tools essential for accessing and engaging with the unconscious. This chapter is designed to bridge the gap between the theoretical underpinnings of psychoanalytic concepts and their practical application in the coaching context. The aim is to equip coaches with a robust set of approaches that not only deepen their practice but also enhance their ability to facilitate transformative change in their coachees.

The exploration of the unconscious is a cornerstone of psychoanalytic coaching, offering a pathway to understanding the hidden motivations, unresolved conflicts, and deep-seated desires that influence behavior and decision-making. However, accessing this rich and complex realm requires more than intuition and empathy; it demands specific techniques and tools that can safely and effectively guide coachees through the depths of their inner worlds.

In this chapter, we will introduce and examine a variety of psychoanalytic techniques and tools, including dream analysis, free association, the interpretation of slips of the tongue, and the use of metaphors and symbols. Each of these methods serves as a unique entry point into the unconscious, allowing coaches and coachees to uncover insights that lie beyond the reach of conscious awareness. These techniques not only reveal the underlying dynamics that shape coachees' perceptions and behaviors but also open up new possibilities for growth and development.

This chapter will highlight the importance of creating a safe and supportive coaching environment, one that encourages openness and vulnerability, allowing coachees to explore their unconscious material without fear of judgment or censure. We will explore the role of the coach as a reflective container, a critical aspect of psychoanalytic coaching that involves holding and processing the coachee's emotional and psychological material to facilitate insight and understanding.

By providing coaches with practical approaches for working with the unconscious, this chapter aims to enhance the efficacy of psychoanalytic coaching. The techniques and tools discussed here are not only valuable for addressing specific coaching goals but are also instrumental in facilitating a deeper, more comprehensive process of change. Through the thoughtful application of these psychoanalytic methods, coaches can support their coachees in achieving not just external success but profound internal transformation, leading to lasting personal and professional fulfillment.

Chapter 7 serves as a practical guide for coaches seeking to incorporate psychoanalytic principles into their coaching practice. It emphasizes the critical role of specific techniques and tools in accessing the unconscious and highlights the transformative potential of psychoanalytic coaching in facilitating deep and lasting change.

Listening with a Third Ear

The concept of "Listening with a Third Ear" is a psychoanalytic listening technique that transcends conventional listening practices, enabling a deeper, more nuanced understanding of communication. This approach involves tuning into the underlying unconscious messages and emotions embedded in what the coachee communicates, going far beyond the explicit content of their words. The term, rich in psychoanalytic tradition, suggests that coaches must listen not only with their ears for what is said but also with an intuitive, inner ear that hears what remains unsaid.

Listening with a Third Ear requires the coach to be highly attuned to the coachee's verbal expressions, non-verbal cues, emotional tone, and the context within which the communication takes place. This form of listening engages the coach's empathy, intuition, and psychological insight, allowing them to perceive the layers of meaning that lie beneath the surface of the coachee's words. It involves an awareness of the coachee's defenses, desires, conflicts, and the relational dynamics that may be at play, including transference and countertransference phenomena.

The technique is based on the understanding that much of our communication is influenced by unconscious processes. Coachees, often unknowingly, express aspects of their inner world through metaphor, tone, choice of words, and even through what they choose not to say. By listening with a Third Ear, coaches can detect these subtle signals and explore them with the coachee, facilitating insights into previously unrecognized thoughts, feelings, and behavioral patterns.

This psychoanalytic listening technique enhances the coaching process in several ways. First, it fosters a deeper empathic connection between coach and coachee, as coachees feel genuinely heard and understood on a profound level. This deep listening also creates a space for coachees to explore and articulate aspects of their experience that they may have been only dimly aware of, promoting greater self-awareness and understanding.

Listening with a Third Ear allows coaches to identify and explore the coachee's resistances and defenses, gently challenging them in a supportive manner. This can lead to breakthrough moments in coaching, where coachees gain new insights into their behavior and motivations, unlocking possibilities for change and growth.

To effectively listen with a Third Ear, coaches must cultivate their self-awareness, manage their countertransference, and remain open and curious. It requires a balance of being fully present with the coachee while also maintaining an analytical perspective, integrating both empathic engagement and psychological insight.

Listening with a Third Ear embodies the depth and complexity of psychoanalytic coaching, offering a powerful tool for facilitating transformative change. Through this nuanced approach to listening, coaches can guide coachees toward a deeper understanding of themselves, fostering personal and professional development that is both profound and lasting.

Developing the skill of Listening with a Third Ear, an essential competency in psychoanalytic coaching, involves cultivating a deep sensitivity to the nuances of unconscious communication. This skill allows coaches to perceive and understand the complex layers of meaning that underlie coachees' words and behaviors. Enhancing this ability requires deliberate practice and a commitment to personal and professional growth. Here are strategies that can aid in developing this nuanced listening skill:

1. Mindfulness Practices: Engaging in mindfulness practices can significantly enhance a coach's ability to listen with a Third Ear. Mindfulness cultivates present-moment awareness and helps coaches attune to their own inner experiences as well as to the subtle cues communicated by coachees. Regular meditation, deep breathing exercises, or mindful observation can train coaches to become more aware of their thoughts and feelings, reducing reactivity and increasing their capacity to listen deeply without judgment.

2. Reflective Journaling: Keeping a reflective journal is another effective strategy for developing this skill. Journaling about coaching sessions can help coaches process their experiences, reflect on their emotional responses, and consider the unconscious dynamics at play. Writing about what was said, the emotions observed, and the coach's intuitive responses can uncover patterns and insights that might not have been apparent in the moment. Reflective journaling encourages a deeper exploration of the coaching relationship and enhances the coach's sensitivity to unconscious communication.

3. Supervision: Regular supervision is invaluable for coaches aiming to deepen their psychoanalytic listening skills.

Supervision provides a space to discuss and reflect on coaching sessions with an experienced practitioner, offering perspectives that can illuminate unconscious processes affecting both the coachee and the coach. Supervisors can help coaches recognize their own countertransference reactions and explore how these may inform their understanding of the coachee's unconscious communication. This reflective process is crucial for integrating psychoanalytic concepts into coaching practice and for developing the capacity to listen beyond the explicit content of conversations.

4. Training and Education: Participating in specialized training programs and workshops that focus on psychoanalytic concepts and listening skills is crucial for coaches. These educational opportunities can provide coaches with the theoretical knowledge and practical techniques needed to effectively listen with a Third Ear. Exposure to case studies, role-playing exercises, and peer discussions can further enhance a coach's ability to detect and interpret unconscious communication.

5. Peer Practice Groups: Joining or forming peer practice groups offers coaches a collaborative environment to refine their listening skills. Practicing with peers allows for the exchange of feedback and insights, enabling coaches to experiment with different listening techniques and to learn from each other's experiences. These groups can simulate coaching scenarios that highlight unconscious communication, providing a safe space for coaches to explore and develop their psychoanalytic listening skills.

Developing the skill of Listening with a Third Ear is a dynamic and ongoing process that enriches a coach's practice and profoundly impacts the coaching relationship. By incorporating mindfulness practices, reflective journaling, supervision, targeted training, and peer learning into their development plan, coaches can enhance their sensitivity to unconscious communication. This, in turn, enables them to facilitate deeper, more transformative coaching outcomes, helping coachees uncover and address the underlying issues that influence their thoughts, feelings, and behaviors.

Listening with a Third Ear in coaching is a transformative skill that enables coaches to access and engage with the deeper layers of the coachee's psyche, revealing insights into their challenges, motivations, and conflicts. This nuanced approach to listening can significantly enhance the effectiveness of coaching interventions by addressing the root causes of issues rather than just their surface manifestations. Here are examples illustrating the power of this skill in action:

Example 1: Uncovering Hidden Motivations

A coachee talks about feeling stuck in their current role but hesitates to seek promotion. Through careful listening, the coach detects a subtle shift in the coachee's tone when discussing the topic of leadership. This cue prompts the coach to explore the coachee's associations with leadership roles, revealing an underlying fear of visibility and exposure rooted in past experiences of being publicly criticized. Recognizing this fear allows the coach to tailor interventions that address the coachee's reluctance to step into more visible positions, focusing on building self-confidence and resilience.

Example 2: Resolving Internal Conflicts

During a session, a coachee repeatedly uses the phrase "I should" when discussing career aspirations, suggesting a conflict between their desires and perceived obligations. By listening with a Third Ear, the coach senses the weight of expectation behind the coachee's words and explores the origin of these "should" statements. This exploration uncovers a deep-seated need to fulfill parental expectations at the expense of the coachee's passions, leading to feelings of dissatisfaction and disengagement. The coach helps the coachee to acknowledge and articulate their own career aspirations, facilitating a process of reconciling internal conflicts and aligning their professional path with personal values.

Example 3: Identifying Emotional Barriers

A coachee describes their difficulty in forming close relationships with team members in a detached manner, minimizing the issue. However, the coach observes a fleeting expression of sadness when the coachee mentions teamwork. Sensing an emotional barrier, the coach gently probes the coachee's past experiences with teamwork, revealing unresolved feelings of betrayal from a previous project. This insight allows the coach to work with the coachee on processing these emotions and developing strategies for building trust and fostering healthy team dynamics.

Example 4: Exploring Resistance to Change

A coachee expresses a desire to change their leadership style but seems resistant to implementing suggested strategies. By listening with a Third Ear, the coach notices a pattern of defensiveness and reluctance when discussing change. This observation leads the coach to explore the coachee's beliefs about change and leadership, uncovering an unconscious association of change with loss of control and vulnerability. Acknowledging this fear enables the coach and coachee to address the resistance directly, creating a more supportive framework for experimenting with new leadership behaviors.

Example 5: Revealing the Impact of Organizational Dynamics

A coachee frequently complains about feeling undervalued at work but insists it's not a significant issue. The coach, listening deeply, picks up on a sense of resignation in the coachee's voice. This prompts an exploration of the coachee's history within the organization, revealing a pattern of unrecognized contributions and a lack of support. Understanding these dynamics, the coach helps the coachee develop strategies for advocating for themselves and seeking environments where their contributions are valued.

In each example, listening with a Third Ear enables the coach to move beyond the explicit content of the coachee's communications, tapping into the rich, often unspoken world of unconscious motivations, conflicts, and emotions. This deep listening fosters a coaching relationship that is profoundly attuned to the coachee's needs, facilitating interventions that are not only more effective but also more meaningful and transformative.

Exploring Dreams, Fantasies, and Slips of the Tongue

Dream analysis, a cornerstone of psychoanalytic theory, offers a unique and profound avenue for exploring the unconscious in coaching. Dreams can serve as windows into the coachee's inner world, revealing insights into their fears, desires, conflicts, and unresolved issues. The process of exploring dreams with coachees involves several key steps, from encouraging the recall and sharing of dreams to using psychoanalytic techniques to interpret their symbolic meanings.

Encouraging Dream Recall and Sharing

The first step in dream analysis is to encourage coachees to pay attention to their dreams and to recall them more vividly. Coaches can suggest keeping a dream journal by the bedside, where coachees can jot down any dreams or fragments of dreams immediately upon waking when they are most vivid. During coaching sessions, creating a safe and non-judgmental space is crucial for coachees to feel comfortable sharing their dreams. Coaches should emphasize the confidentiality of the process and reassure coachees that all dreams, regardless of their content, offer valuable insights.

Initial Exploration of the Dream

Once a dream is shared, the coach begins its exploration by asking the coachee to describe the dream in detail, including the setting, characters, events, and emotions experienced. Coaches should listen attentively, not only to the content but also to the emotions and associations that arise as the coachee recounts the dream. This step is crucial for setting the stage for deeper analysis, as it allows the coach to gather comprehensive information about the dream and how the coachee relates to it.

Identifying Symbols and Themes

Dreams are rich in symbols and metaphors that carry individual meanings unique to the coachee's experiences and psyche. The coach's role is to help the coachee explore these symbols, considering their personal significance and any emotions or memories they evoke. This exploration involves asking open-ended questions that encourage coachees to reflect on the symbolic elements of the dream and their possible connections to their waking life, relationships, and current challenges.

Exploring Emotional Reactions and Associations

An essential part of dream analysis is exploring the coachee's emotional reactions both within the dream and upon recalling it. Coaches should inquire about how the coachee felt during different parts of the dream and any changes in emotion throughout the dream narrative. Additionally, discussing the coachee's immediate emotional response upon waking can offer clues to the dream's significance. This emotional exploration helps to reveal the underlying issues or conflicts that the dream may be addressing.

Connecting Dream Insights to Coaching Goals

The final step is to integrate the insights gained from the dream analysis into the broader context of the coachee's coaching goals and personal development journey. This involves discussing how the themes, conflicts, and emotions revealed in the dream relate to the coachee's waking life, identifying areas for growth, and exploring potential actions or reflections. Coaches can guide coachees in considering how the insights from their dreams might inform their understanding of themselves, their behaviors, and their relationships, facilitating a deeper level of self-awareness and transformation.

Dream analysis in coaching is a delicate process that requires sensitivity, patience, and skill. Coaches must navigate the coachee's dreamscapes with respect for their complexity and personal significance, using psychoanalytic techniques to unearth the valuable insights they hold. By engaging with dreams in this thoughtful and exploratory manner, coaches can help coachees access profound unconscious material, enriching the coaching process and supporting coachees in achieving transformative change.

Fantasies and daydreams are rich sources of insight into the coachee's inner world, revealing desires, fears, and unconscious conflicts that might not be easily accessible through direct conversation. Unlike dreams, which occur in sleep, fantasies and daydreams unfold in the coachee's waking mind, often serving as a window into their hopes, aspirations, and the psychological defenses they employ to manage inner turmoil or external challenges. Exploring these narratives within the coaching context can provide valuable clues to the coachee's emotional and psychological landscape, offering pathways to deeper self-understanding and personal growth.

Fantasies and daydreams often represent the coachee's attempts to solve problems, achieve desires, or manage emotions in a symbolic manner. They can embody idealized scenarios, wish fulfillments, or rehearsed confrontations, reflecting the individual's deeper needs, values, and unresolved issues. By paying attention to the content and emotional tone of these fantasies, coaches can gain insights into the coachee's motivational drivers, the conflicts they experience, and the defenses they might be using to cope with reality.

To explore fantasies and daydreams effectively, coaches should first establish a trusting and supportive environment where coachees feel safe to share these inner narratives without fear of judgment. Coaches can introduce the topic by inquiring about the coachee's recent daydreams or asking if they ever imagine alternative scenarios related to their goals, challenges, or relationships. It's important for coaches to approach these conversations with curiosity and openness, framing fantasies and daydreams as normal and valuable aspects of the coachee's psychological experience.

Coaches can encourage coachees to reflect on their fantasies by asking them to describe these narratives in detail, including the emotions they evoke and the outcomes they imagine. Questions might focus on what these fantasies reveal about the coachee's desires, fears, or areas of dissatisfaction in their current reality. Coaches can also explore how these daydreams might serve as coping mechanisms, providing temporary relief from stress or anxiety, or how they might represent internal conflicts that require resolution.

Integrating the insights gained from exploring fantasies and daydreams into the broader coaching goals is a critical step. Coaches can help coachees recognize patterns in their fantasies that relate to their aspirations or obstacles, facilitating discussions on how these insights can inform their personal development plan. For instance, if a coachee frequently fantasizes about being recognized for their work, this might highlight a need for validation or a fear of insignificance, which could become areas of focus in the coaching sessions.

Fantasies and daydreams can also be used proactively as tools for growth and creativity. Coaches can guide coachees in harnessing the creative energy of their daydreams to envision new possibilities, set inspiring goals, or develop creative solutions to challenges. This positive engagement with fantasies can empower coachees to transform their daydreams into actionable steps towards their desired future.

Exploring fantasies and daydreams offers a unique lens through which coaches can understand and support their coachees. By gently navigating these narratives, coaches can uncover profound insights into the coachee's desires, fears, and unconscious conflicts, facilitating a coaching process that is deeply attuned to the coachee's psychological needs and aspirations for change.

Slips of the tongue, often referred to as Freudian slips, are inadvertent verbal mistakes that are believed to reveal underlying, unconscious thoughts and feelings. These slips can be particularly illuminating in the coaching context, as they offer glimpses into the coachee's inner world, including their desires, fears, and unresolved conflicts. When a coachee misspeaks, substitutes one word for another, or inadvertently reveals a thought they intended to keep private, it can provide valuable clues to their psychological state and the issues they are grappling with, perhaps even those they are not consciously aware of or are reluctant to address directly.

Understanding and interpreting Freudian slips requires a coach to be highly attuned to the coachee's language and the nuances of their communication. This level of attunement allows the coach to notice when a slip of the tongue occurs and to consider its potential significance within the broader context of the coachee's expressions and behaviors. It's important for coaches to approach these slips with curiosity rather than assumption, recognizing that each slip may have multiple interpretations or may sometimes be simply a verbal mistake without deeper psychological implications.

Strategies for sensitively addressing slips of the tongue in coaching sessions include:

1. Creating a supportive environment where coachees feel safe to explore the meanings behind their slips without fear of judgment or embarrassment. This involves building a strong foundation of trust and rapport from the outset of the coaching relationship.

2. When a slip occurs, gently bringing it to the coachee's attention without implying that it necessarily has a significant unconscious meaning. Coaches might say something like, "I noticed you said 'X' just now, does that resonate with you in any way?" This open-ended approach invites the coachee to reflect on the slip and its possible meanings without imposing an interpretation.

3. Encouraging coachees to explore their immediate thoughts and feelings about the slip, as well as any associations or memories it might evoke. This exploration can uncover

connections to deeper emotional issues or conflicts that the coachee may not have been aware of.

4. Being mindful of the coach's own reactions and interpretations of the slip, recognizing that their understanding may be influenced by their own biases or countertransference. It's crucial for coaches to maintain an objective stance, using supervision and self-reflection to explore their responses to coachees' slips.

5. Integrating the insights gained from exploring slips of the tongue into the broader coaching process, linking them to the coachee's goals, challenges, and areas for development. This might involve identifying patterns in the slips that relate to specific themes in the coachee's life or work and using these insights to inform coaching interventions.

Freudian slips can be a rich source of insight into the coachee's unconscious mind, offering clues to their innermost thoughts and feelings. By noticing and sensitively addressing these slips in coaching sessions, coaches can deepen their understanding of the coachee, facilitating a more nuanced and effective coaching process. This approach underscores the importance of listening not just to what is said, but also to what is inadvertently revealed, harnessing the transformative potential of the unconscious in promoting personal growth and development.

Working with Resistance and Defense Mechanisms

In the psychoanalytic context, resistance refers to the coachee's unconscious attempts to avoid confronting painful or difficult aspects of their psyche. This defense mechanism is a natural part of the human psyche's way of protecting itself from emotional discomfort or anxiety that may arise from facing unresolved conflicts, traumatic memories, or undesirable truths about oneself. In coaching, resistance can manifest in various forms, including reluctance to discuss certain topics, rationalizing behaviors, frequent cancellations or lateness, and deflecting questions with humor or changing the subject.

Identifying resistance is crucial in coaching, as it can signal important underlying issues that need to be addressed for the coachee to move forward. Here are techniques for identifying resistance in coaching sessions:

1. Notice Patterns of Avoidance: Pay attention to topics or questions that the coachee consistently avoids or responds to with superficial answers. Patterns of avoidance can indicate areas of discomfort that the coachee may be unconsciously resisting exploring.

2. Observe Changes in Emotional State: Resistance can often be accompanied by a noticeable change in the coachee's emotional state or energy level. For instance, a coachee may become more anxious, defensive, or disengaged when approaching a sensitive topic.

3. Listen for Repeated Rationalizations: Coachees demonstrating resistance might frequently rationalize behaviors or situations in ways that prevent deeper examination. These rationalizations often serve to justify actions or to minimize the significance of certain feelings or events.

4. Be Attuned to Non-Verbal Cues: Non-verbal cues such as body language, facial expressions, and tone of voice can provide valuable clues to resistance. For example, crossing arms, looking away, or a sudden shift in tone might indicate discomfort and resistance to the topic at hand.

5. Monitor the Coaching Process: Resistance can also manifest as a disruption in the coaching process itself, such as recurring cancellations, lateness, or a reluctance to complete agreed-upon tasks or reflections between sessions.

Once resistance is identified, addressing it sensitively and constructively becomes crucial. Techniques to work through resistance include:

- Creating a Safe Space: Reinforce the coaching environment as a safe, non-judgmental space. Emphasizing confidentiality and the non-directive nature of coaching can help coachees feel more comfortable opening up.

- Reflecting Observations: Gently reflect your observations back to the coachee without judgment. For example, "I've noticed a change in your energy when we discuss this topic. Can you share more about what you're feeling right now?"

- Exploring Resistance Directly: Sometimes, directly exploring the resistance itself can be insightful. Asking questions like, "What makes this topic challenging for you to discuss?" can open up a conversation about the resistance.

- Pacing the Coaching: Respect the coachee's pace and readiness to confront difficult topics. Pushing too hard can increase resistance, while a more patient approach can allow coachees to gradually feel more comfortable and open.

- Encouraging Self-Compassion: Help coachees develop self-compassion, understanding that resistance is a normal part of the process and not a failure on their part.

Identifying and working through resistance is a delicate part of the coaching process, requiring patience, empathy, and skill. By recognizing resistance as a clue to deeper underlying issues and navigating it thoughtfully, coaches can support coachees in achieving meaningful insights and transformative growth.

Understanding defense mechanisms is crucial in the coaching process, as these unconscious psychological strategies play a significant role in how coachees perceive and interact with the world around them. Defense mechanisms protect individuals from feelings of anxiety or guilt by distorting reality in various ways. Common defense mechanisms include denial, projection, and rationalization, each serving as a way to cope with uncomfortable emotions or situations.

Denial involves refusing to accept reality or facts, acting as if a painful event, thought, or feeling did not exist. It is one of the most primitive defense mechanisms, often leading to a significant discrepancy between what is true and what is believed. In coaching, denial might manifest as a coachee insisting a problem doesn't exist or minimizing the impact of their actions. Recognizing denial involves noticing discrepancies between a coachee's perception and objective reality, often requiring gentle confrontation and the presentation of evidence in a supportive, non-threatening manner.

Projection involves attributing one's unacceptable thoughts, feelings, or impulses onto another person. Instead of acknowledging uncomfortable feelings like jealousy or anger, an individual might claim that someone else is feeling these emotions towards them. In the coaching context, projection can be identified when a coachee consistently blames others for their own challenges or describes others in ways that seem to reflect their unconscious feelings. Understanding projection involves exploring the feelings the coachee attributes to others and gently encouraging self-reflection to uncover the true source of these emotions.

Rationalization involves justifying behaviors or feelings with logical, plausible explanations, often avoiding the true reasons for an action. This defense mechanism can make it challenging to address underlying issues because the coachee may provide a seemingly logical explanation for irrational or harmful behavior. Recognizing rationalization requires listening for explanations that don't fully account for a behavior or that seem to mask deeper emotions. Coaches can address rationalization by inviting coachees to explore alternative explanations for their actions and to consider their feelings more deeply.

In the coaching process, understanding and recognizing these defense mechanisms is vital for facilitating self-awareness and growth. Coaches must approach these dynamics with sensitivity, employing techniques such as reflective listening, open-ended questioning, and the exploration of inconsistencies in the coachee's narrative. By creating a safe and supportive environment, coaches can encourage coachees to confront and understand their use of defense mechanisms, leading to more authentic and fulfilling ways of being.

Addressing defense mechanisms in coaching involves a delicate balance of challenge and support, requiring coaches to be attuned to the coachee's readiness to engage with deeper psychological work. Through this process, coachees can learn to identify and modify their defensive responses, opening up new possibilities for personal development and more adaptive coping strategies.

Defense mechanisms play a pivotal role in how individuals navigate emotional discomfort and protect their sense of self. Understanding these mechanisms—denial, projection, and rationalization—is essential in the coaching process, as it allows for a deeper exploration of the coachee's internal world and their interactions with external realities.

Denial is the outright refusal to accept reality or facts, creating a significant gap between what is true and what an individual chooses to believe. This mechanism can manifest in coaching when a coachee refuses to acknowledge the existence of a problem or the consequences of their actions. Recognizing denial involves observing the disparities between the coachee's perceptions and the objective situation, often requiring the coach to navigate these conversations with care, aiming to bridge the gap between denial and acceptance.

Projection involves attributing one's own undesirable thoughts, feelings, or motivations to someone else rather than admitting to them. This mechanism can be identified in a coaching context when a coachee consistently assigns their own feelings or shortcomings to others, portraying themselves as the recipient of these undesired traits. Understanding projection in coaching sessions involves gently challenging the coachee to consider the origins of these attributions, fostering a space for introspection and the reclamation of projected aspects of the self.

Rationalization is the process of concocting logical reasons for actions or feelings that stem from less acceptable motives. This mechanism can make it difficult to address deeper issues since the coachee might present seemingly reasonable explanations for behaviors that are actually driven by unconscious motives. Spotting rationalization requires attentive listening for justifications that seem to skirt around the deeper emotional truth. Coaches can work through rationalization by encouraging coachees to explore the fuller emotional landscape behind their rationalized actions, promoting a richer understanding of their motivations.

In addressing these defense mechanisms, the coaching process becomes an invaluable tool for self-awareness and personal growth. Coaches must approach these unconscious strategies with empathy and patience, creating an environment where coachees feel safe to confront and work through the complexities of their inner lives. This involves a nuanced balance of challenging coachees to face their defenses while providing unwavering support as they navigate this transformative journey. Through such sensitive exploration, coachees can learn to recognize and adjust their defensive responses, paving the way for more authentic engagement with themselves and the world around them.

Enhancing Self-Reflection and Insight

Engaging coachees in self-reflection is a powerful way to explore their unconscious motivations and foster personal growth. Reflective practices can help coachees uncover insights about their thoughts, feelings, and behaviors, facilitating a deeper understanding of themselves. Here are some exercises and practices that can encourage this process:

1. Reflective Writing: Encourage coachees to keep a reflective journal where they can write about their experiences, thoughts, and feelings. Prompt them with specific questions related to their goals, challenges, and the emotions these evoke. This practice can help coachees articulate and explore aspects of

their psyche that they might not have been consciously aware of. Encouraging them to reflect on their reactions to certain events or decisions can also reveal underlying beliefs and assumptions that influence their behavior.

2. Guided Imagery: Guided imagery exercises can help coachees access and explore their unconscious mind in a safe and structured way. Coaches can guide coachees through visualizations that tap into their inner desires, fears, and unresolved conflicts. For example, asking coachees to imagine themselves in a place where they feel completely safe and then to visualize confronting a current challenge can reveal new insights into their emotional responses and coping mechanisms.

3. Mindfulness Meditation: Mindfulness meditation encourages coachees to observe their thoughts and feelings without judgment, fostering an awareness of the present moment. This practice can help coachees become more attuned to their internal experiences, including unconscious motivations that might surface during meditation. Encouraging coachees to practice mindfulness regularly can enhance their ability to notice and reflect on patterns in their thoughts and emotions that relate to deeper aspects of their personality and behavior.

4. Dialogue with Parts of Self: Invite coachees to engage in dialogues with different parts of themselves, such as the inner critic, the fearful self, or the ambitious self. This exercise can be done through writing or speaking and involves asking these parts questions to understand their concerns, desires, and motivations. Such dialogues can help coachees recognize and reconcile conflicting internal voices, leading to greater self-compassion and integration.

5. Exploring Dreams and Daydreams: As previously discussed, dreams and daydreams can provide valuable insights into the coachee's unconscious. Encouraging coachees to record and reflect on their dreams and daydreams can open up discussions about their symbolic meanings and the emotions they evoke.

Coaches can ask coachees to describe these narratives in detail and explore any connections to their waking life.

6. Emotion Tracking: Suggest that coachees keep an emotion diary, where they note down their emotions throughout the day and the context in which these feelings arose. This practice can help coachees identify triggers for certain emotions and recognize patterns in their emotional responses. Over time, this can lead to insights into unconscious motivations and the opportunity to work through unresolved emotional issues.

Engaging coachees in these reflective practices can significantly enrich the coaching process, providing a deeper understanding of their inner world. By encouraging self-reflection and the exploration of unconscious motivations, coaches can support coachees in achieving meaningful and lasting change.

Facilitating moments of insight for coachees involves guiding them to connect with and understand the unconscious roots of their thoughts, emotions, and behaviors, a process that is central to transformative coaching. The journey to these moments begins with the creation of a safe and trusting environment where coachees feel valued and understood, laying the groundwork for deep exploration. Active listening and reflective feedback play crucial roles in this context, as they help coachees to hear their own narratives from a fresh perspective, often illuminating hidden beliefs or contradictions.

The art of asking powerful questions that provoke deep reflection is another key tool for coaches. By exploring the motivations behind actions, the emotions linked to specific thoughts, or the origins of recurrent life themes, coachees are encouraged to delve into the deeper layers of their psyche. Similarly, resistance, when approached with curiosity and empathy, can reveal underlying fears, beliefs, or past experiences shaping current behaviors.

Imagery and metaphors offer a creative avenue for coachees to express complex emotions and situations, providing insights into their unconscious mind. Coaches can further facilitate insight by helping coachees recognize and reflect on patterns in their lives, illuminating the unconscious motivations driving these recurrent dynamics.

Dream analysis presents a direct pathway to the unconscious, with coaches guiding coachees through the symbolic and often emotional landscapes of their dreams. This exploration can uncover significant aspects of the coachee's inner world that might remain obscured in waking life. Additionally, promoting mindfulness practices enhances coachees' self-awareness, allowing them to observe their internal processes more clearly and without immediate judgment. This increased awareness can lead to significant insights as coachees begin to notice how unconscious material influences their daily experiences.

Through these nuanced approaches, coaches skillfully guide coachees toward greater self-understanding, encouraging the integration of unconscious material into conscious awareness. This deep level of insight is foundational for authentic change, empowering coachees to address the root causes of their challenges and move toward more fulfilling lives. The process of facilitating insight is both an art and a science, requiring patience, expertise, and a profound understanding of human psychology. It is through this careful and considered guidance that coaches can support coachees in achieving transformative personal growth and development.

Ethical Use of Psychoanalytic Techniques

Maintaining clear boundaries in the coaching relationship is especially crucial when employing psychoanalytic techniques, due to the depth of personal exploration and vulnerability involved. These boundaries ensure that the relationship remains professional, ethical, and focused on the coachee's goals, while providing a safe space for the exploration of deep-seated thoughts, emotions, and behaviors. The intimate nature of delving into unconscious material demands a structured framework within which both coach and coachee understand their roles and the limits of their engagement.

Clear boundaries help in delineating the scope of the coaching relationship, distinguishing it from therapeutic or personal relationships. This distinction is important because it helps coachees understand the purpose of the coaching process—to foster personal and professional development rather than to diagnose or treat psychological disorders. By establishing these boundaries, coaches underscore the goal-oriented nature of the engagement, focusing on the coachee's objectives and how unconscious insights can support their attainment.

Boundaries also protect the coachee's psychological well-being. Exploring unconscious material can sometimes bring to the surface unresolved conflicts or painful memories. A well-defined boundary ensures that such exploration is conducted with care and sensitivity, preventing harm and ensuring that the coachee does not become overly dependent on the coach for emotional support. It encourages self-reliance and empowers coachees to take responsibility for their growth, with the coach acting as a facilitator rather than a caretaker.

Maintaining professional boundaries prevents the blurring of roles that can occur when deep psychological work is involved. It helps in managing transference and countertransference dynamics effectively, ensuring that any feelings or reactions that arise in the context of the coaching relationship are acknowledged and explored in a way that benefits the coachee's development. This clarity around roles and expectations prevents confusion and maintains the integrity of the coaching process.

For coaches, respecting boundaries involves continuous self-reflection and supervision to navigate the complex dynamics that psychoanalytic techniques can unearth. It requires a clear communication of the coaching process, confidentiality, and the limits of the coaching relationship from the outset. Regular check-ins with the coachee to revisit goals, progress, and the nature of the coaching relationship can also reinforce these boundaries.

The importance of maintaining clear boundaries when using psychoanalytic techniques in coaching cannot be overstated. These boundaries ensure that the coaching relationship remains professional, focused, and ethically sound, providing a secure framework within which coachees can safely explore and integrate insights from their unconscious, thereby supporting their journey towards achieving their personal and professional goals.

Handling sensitive material that emerges from working with the unconscious demands a high level of ethical consideration and sensitivity. As coaches delve into the deeper layers of a coachee's psyche, they may encounter emotional and vulnerable content that requires careful navigation. The following guidelines can help ensure that such material is handled ethically and sensitively:

- Establish a Safe Environment: Creating a safe and supportive coaching environment is paramount. Coachees should feel secure in sharing their thoughts and emotions without fear of judgment. This involves setting clear expectations about the confidentiality of the sessions, actively listening, and demonstrating empathy and respect for the coachee's experiences.

- Communicate Clear Boundaries: It's essential to clarify the scope and limitations of the coaching relationship, especially when psychoanalytic techniques are employed. Coaches should communicate that while they can provide support in exploring unconscious material, they are not psychotherapists unless specifically trained and licensed as such. If psychological issues requiring therapeutic intervention are uncovered, coaches should be prepared to refer coachees to appropriate mental health professionals.

- Handle Disclosure with Care: When coachees disclose sensitive or emotionally charged information, respond with acknowledgment and validation. Recognize the courage it takes to share such material and express appreciation for their trust. Avoid offering quick solutions or judgments; instead, focus on exploring the implications and meanings of these disclosures in the context of the coachee's goals and development.

- Maintain Professionalism and Objectivity: While empathy is crucial, maintaining a professional distance is equally important. Coaches should be wary of becoming overly involved emotionally, as this can cloud judgment and hinder the coachee's progress. Staying objective helps in managing transference and countertransference dynamics effectively, ensuring that the coach's personal reactions do not interfere with the coachee's exploration of their unconscious material.

- Practice Self-Reflection and Supervision: Engaging in regular self-reflection and seeking supervision are vital practices for coaches working with unconscious material. These practices provide opportunities to examine one's own reactions and biases, ensuring they do not impact the coaching relationship negatively. Supervision offers a valuable external perspective and support in handling complex emotional material ethically and sensitively.

- Promote Coachee Autonomy: Empower coachees to take ownership of their exploration of unconscious material. Encourage them to reflect on their insights and how these may inform their actions and decisions. Facilitating autonomy supports coachees in integrating their discoveries into their lives in meaningful ways.

- Be Prepared for Emotional Intensity: The exploration of unconscious material can sometimes lead to intense emotional reactions. Coaches should be prepared to manage these situations calmly and supportively, helping coachees navigate their emotions without becoming overwhelmed. Techniques such as grounding exercises or mindfulness can be useful tools in these moments.

Handling sensitive and vulnerable material that emerges from the unconscious is a profound responsibility. By following these guidelines, coaches can ensure that they approach this aspect of coaching with the ethical consideration and sensitivity it requires. This careful approach not only protects the coachee's psychological well-being but also enhances the transformative potential of the coaching process.

Conclusion

This chapter has highlighted the significant value of integrating psychoanalytic techniques and tools into coaching practice, underscoring their effectiveness in accessing deeper levels of understanding and facilitating significant personal growth. Through the exploration of the unconscious, coaches are equipped with a powerful means to uncover the hidden motivations, conflicts, and desires that shape coachees' thoughts, behaviors, and emotional responses. Techniques such as dream analysis, reflective writing, guided imagery, and the attentive interpretation of slips of the tongue and resistance patterns enable coaches to delve into the rich, often uncharted territories of the coachee's psyche.

The use of psychoanalytic tools in coaching extends beyond mere problem-solving; it opens up a transformative space for coachees to engage in profound self-exploration. This process not only brings to light the underlying issues impacting their personal and professional lives but also empowers coachees to confront and work through these challenges in a supportive and non-judgmental environment. The chapter has emphasized the importance of creating a safe and trusting space where coachees feel comfortable to share and explore sensitive and sometimes vulnerable material. It has also underscored the necessity of clear boundaries and ethical considerations, ensuring that the coaching relationship remains professional, focused, and conducive to the coachee's growth.

The chapter discussed the critical role of the coach in facilitating this exploratory process, highlighting the need for coaches to maintain an empathetic, yet objective stance. Coaches' self-awareness, continuous self-reflection, and engagement in supervision are essential in managing the complex dynamics that psychoanalytic techniques can evoke, such as transference and countertransference. These practices not only safeguard the integrity of the coaching process but also enhance the coach's ability to navigate the emotional depths of psychoanalytic exploration effectively.

Integrating psychoanalytic techniques and tools into coaching practice offers a profound avenue for achieving deep-seated change and personal growth. By engaging with the unconscious, coaches and coachees embark on a journey of discovery that can lead to transformative insights and lasting improvements in personal and professional fulfillment. This chapter serves as a guide for coaches seeking to enrich their practice with psychoanalytic principles, providing them with the knowledge and strategies to navigate the intricate landscape of the human psyche with sensitivity, insight, and professionalism.

Coaches are encouraged to approach psychoanalytic techniques with a sense of curiosity, a deep respect for the coachee's individual process, and a steadfast commitment to ongoing learning and self-development. These attitudes are foundational to effectively utilizing psychoanalytic approaches in coaching and facilitating profound personal growth for coachees.

Curiosity opens the door to exploring the depths of the coachee's unconscious mind, inviting a journey into uncharted territories of thoughts, emotions, and desires. This exploratory mindset allows coaches to uncover insights that lie beneath the surface of conscious awareness, fostering a deeper understanding of the coachee's inner world. Approaching coaching with curiosity also means being open to the unexpected and being prepared to navigate the complexities of the human psyche with flexibility and openness.

Respecting the coachee's process is paramount in psychoanalytic coaching. Every individual's journey through self-exploration and personal growth is unique, with its own pace, challenges, and breakthroughs. Coaches must honor this individuality, providing support and guidance while allowing coachees the space to discover and work through their unconscious material in their own time. This respect fosters a safe and trusting coaching relationship, crucial for engaging in deep psychological work.

A commitment to ongoing learning and self-development is essential for coaches employing psychoanalytic techniques. The field of psychoanalysis is rich and complex, offering endless opportunities for professional growth and enhanced understanding. Engaging in continuous education, whether through formal training, supervision, or personal psychoanalytic work, enriches a coach's practice and ensures that they are well-equipped to navigate the intricacies of unconscious exploration with coachees.

A coaches' commitment to their own self-development serves as a model for coachees, demonstrating the value of introspection, self-awareness, and lifelong learning. As coaches deepen their understanding of psychoanalytic principles and refine their skills, they become more effective in facilitating transformative change, helping coachees to achieve greater self-understanding, resolve inner conflicts, and pursue their goals with renewed insight and motivation.

Approaching psychoanalytic techniques in coaching with curiosity, respect for the coachee's process, and a commitment to ongoing learning and self-development is crucial for maximizing the efficacy of these approaches. By embodying these principles, coaches can enhance their ability to facilitate deep and lasting personal growth, making a meaningful impact on the lives of their coachees.

Chapter 8: Addressing Leadership Challenges Psychoanalytically

Chapter 8 delves into the nuanced realm of addressing common leadership challenges through the lens of psychoanalytic principles, offering a profound and insightful approach to understanding and navigating the complex psychological landscapes that leaders often face. This chapter illuminates how psychoanalytic concepts can be applied to dissect and address the underlying issues that manifest as leadership challenges, including navigating power dynamics and authority issues, enhancing emotional intelligence and relational skills, and overcoming imposter syndrome and leadership anxieties.

Leadership, inherently laden with responsibilities and expectations, can evoke a range of unconscious responses and defense mechanisms in individuals. By applying psychoanalytic principles, coaches can help leaders uncover the root causes of their challenges, whether they stem from past experiences, deep-seated fears, or unresolved conflicts. This exploration offers leaders a unique opportunity to achieve greater self-awareness and insight into their behaviors and motivations, paving the way for more authentic and effective leadership.

The chapter emphasizes the significance of understanding power dynamics and authority issues through a psychoanalytic perspective. It explores how leaders can unconsciously replicate or react against patterns of authority and power learned in early life experiences, impacting their leadership style and relationships with subordinates. By bringing these unconscious influences to light, leaders can develop healthier, more balanced approaches to power and authority, fostering a more collaborative and empowering organizational culture.

Enhancing emotional intelligence and relational skills is another focal point of the chapter. Psychoanalytic techniques offer leaders tools to better understand their own emotional responses and those of others, improving empathy, communication, and conflict resolution skills. This enhanced emotional intelligence supports leaders in building stronger, more positive relationships with their teams, crucial for effective leadership.

The chapter addresses the pervasive challenges of imposter syndrome and leadership anxieties. Many leaders, regardless of their successes, grapple with feelings of inadequacy and fear of exposure as frauds. Psychoanalytic exploration can reveal the origins of these anxieties, often tied to unconscious beliefs about self-worth and competence. By confronting and working through these issues, leaders can overcome imposter syndrome, embrace their strengths, and lead with confidence.

Chapter 8 underscores the transformative potential of integrating psychoanalytic principles into leadership coaching. It offers a roadmap for leaders and coaches alike to navigate the psychological underpinnings of leadership challenges, enabling leaders to achieve not only professional growth but also personal fulfillment. Through this psychoanalytic journey, leaders are equipped to face their roles with greater insight, resilience, and effectiveness, ultimately contributing to the creation of more dynamic, healthy organizational environments.

Understanding the unconscious aspects of leadership challenges is essential for achieving more profound and lasting solutions. The unconscious mind, with its complex web of desires, fears, and unresolved conflicts, significantly influences leadership behaviors, decision-making processes, and interpersonal dynamics. By delving into these unconscious aspects, leaders can uncover the root causes of their challenges, moving beyond superficial fixes to initiate deep-seated and enduring change.

The exploration of the unconscious allows for a comprehensive understanding of why certain patterns of behavior persist, why particular interpersonal dynamics unfold as they do, and why some leadership challenges seem insurmountable. It reveals that what might appear as a professional impediment often has deeper psychological underpinnings, rooted in early experiences, unconscious beliefs, and internalized narratives about authority, power, and self-worth.

Addressing leadership challenges at this level requires courage and openness from leaders, as it involves confronting aspects of themselves that may have been long hidden from their conscious awareness. However, this journey into the unconscious is not undertaken alone; it is facilitated by a skilled coach who can guide the leader through the process with empathy, insight, and professionalism. Through techniques such as reflective listening, dream analysis, and the exploration of resistance and defense mechanisms, coaches help leaders to bring unconscious material into consciousness, where it can be examined, understood, and integrated.

This deep level of understanding fosters more authentic and adaptive leadership styles. Leaders become more self-aware and emotionally intelligent, better equipped to manage their reactions and relationships effectively. They gain insights into their motivations and fears, allowing them to lead with greater confidence and resilience. Moreover, by addressing the unconscious roots of imposter syndrome and leadership anxieties, leaders can shed the burdens of self-doubt and fear of exposure, stepping into their roles with a newfound sense of legitimacy and authority.

The significance of understanding the unconscious aspects of leadership challenges cannot be overstated. It is the key to unlocking more meaningful, sustainable solutions that not only enhance individual leadership effectiveness but also contribute to the creation of healthier, more dynamic organizational cultures. This profound approach to leadership development promises not just professional growth but personal transformation, leading to leadership that is both effective and deeply fulfilling.

Navigating Power Dynamics and Authority Issues

Understanding power and authority through a psychoanalytic lens involves delving into the complex, often unconscious factors that influence how leaders exercise power and respond to authority. Psychoanalytic theory suggests that individuals' experiences with power and authority are deeply rooted in their earliest relationships and experiences, particularly those with primary caregivers. These early interactions can shape an individual's attitudes towards power and authority, influencing their leadership style and behavior in profound ways.

From a psychoanalytic perspective, the exercise of power and response to authority can be seen as manifestations of unconscious dynamics, including unresolved conflicts, internalized values, and the re-enactment of past relationships. Leaders may unconsciously replicate the patterns of authority they experienced in childhood, whether by adopting a similar style or reacting against it. For example, a leader who experienced authoritarian parenting might unconsciously model their leadership after this style, exerting control and demanding obedience, or they may swing to the opposite extreme, avoiding the exercise of authority altogether to not replicate their parent's behavior.

Psychoanalytic theory highlights the role of defense mechanisms in how leaders deal with power and authority. Leaders might use projection, projecting their own feelings of inadequacy or desires for power onto others, or they might engage in denial, refusing to acknowledge the impact of their authority on their team. Such mechanisms can distort a leader's perception of power dynamics, leading to challenges in effectively managing relationships and authority within their organizations.

The concept of transference and countertransference is also crucial in understanding the psychoanalytic perspective on power and authority. Leaders and their followers might experience transference, unconsciously transferring feelings and expectations from past authority figures onto each other. This can complicate the leader-follower relationship, as reactions and expectations may be based more on past experiences than on the current reality. Similarly, leaders might experience countertransference, reacting to their followers based on their own unconscious biases and past experiences, rather than responding to the followers' actual behaviors or needs.

Understanding these unconscious factors requires leaders to engage in deep self-reflection and exploration, often with the help of a skilled coach or psychotherapist. By bringing unconscious material into consciousness, leaders can gain insights into their attitudes and behaviors related to power and authority. This awareness allows them to modify their leadership style in more adaptive and effective ways, fostering healthier relationships and organizational dynamics. The psychoanalytic perspective offers a rich framework for understanding the unconscious factors that influence leaders' exercise of power and response to authority. By exploring these deep-seated dynamics, leaders can achieve a more nuanced understanding of their leadership style, enabling them to lead with greater self-awareness, empathy, and effectiveness. This approach not only enhances individual leadership capabilities but also contributes to the development of more collaborative, empowered, and psychologically healthy organizations.

The interplay of power dynamics within the context of leadership and followership is significantly influenced by unconscious factors, many of which stem from individuals' past experiences, particularly their early relationships with authority figures. These foundational relationships, often established in childhood with parents, teachers, and other caretakers, serve as the initial blueprint for understanding and interacting with power and authority. This early imprinting shapes perceptions and behaviors related to power dynamics in profound and often unconscious ways, affecting how individuals navigate their roles as leaders and followers in the workplace.

For leaders, early experiences with authority figures can influence their approach to wielding power. A leader who experienced authoritative parenting, characterized by strict rules and high expectations, may unconsciously adopt a similar style, equating leadership with control and discipline. Conversely, if early authority figures were permissive or absent, a leader might struggle with asserting authority, fearing being perceived as overbearing or might excessively seek approval from their team to avoid conflict. These patterns reveal how past experiences can shape a leader's comfort with and style of exercising power, often without the leader being consciously aware of these influences.

Followers, on the other hand, bring their own set of unconscious expectations and reactions to power dynamics based on their historical interactions with authority figures. A follower who was encouraged to be independent and question authority might find it challenging to accept hierarchical structures or directive leadership styles. Alternatively, someone used to rigid authority structures might feel more comfortable in clearly defined, traditional power dynamics and may struggle in more collaborative or flat organizational cultures. These unconscious preferences and aversions influence how followers perceive their leaders, respond to directives, and navigate their roles within the team and organization.

The unconscious influences on power dynamics are also evident in phenomena such as transference and projection. Leaders and followers might unconsciously transfer feelings, expectations, or unresolved conflicts from past authority figures onto their current professional relationships. For example, a follower might project feelings of rebellion against a parent onto a leader, while a leader might transfer parental expectations of obedience and respect onto their followers. These projections can distort the reality of the professional relationship, leading to misunderstandings, conflicts, or unmet expectations.

Recognizing and addressing these unconscious influences requires a deliberate and reflective approach. Leaders can benefit from engaging in self-exploration, whether through coaching, therapy, or reflective practices, to uncover and understand the origins of their attitudes and behaviors towards power and authority. By bringing these unconscious influences into awareness, leaders and followers alike can work towards more consciously chosen and adaptive ways of interacting with power dynamics.

The unconscious influences stemming from early relationships with authority figures play a critical role in shaping current perceptions and behaviors related to power and authority in the workplace. Understanding and addressing these influences can lead to healthier power dynamics, improved leader-follower relationships, and more effective organizational leadership. This exploration not only enhances individual self-awareness and growth but also contributes to creating a more cohesive, empowered, and psychologically aware organizational culture.

Psychoanalytically informed strategies can provide leaders with valuable insights into recognizing and modifying unconscious patterns that affect their approach to power and authority. By engaging with these strategies, leaders can foster a more balanced and effective leadership style, characterized by healthier power dynamics within their teams and organizations. Here are several approaches to consider:

1. Engage in Reflective Practice: Leaders should cultivate a habit of regular self-reflection to examine their feelings, thoughts, and behaviors related to power and authority. Reflective practices such as journaling about leadership experiences, decisions, and interactions can help leaders identify recurring patterns and themes that may indicate underlying unconscious influences.

2. Seek Feedback and Open Dialogue: Encouraging feedback from peers, mentors, and team members can provide leaders with external perspectives on their leadership style and power dynamics. Open dialogue about power and authority within the team can also reveal how a leader's approach is perceived and the impact it has on others, offering insights into areas for improvement.

3. Explore Early Relationships with Authority: Leaders can benefit from exploring their early relationships with authority figures, such as parents or teachers, to understand the origins of their beliefs and attitudes towards power and authority.

Psychotherapy or coaching with a psychoanalytic orientation can facilitate this exploration, helping leaders to connect past experiences with present behaviors.

4. Understand and Address Transference and Countertransference: Becoming aware of transference and countertransference dynamics in the workplace can help leaders recognize when their reactions to team members or situations are influenced by past relationships rather than the current reality. Acknowledging and addressing these dynamics can lead to clearer and more effective communication and decision-making.

5. Develop Emotional Intelligence: Enhancing emotional intelligence is crucial for leaders aiming to improve their approach to power and authority. Skills such as empathy, self-awareness, and emotional regulation can help leaders understand and manage their own emotional responses as well as those of their team members, leading to more compassionate and balanced leadership.

6. Practice Mindfulness: Mindfulness practices can increase a leader's awareness of their moment-to-moment experiences, including their reactions to power dynamics and authority issues. This heightened awareness can facilitate a more deliberate and thoughtful approach to leadership, allowing leaders to choose responses that align with their values and goals rather than reacting unconsciously.

7. Foster a Culture of Collaboration: Leaders can work to create an organizational culture that values collaboration and shared power. By involving team members in decision-making processes and encouraging autonomy, leaders can shift away from hierarchical power dynamics towards a more inclusive and empowering model.

8. Seek Professional Development: Participating in leadership development programs that focus on psychoanalytic concepts can provide leaders with deeper insights into the psychological aspects of leadership and power dynamics. These programs

can offer practical tools and strategies for addressing unconscious patterns and fostering healthier relationships within teams.

By employing these psychoanalytically informed strategies, leaders can begin to recognize and modify unconscious patterns that negatively affect their approach to power and authority. This process not only enhances personal growth and leadership effectiveness but also contributes to the development of healthier, more productive power dynamics within organizations, ultimately leading to a more positive and empowering workplace environment.

Enhancing Emotional Intelligence and Relational Skills

The role of unconscious processes, including mechanisms like projection and transference, plays a significant part in shaping a leader's emotional intelligence and relational skills. These deep-seated psychological dynamics can profoundly influence how leaders perceive, relate to, and interact with others, often without their conscious awareness. Understanding these processes can provide valuable insights into the complexities of leadership behavior, particularly in the realms of emotional intelligence and interpersonal relationships.

Projection involves the unconscious attribution of one's unacceptable feelings, desires, or impulses onto another person. For leaders, this might mean attributing their own insecurities, fears, or motivations to their team members or colleagues, leading to misinterpretations of others' actions and intentions. Such misattributions can hinder a leader's ability to accurately empathize with and understand the emotional states of others, a core component of emotional intelligence. For example, a leader who unconsciously feels inadequate might perceive criticism where there is none, reacting defensively to feedback and thereby straining relationships.

Transference, on the other hand, refers to the redirection of feelings and desires from one person to another, particularly in a new relationship that resembles one from the past. Leaders might experience transference when they unconsciously replicate dynamics from previous authority relationships with current team members, affecting their leadership style and decision-making. This can lead to skewed perceptions of team members' capabilities and motivations, potentially resulting in leadership decisions that are more reflective of the leader's past experiences than the present situation.

Both projection and transference can significantly impact a leader's emotional intelligence, particularly in the areas of self-awareness, self-regulation, empathy, and social skills. A lack of awareness of these unconscious processes can lead to misunderstandings, conflict, and ineffective leadership. Leaders might struggle to form genuine connections, misinterpret emotions, or respond inappropriately to team dynamics, undermining their relational skills and emotional intelligence.

To mitigate the impact of unconscious processes on emotional intelligence and relational skills, leaders can benefit from engaging in self-reflective practices that increase self-awareness. This might involve psychotherapy, coaching, or mindfulness practices that help leaders recognize and understand their unconscious motivations, fears, and biases. Developing a deeper understanding of oneself allows leaders to better regulate their emotional responses, improve their empathy, and enhance their interpersonal skills.

Creating opportunities for open feedback and dialogue within teams can help leaders become more attuned to the perspectives and emotional states of others, further developing their emotional intelligence. By acknowledging and addressing the influence of unconscious processes on their behavior, leaders can foster healthier, more productive relationships, and cultivate a leadership style characterized by emotional awareness, adaptability, and genuine connection.

The unconscious processes of projection and transference can significantly impact a leader's emotional intelligence and relational skills. By becoming aware of and addressing these unconscious dynamics, leaders can enhance their ability to connect with, understand, and effectively lead their teams, ultimately contributing to more empathetic and emotionally intelligent leadership.

Developing self-awareness and empathy is crucial for leaders aiming to enhance their leadership effectiveness and foster positive relationships within their teams. These competencies allow leaders to understand their own motivations and emotional responses, as well as to connect with the feelings and perspectives of others. Several techniques can support leaders in cultivating these vital skills, focusing on reflective practices and the exploration of unconscious emotional responses.

- Engage in Regular Reflective Practices: Leaders can benefit from setting aside time for regular self-reflection. This could involve journaling about daily experiences, decisions made, interactions with team members, and the emotions those interactions evoked. Reflective writing helps leaders identify patterns in their thoughts and behaviors, offering insights into their unconscious motivations and emotional triggers.

- Practice Mindfulness and Meditation: Mindfulness meditation is a powerful tool for developing self-awareness. By focusing on the present moment and observing thoughts and feelings without judgment, leaders can become more attuned to their internal emotional landscape. This practice enhances the ability to manage emotions effectively and respond to situations with greater clarity and compassion.

- Seek Feedback from Others: Soliciting feedback from peers, mentors, and team members can provide valuable perspectives on a leader's behavior and its impact on others. Constructive feedback helps leaders identify areas for improvement, including aspects of their emotional intelligence and empathy they may not have been aware of.

- Participate in Coaching or Therapy: Working with a coach or therapist, especially one with a psychoanalytic background, can facilitate deeper self-exploration. These professionals can guide leaders in uncovering unconscious emotional responses and unresolved issues that may be influencing their leadership style. Through this exploration, leaders can gain insights into their behavior and develop strategies to enhance their self-awareness and empathy.

- Explore Emotional Triggers: Leaders should strive to identify and understand their emotional triggers—specific situations or behaviors that elicit strong emotional responses. Recognizing these triggers and reflecting on their origins can help leaders manage their reactions more effectively, leading to more empathetic interactions with others.

- Develop Active Listening Skills: Active listening involves fully concentrating on what is being said, rather than passively hearing the message of the speaker. By practicing active listening, leaders can better understand the perspectives and emotions of their team members, fostering empathy and strengthening relationships.

- Use Role-Playing or Simulation Exercises: Engaging in role-playing or simulation exercises can help leaders put themselves in their team members' shoes, enhancing empathy. These exercises can be particularly effective in exploring different viewpoints and emotional experiences, enabling leaders to appreciate the diversity of perspectives within their teams.

- Cultivate a Culture of Openness: By fostering an environment where emotions and vulnerabilities can be openly shared, leaders model the value of emotional awareness and empathy. Encouraging team members to express their feelings and share their experiences can enrich a leader's understanding of the emotional dynamics within the team.

Developing self-awareness and empathy requires ongoing effort and dedication. By employing these techniques, leaders can enhance their ability to connect with their own emotions and those of others, leading to more effective, compassionate, and emotionally intelligent leadership.

Applying psychoanalytic insights to leadership practices offers a profound approach to enhancing interpersonal relationships, team cohesion, and conflict resolution skills. By delving into the unconscious motivations, emotions, and defense mechanisms that influence behavior, leaders can gain a deeper understanding of themselves and their team members, fostering a more empathetic and effective leadership style.

One practical way leaders can use psychoanalytic insights is by exploring their own reactions and responses to team dynamics. Understanding the origins of these reactions—whether they stem from past experiences or unconscious biases—allows leaders to manage their behavior more effectively, reducing the potential for misunderstandings and improving communication. For instance, recognizing a tendency to project one's own insecurities onto team members can lead to more objective assessments of their performance and contributions.

Leaders can also apply psychoanalytic insights to understand the underlying causes of team conflicts. Conflicts often arise not just from surface disagreements but from deeper emotional undercurrents or unresolved issues within the team. By exploring these deeper layers, leaders can address the root causes of conflict, facilitating more meaningful and lasting resolutions. This might involve acknowledging and discussing the emotional aspects of a conflict or exploring the team's dynamics to uncover hidden tensions or alliances.

Psychoanalytic insights are particularly valuable in enhancing team cohesion. Leaders can use their understanding of transference and countertransference to navigate the complex emotional relationships within the team, fostering an environment where team members feel seen, understood, and valued. This might involve creating opportunities for team members to explore their own motivations and relationships within the team, such as through team-building exercises or reflective group discussions that encourage openness and vulnerability.

Leaders can apply psychoanalytic concepts to improve their empathy and relational skills. By becoming more attuned to the unconscious emotions and motivations of team members, leaders can tailor their communication and leadership approach to meet the individual needs of their team. This heightened empathy can lead to stronger, more positive relationships, where team members feel genuinely supported and motivated.

In terms of developing conflict resolution skills, psychoanalytic insights offer leaders tools to approach conflicts with a deeper understanding of the emotional factors at play. Instead of focusing solely on the practical aspects of a disagreement, leaders can explore the emotional narratives and unconscious dynamics underlying the conflict. This approach allows for more compassionate and comprehensive conflict resolution strategies that address both the immediate issue and the emotional well-being of the team members involved.

Applying psychoanalytic insights to leadership practices provides leaders with a powerful framework for enhancing interpersonal relationships, team cohesion, and conflict resolution skills. By exploring the unconscious dimensions of behavior and relationships, leaders can foster a work environment characterized by deep mutual understanding, empathy, and effective collaboration. This not only improves team dynamics but also contributes to a more inclusive, supportive, and productive organizational culture.

Overcoming Imposter Syndrome and Leadership Anxieties
Imposter syndrome and leadership anxieties, while common in the professional world, often have their roots in deep psychoanalytic processes. These feelings of doubt and fraudulence, despite external evidence of competence, can be profoundly influenced by unconscious beliefs and past experiences. Psychoanalytic theory

provides a lens through which to understand these phenomena, revealing how they are not merely surface-level concerns but are tied to deeper psychological dynamics.

At the heart of imposter syndrome lies a conflict between the ego and the superego—the part of the psyche that holds internalized standards, ideals, and critical judgments. Individuals suffering from imposter syndrome often have a superego that is overly critical, a condition that can stem from early experiences with demanding or perfectionistic authority figures. These early interactions can lead to the internalization of unrealistic standards and a pervasive sense of never being good enough, regardless of achievements or qualifications.

Unconscious beliefs about self-worth and competence play a significant role in imposter syndrome and leadership anxieties. These beliefs are often formed in childhood and can be rooted in experiences of conditional love or acceptance, where worth was tied to achievement or behavior. As adults, this can translate into a deep-seated fear of being exposed as a "fraud" if one fails to meet these internalized standards, even in the face of contrary evidence.

Psychoanalytic theory also highlights the role of defense mechanisms in imposter syndrome. Mechanisms such as projection can cause individuals to attribute their own feelings of inadequacy to others, believing that those around them also see them as frauds. Similarly, rationalization might lead individuals to dismiss their accomplishments as luck or timing, rather than acknowledging their own competence and effort.

Transference dynamics can further complicate imposter syndrome, with individuals unconsciously transferring feelings and expectations from past authority figures onto current colleagues or superiors. This can exacerbate feelings of being judged or exposed, as the individual projects onto others the critical voices of their past.

Addressing imposter syndrome and leadership anxieties from a psychoanalytic perspective involves bringing these unconscious beliefs and dynamics into consciousness. Through psychoanalytic coaching or therapy, individuals can explore their early relationships, internalized standards, and the origins of their critical self-beliefs. This exploration allows for the identification and challenging of these unconscious patterns, facilitating a more compassionate and realistic self-assessment.

Developing a more secure sense of self and self-worth is key in overcoming imposter syndrome. This involves not only recognizing and valuing one's achievements and competencies but also accepting imperfection and vulnerabilities as inherent aspects of being human. By understanding the psychoanalytic underpinnings of imposter syndrome and leadership anxieties, individuals can begin to free themselves from the grip of these unconscious beliefs and fears, stepping into their roles with greater confidence and authenticity.

Addressing the root causes of imposter syndrome and leadership anxieties with psychoanalytic techniques requires a multifaceted approach that delves into the unconscious beliefs, fears, and self-doubts underpinning these feelings. This journey begins with encouraging leaders to undertake deep self-reflection, possibly through journaling, to uncover the unconscious narratives driving their sense of inadequacy. Such introspection helps in identifying moments of feeling like an imposter, allowing for an exploration of the associated emotions and thoughts.

Exploring early life experiences is also pivotal, as psychoanalytic theory points to the significant impact of these formative years on the development of self-worth and identity. Leaders are guided to revisit their relationships with early authority figures and pivotal life events that have shaped their self-perception. This exploration can shed light on the origins of their imposter feelings and leadership anxieties.

A critical aspect of this process involves identifying and challenging negative self-talk, which often stems from unconscious beliefs. Recognizing patterns of self-criticism and their triggers enables leaders to begin reframing these thoughts more positively, employing techniques such as cognitive restructuring to challenge and change the underlying beliefs.

Defense mechanisms like projection and rationalization can exacerbate feelings of fraudulence and anxiety by distorting reality. By becoming aware of these unconscious defenses, leaders can question the validity of their fears and the authenticity of their self-doubts, gradually dismantling the barriers to a more secure self-image.

Addressing transference issues, where past feelings are redirected onto present figures, can also influence how leaders view themselves and interact with others. Psychoanalytically informed coaching can assist in recognizing and working through these dynamics, lessening their impact on interpersonal relationships and self-perception.

Developing a stronger, more integrated sense of self is essential in overcoming imposter syndrome and leadership anxieties. This entails not only recognizing and valuing one's achievements but also accepting and integrating more vulnerable aspects of the self. Techniques that promote self-compassion and acceptance are invaluable in this regard, helping leaders to see themselves in a more balanced and forgiving light.

For those grappling with deep-seated issues, seeking the assistance of a psychoanalytically trained coach or therapist can offer the structured support necessary for exploring and addressing the unconscious roots of their anxieties. This professional guidance provides a safe and confidential space for leaders to be vulnerable, facilitating a deeper exploration of their unconscious material and the development of effective strategies to challenge limiting self-beliefs.

Through this comprehensive psychoanalytic approach, leaders can gain profound insights into themselves and their behaviors, enabling a transformative shift in self-perception and leadership style. This deeper understanding allows for a more confident, resilient, and authentic approach to leadership, transforming not only the leaders themselves but also the teams and organizations they lead.

Building authentic confidence for leaders, particularly those grappling with imposter syndrome and leadership anxieties, involves a process of integrating newfound insights into their self-concept and leadership practices. This journey towards authentic confidence is marked by self-acceptance, continuous learning, and the practical application of insights into daily leadership activities. Here are ways leaders can embark on this transformative path:

- Integrate Insights into Self-Concept: Leaders should start by consciously incorporating their psychoanalytic discoveries about unconscious beliefs and past experiences into their understanding of themselves. This involves acknowledging both strengths and vulnerabilities, and recognizing how these elements contribute to their unique leadership style. By understanding the origins of their imposter syndrome and anxieties, leaders can reframe these experiences, viewing them as opportunities for growth rather than signs of inadequacy.

- Practice Self-Compassion: Cultivating self-compassion is crucial in overcoming harsh self-judgments that fuel imposter feelings. Leaders can practice self-compassion by speaking to themselves as they would to a close friend, with kindness and understanding, especially in moments of doubt or failure. This practice helps in developing a more forgiving and supportive internal dialogue, which is essential for building authentic confidence.

- Set Realistic Goals and Celebrate Achievements: Leaders should set achievable goals that align with their values and strengths. By setting and accomplishing these goals, they can gather evidence of their competencies and contributions, countering feelings of fraudulence. Celebrating these achievements, both big and small, reinforces their sense of efficacy and value as leaders.

- Seek Supportive Feedback: Regularly seeking feedback from trusted peers, mentors, or coaches can provide leaders with perspectives that affirm their abilities and highlight areas for improvement. This feedback can bolster their confidence by validating their progress and helping them see how they are perceived by others, often more positively than they perceive themselves.

- Embrace Lifelong Learning: Adopting a mindset of continuous learning and growth allows leaders to view challenges and setbacks as learning opportunities rather than evidence of inadequacy. Engaging in professional development activities, reading widely, and staying curious can help leaders build expertise and confidence in their leadership abilities.

- Apply Insights in Leadership Practices: Leaders can apply their psychoanalytic insights by adopting leadership practices that foster openness, empathy, and inclusivity. This might involve creating spaces for team members to share their own experiences and vulnerabilities, promoting a culture where authenticity and mutual support are valued. Demonstrating vulnerability, when appropriate, can also strengthen connections with team members and enhance team cohesion.

- Reflect on Leadership Impact: Regular reflection on the impact of their leadership on their team and organization can help leaders appreciate the positive influence they have. Considering the growth and achievements of their team members as a result of their leadership can provide tangible proof of their effectiveness, reinforcing their confidence.

Building authentic confidence is a dynamic and ongoing process that requires patience, effort, and a willingness to confront and transform deeply ingrained beliefs and behaviors. By integrating psychoanalytic insights into their self-concept and leadership practices, leaders can develop a sense of confidence that is rooted in a deep understanding of themselves and their value as leaders. This authentic confidence enables them to overcome imposter syndrome and leadership anxieties, leading with greater assurance, resilience, and impact.

Case Studies and Practical Applications

Due to the confidential nature of psychoanalytic coaching and the personal journey of self-exploration, specific real-life examples of leaders who have navigated power dynamics, enhanced emotional intelligence, and overcome imposter syndrome are anonymized and generalized to maintain privacy. These composite case studies illustrate the transformative potential of psychoanalytic coaching and self-exploration in leadership development.

Case Study 1: Navigating Power Dynamics

Alex, a mid-level manager in a technology firm, struggled with asserting authority, leading to challenges in team performance and personal stress. Through psychoanalytic coaching, Alex explored early life experiences with authoritative parents, where expressing autonomy was often met with criticism. This exploration revealed Alex's unconscious fear of replicating such authoritative behaviors, leading to a reluctance to assert power. By acknowledging and working through these fears, Alex developed a more balanced leadership style, confidently setting boundaries and expectations while maintaining openness and approachability. This shift not only improved team performance but also enhanced Alex's satisfaction with their leadership role.

Case Study 2: Enhancing Emotional Intelligence
Jordan, a high-performing executive, faced difficulties in connecting with their team on an emotional level, impacting team morale and collaboration. Psychoanalytic coaching helped Jordan uncover a pattern of emotional detachment, a defense mechanism developed in response to early emotional vulnerabilities. By engaging in reflective practices and mindfulness, Jordan became

more attuned to their own emotions and those of their team members. This newfound emotional awareness allowed Jordan to foster a more supportive and empathetic team environment, leading to improved collaboration and team cohesion.

Case Study 3: Overcoming Imposter Syndrome

Taylor, a CEO of a startup, experienced persistent imposter syndrome despite the company's success, leading to overwork and anxiety. Psychoanalytic coaching provided a space to explore the roots of Taylor's feelings of inadequacy, tracing them back to a childhood marked by high expectations and conditional praise. Through understanding the impact of these early experiences on their self-concept, Taylor worked to internalize their achievements and develop a more compassionate self-view. By embracing vulnerability and practicing self-compassion, Taylor overcame the paralyzing effects of imposter syndrome, leading with greater authenticity and resilience.

These case studies highlight the power of psychoanalytic coaching and self-exploration in addressing deep-seated leadership challenges. By engaging with unconscious motivations, past experiences, and emotional patterns, leaders like Alex, Jordan, and Taylor have successfully navigated complex power dynamics, enhanced their emotional intelligence, and overcome imposter syndrome. These transformations not only benefit individual leaders but also have a profound impact on their teams and organizations, fostering environments of greater understanding, collaboration, and effectiveness.

The chapter on psychoanalytic principles in addressing leadership challenges offers a wealth of practical applications for leaders seeking to navigate the complexities of their roles with greater insight and effectiveness. By integrating psychoanalytic concepts into their leadership approach, leaders can achieve profound understanding and transformation in several key areas:

1. Understanding and Navigating Power Dynamics: Leaders can use psychoanalytic insights to explore their own beliefs and

feelings about power and authority, which may be rooted in early life experiences. Reflecting on how these unconscious influences shape their leadership style can help leaders develop more balanced and effective ways of wielding power. For instance, leaders who recognize a tendency to either shy away from or over-exert authority can seek to find a middle ground that fosters respect without creating distance or resentment.

2. Enhancing Emotional Intelligence: Psychoanalytic principles can be applied to deepen leaders' emotional intelligence by encouraging self-exploration of their emotional reactions and triggers. Leaders can become more attuned to their own emotional states and those of their team members by practicing mindfulness and reflective listening. This heightened emotional awareness can improve empathy, communication, and conflict resolution skills, leading to stronger, more cohesive teams.

3. Overcoming Imposter Syndrome: By delving into the unconscious roots of imposter syndrome, leaders can confront and challenge the deep-seated fears and self-doubts that fuel feelings of inadequacy. Techniques such as journaling about achievements and moments of doubt and exploring the origins of these feelings in therapy or coaching, can help leaders reframe their self-perception and build authentic confidence in their capabilities.

4. Addressing Leadership Anxieties: Leaders can use psychoanalytic insights to understand and mitigate anxieties related to leadership responsibilities, decision-making, and personal visibility. Recognizing that such anxieties may stem from past experiences and internalized pressures allows leaders to address them more directly. Strategies may include setting realistic expectations, seeking supportive feedback, and engaging in self-care practices that reduce stress and build resilience.

5. Developing Self-Awareness: Psychoanalytic principles emphasize the importance of self-awareness in effective leadership. Leaders can engage in regular self-reflection, perhaps through meditation or therapy, to uncover and understand their motivations, biases, and behavioral patterns. This ongoing process of self-discovery can inform more mindful and authentic leadership practices.

6. Fostering Team Dynamics: Understanding the unconscious dynamics within teams, such as transference and projection, can help leaders navigate interpersonal relationships and team conflicts more effectively. Leaders can create environments that encourage open communication and vulnerability, helping team members explore and address their own unconscious influences on team dynamics.

7. Practicing Reflective Leadership: Leaders can embody psychoanalytic principles by adopting a reflective leadership style that values introspection, continuous learning, and the psychological well-being of both themselves and their team members. This approach encourages a culture of mutual understanding, personal growth, and adaptive change.

The practical applications of psychoanalytic principles in leadership contexts offer powerful tools for addressing and overcoming common leadership challenges. By fostering a deeper understanding of the unconscious factors that influence behavior and relationships, leaders can enhance their effectiveness, build stronger teams, and lead with greater authenticity and resilience.

Conclusion

This chapter has illuminated the profound value of a psychoanalytic approach in comprehensively addressing leadership challenges, emphasizing that true understanding and transformation require leaders to courageously explore the unconscious dimensions of their experiences and behaviors. By delving into the depths of the unconscious, leaders can uncover the root causes of their challenges, such as imposter syndrome, leadership anxieties, difficulties in navigating power dynamics, and issues in emotional intelligence and relational skills.

A psychoanalytic approach provides leaders with the tools to examine how past experiences, particularly early relationships with authority figures, shape their perceptions of power and authority. This exploration allows leaders to understand the unconscious influences on their leadership style, enabling them to modify their approach for more balanced and effective leadership.

Psychoanalytic principles shed light on the complex interplay between a leader's self-concept and their professional role. By confronting and working through unconscious conflicts, leaders can overcome deep-seated fears and self-doubts, leading to the development of authentic confidence. This process not only enhances their capacity for self-awareness and empathy but also improves their ability to form genuine connections with team members, fostering a positive and collaborative team environment.

The chapter also highlights the significance of addressing unconscious dynamics within teams, such as transference and projection, which can impact team cohesion and conflict resolution. Leaders equipped with psychoanalytic insights are better positioned to navigate these dynamics sensitively, promoting a culture of openness and mutual understanding.

The psychoanalytic approach advocates for reflective practices that encourage continuous self-exploration and growth. Leaders are encouraged to engage in activities such as journaling, mindfulness, and seeking feedback, which support the integration of newfound insights into their leadership practices. This commitment to self-development not only benefits leaders individually but also serves as a model for their teams, contributing to a more introspective, resilient, and adaptive organizational culture.

The chapter underscores that a psychoanalytic approach offers a comprehensive and deeply insightful framework for addressing leadership challenges. By being willing to explore the unconscious dimensions of their experiences and behaviors, leaders can achieve a level of understanding and transformation that transcends conventional leadership development methods. This deeper exploration facilitates lasting change, enabling leaders to navigate their roles with greater authenticity, effectiveness, and emotional intelligence, ultimately leading to healthier and more productive organizational environments.

Leaders and coaches are encouraged to continue exploring psychoanalytic principles and techniques, recognizing them as invaluable resources for personal growth and addressing the myriad leadership challenges discussed in this chapter. The journey into the psychoanalytic realm offers a unique opportunity to delve deeply into the unconscious aspects of one's psyche, unveiling the intricate web of motivations, fears, and desires that influence leadership behavior and interpersonal dynamics.

Engaging with psychoanalytic principles enables leaders to confront and understand the root causes of various leadership challenges, such as navigating complex power dynamics, enhancing emotional intelligence, overcoming imposter syndrome, and improving relational skills. This exploration fosters a profound level of self-awareness and empathy, crucial qualities for effective, authentic leadership.

For coaches, incorporating psychoanalytic techniques into their practice provides a powerful framework for facilitating transformative change in leaders. By guiding leaders through the process of self-discovery, coaches can help them uncover and address unconscious patterns and beliefs that may be hindering their leadership potential. This not only aids in resolving specific leadership challenges but also contributes to the leader's overall personal and professional development.

The path of psychoanalytic exploration is one of continuous learning and growth. As such, leaders and coaches are encouraged to pursue further education and training in psychoanalytic theories and techniques, seek supervision from experienced practitioners, and engage in their own psychoanalytic work. This commitment to ongoing exploration not only enhances their ability to navigate leadership challenges but also enriches their personal lives and relationships.

Fostering a culture of introspection and psychological awareness within organizations can have a ripple effect, encouraging teams and entire organizations to engage in their own processes of reflection and growth. This culture shift can lead to more adaptive, resilient, and emotionally intelligent organizational environments, where challenges are approached with depth, understanding, and creativity.

In embracing the psychoanalytic approach, leaders and coaches embark on a path that promises not only the resolution of immediate leadership challenges but also a journey toward deeper personal fulfillment and effectiveness. This exploration is an invitation to transform not just the way one leads but also how one lives, offering insights and tools that have the power to catalyze profound change.

Part IV: Case Studies and Practical Applications

In part IV we explore Case Studies and Integration of material starting with chapter 9 that dives into the real-world impact of psychoanalytic principles on leadership development, offering a compelling look at how these concepts are applied in practice. Through detailed case studies and practical applications, this section illuminates the transformative power of psychoanalytic leadership coaching, providing readers with concrete examples of how deep psychological insights can lead to significant personal and professional growth.

Chapter 9: Case Studies in Psychoanalytic Leadership Coaching serves as a foundational piece in this exploration, presenting a series of case studies that showcase the application of psychoanalytic techniques in addressing complex leadership challenges. This chapter offers a glimpse into the journeys of various leaders who have engaged in psychoanalytic coaching to overcome issues such as imposter syndrome, ineffective communication, unresolved power dynamics, and emotional intelligence barriers.

Each case study details the specific challenges faced by the leader, the psychoanalytic interventions employed by the coach, and the outcomes of the coaching process. Through these narratives, readers gain insight into the nuanced ways in which unconscious factors influence leadership behavior and how targeted psychoanalytic coaching can bring these factors to light, facilitating profound change.

The case studies underscore the value of a psychoanalytic approach in uncovering the root causes of leadership challenges, moving beyond surface-level solutions to effect lasting transformation. By engaging with these real-life examples, leaders and coaches alike can better understand the potential of psychoanalytic coaching to enhance leadership effectiveness, improve team dynamics, and foster personal growth.

Chapter 9 sets the stage for subsequent chapters in Part IV, which delve further into practical applications and strategies for integrating psychoanalytic principles into leadership development. Through this comprehensive exploration, readers are equipped with the knowledge and tools necessary to apply psychoanalytic insights to their own leadership challenges, paving the way for more insightful, empathetic, and effective leadership practices.

Following this, Chapter 10: Integrating Psychoanalytic Approach in Executive Coaching Programs aims to guide the integration of psychoanalytic approaches into executive coaching programs. This chapter emphasizes the value of deep psychological insights in elevating coaching effectiveness and leadership development. It discusses the careful design of psychoanalytically informed coaching programs, highlighting foundational principles such as the exploration of unconscious processes and the dynamics of transference and countertransference. The chapter underscores the importance of tailoring programs to meet individual leaders' needs, ensuring that coaching is sensitive to their psychological makeup and professional context.

Ethical considerations and boundaries are addressed, stressing the necessity of maintaining professionalism, confidentiality, and informed consent, especially when delving into deep psychological issues. This ensures a safe and supportive coaching environment, fostering trust and openness in the coaching relationship.

The chapter further explores the crucial role of supervision and continuing professional development for coaches. It advocates for ongoing learning and self-reflection, encouraging coaches to deepen their understanding of psychoanalytic theory and practice. Supervision, whether individual or group, is presented as essential for navigating the complexities of psychoanalytically informed coaching, offering support and guidance to coaches.

Illustrative case studies and best practices are shared, demonstrating the successful integration of psychoanalytic approaches in executive coaching. These examples highlight the process, challenges, and outcomes of psychoanalytically informed coaching interventions, providing practical insights for coaches looking to adopt this approach.

Chapter 10 reinforces the significant benefits of incorporating psychoanalytic principles into executive coaching. It encourages coaches to approach this integration with diligence, ethics, and a commitment to ongoing professional development. By doing so, coaches can enhance their effectiveness and contribute to the profound growth and development of leaders, ultimately leading to more insightful, empathetic, and effective leadership practices across organizations.

Chapter 9: Case Studies in Psychoanalytic Leadership Coaching

Chapter 9 stands as a pivotal exploration within the broader discourse on psychoanalytic leadership coaching, dedicated to presenting detailed case studies that vividly illustrate the practical application of psychoanalytic concepts in the realm of leadership development. This chapter aims to bridge the theoretical underpinnings of psychoanalysis with the tangible, day-to-day challenges leaders face, offering a window into the transformative power of psychoanalytic coaching.

The purpose of this chapter is multifaceted: to demystify the often-abstract principles of psychoanalysis by grounding them in real-world contexts, to showcase the depth and breadth of change possible when leaders engage in this introspective work, and to provide coaches and leaders alike with concrete examples of how psychoanalytic techniques can be applied to foster growth, overcome obstacles, and enhance leadership effectiveness.

Each case study within the chapter is carefully selected to cover a diverse range of leadership challenges, from navigating complex power dynamics and managing emotions effectively to confronting imposter syndrome and enhancing relational skills. Through these narratives, readers will gain insights into the nuanced process of psychoanalytic coaching, including the initial identification of unconscious patterns, the exploration and interpretation of these dynamics, and the integration of newfound insights into more adaptive leadership practices.

The chapter illuminates the critical role of the coach-client relationship in psychoanalytic leadership coaching, highlighting how trust, empathy, and understanding form the foundation for deep psychological exploration and change. It underscores the importance of ethical considerations, such as confidentiality and informed consent, in creating a safe and supportive environment conducive to self-discovery and transformation.

Chapter 9 serves as both a testament to the efficacy of psychoanalytic leadership coaching and a practical guide for those interested in applying these principles to their own leadership development or coaching practice. It invites readers into a journey of discovery, illustrating how the exploration of the unconscious can unlock profound insights and catalyze lasting growth for leaders committed to their personal and professional evolution.

The inclusion of real-world examples in demonstrating the application of psychoanalytic principles to leadership coaching is invaluable. These examples serve as tangible evidence of how deep-seated, often unconscious, factors influence leadership behavior, decision-making, and interpersonal dynamics. Through the lens of actual case studies, the abstract and complex theories of psychoanalysis become accessible and relatable, illustrating their practical relevance to everyday leadership challenges.

Real-world examples highlight the nuanced process of psychoanalytic coaching, showing how an exploration of a leader's unconscious motivations, fears, and desires can lead to significant personal growth and enhanced leadership effectiveness. They provide a concrete framework for understanding the transformative journey from self-awareness to action, showcasing the steps involved in identifying unconscious patterns, interpreting their impact on leadership, and integrating insights to foster change.

These examples underscore the value of psychoanalytic coaching in addressing a wide range of leadership challenges. From overcoming imposter syndrome and managing leadership anxieties to navigating power dynamics and improving emotional intelligence, real-world case studies demonstrate the breadth of issues psychoanalytic principles can help resolve. They show that by delving into the unconscious, leaders can gain profound insights into their behavior and relationships, leading to more authentic, empathetic, and effective leadership.

The use of real-world examples in illustrating the application of psychoanalytic principles to leadership coaching is essential. They not only bring psychoanalytic theories to life but also highlight the potential for deep, transformative change. By showcasing the impact of psychoanalytic coaching on individual leaders and their organizations, these examples reinforce the value of exploring the unconscious as a powerful tool for personal growth and leadership development.

Case Study 1: Navigating Power Dynamics in a Family-Owned Business

In the intricate landscape of a family-owned business, power dynamics and succession planning can intertwine with deep personal relationships, creating unique challenges for leadership. This case study revolves around a leader at the helm of such a business, where the lines between family roles and business roles blur, complicating decision-making and authority.

The leader in focus inherited the business from a previous generation, stepping into a role fraught with expectations and unspoken rules about leadership and authority shaped by the family's history. The business was at a crucial juncture, facing the need for a clear succession plan amidst underlying tensions about the future direction and leadership of the company.

The psychoanalytic coaching process began with an exploration of the leader's unconscious beliefs about authority and power, deeply ingrained in the family dynamics from which they emerged. Concepts such as transference and the influence of early authority figures were key in understanding how past family relationships impacted the leader's approach to power within the business. The leader's narratives about their predecessors in the business and their own role within the family provided rich material for analysis, revealing unconscious patterns influencing their leadership style.

Through a series of coaching sessions, interventions were carefully chosen to delve into the leader's psyche. Dream analysis offered insights into unconscious fears and desires related to the business and its future, while discussions around transference phenomena helped the leader recognize how familial relationships were being replicated in the business context, affecting both decision-making and interpersonal dynamics within the company. By exploring these unconscious dynamics, the coaching process aimed to untangle the personal from the professional, providing the leader with a clearer perspective on their authority and role.

The outcome of the psychoanalytic coaching was multifaceted. The leader developed a profound understanding of their unconscious motivations and how these shaped their approach to leadership and succession planning. This insight allowed for a reevaluation of their leadership style, fostering more open and effective communication within both the family and the business. As a result, relationships improved, and a clear succession plan was established, aligning with both the business's needs and the family's values. The leader reflected on the coaching process as a transformative journey that not only addressed immediate challenges but also facilitated personal growth and a deeper understanding of their role within the complex dynamics of a family-owned business.

This case study exemplifies the power of psychoanalytic coaching in navigating the nuanced challenges of leadership within a family-owned business. By addressing the unconscious underpinnings of power dynamics and succession planning, the leader was able to move forward with clarity and confidence, ensuring the business's continuity and strengthening family relationships.

Case Study 2: Enhancing Emotional Intelligence in a High-Tech Company

In the fast-paced environment of a high-tech company, a leader found themselves at a crossroads, grappling with challenges in team management and interpersonal relationships. These difficulties stemmed from a noted lack of emotional intelligence, which hindered effective communication, empathy, and ultimately, team cohesion and performance.

The leader, skilled in technical aspects, faced hurdles in understanding and managing emotions—both their own and those of their team members. This gap in emotional intelligence led to miscommunications, unresolved conflicts, and a noticeable impact on team morale and productivity.

The psychoanalytic approach to coaching offered a pathway to explore the deeper, unconscious emotional blocks and past experiences that were influencing the leader's ability to connect with and understand others. The coaching process began with an exploration of the leader's early life experiences and relationships, particularly those with significant authority figures, to uncover patterns and beliefs that shaped their current emotional responses and interactions.

Interventions included reflective listening exercises, where the leader was encouraged to actively listen and respond to emotional cues in conversations, both within and outside the coaching sessions. These exercises aimed to enhance the leader's empathy and understanding of others' perspectives. Additionally, the leader engaged in exercises exploring their childhood experiences, examining how these formative years influenced their understanding of emotions and their expression. This exploration was pivotal in identifying and addressing the unconscious roots of the leader's struggles with emotional intelligence.

The outcomes of this psychoanalytic coaching process were profound. The leader demonstrated significant improvement in their emotional intelligence, marked by an increased ability to recognize and manage emotions, both in themselves and in their team members. This newfound emotional awareness and sensitivity led to improved communication, conflict resolution, and interpersonal relationships within the team. Team dynamics transformed, with increased collaboration, trust, and performance, as the leader applied their enhanced emotional intelligence to foster a more supportive and cohesive work environment.

Reflecting on the transformation process, the leader acknowledged the pivotal role of psychoanalytic coaching in facilitating their personal growth and development. This journey not only addressed the immediate challenges of team management but also contributed to the leader's overall self-awareness and emotional maturity. The exploration of unconscious emotional blocks and past experiences provided the leader with invaluable insights into their behavior and interactions, equipping them with the tools to continue building on their emotional intelligence.

This case study underscores the value of integrating psychoanalytic principles and techniques in coaching to enhance emotional intelligence in leadership. By delving into the unconscious factors that impact emotional awareness and expression, leaders can achieve lasting change, leading to more effective leadership and healthier team dynamics.

Case Study 3: Overcoming Imposter Syndrome in a Corporate Executive

In the competitive realm of corporate leadership, a high-achieving executive found themselves grappling with the pervasive challenge of imposter syndrome, coupled with deep-seated leadership anxieties. Despite a track record of success, this executive was plagued by a persistent fear of being exposed as a fraud, a feeling that their accomplishments were not truly deserved but rather the result of luck or deception. This psychological struggle threatened not only their personal well-being but also their effectiveness as a leader.

The psychoanalytic approach to coaching provided a framework for unraveling the complex web of unconscious drivers fueling the executive's imposter syndrome. Central to this exploration were the executive's early life experiences and the familial expectations placed upon them. Delving into the executive's upbringing revealed a pattern of high achievement being met with conditional approval, setting the stage for a belief system wherein self-worth was intricately tied to performance and external validation.

The coaching process employed a range of psychoanalytic techniques tailored to addressing the executive's specific challenges. Dream analysis became a key tool, offering insights into the executive's unconscious fears and desires. Dreams depicting scenarios of failure or exposure were dissected to understand their symbolic meanings, shedding light on the deep-seated feelings of inadequacy the executive harbored. Additionally, the exploration of transference and countertransference dynamics within the coaching relationship and in the executive's interactions with others in the corporate environment provided valuable clues to the unconscious patterns affecting their leadership style and self-perception.

The outcome of this psychoanalytic coaching journey was transformative. The executive emerged with a newfound sense of confidence, rooted not in external achievements but in a deeper understanding and acceptance of their intrinsic worth. This shift in self-perception led to a significant improvement in leadership effectiveness, as the executive now led with authenticity and vulnerability, inspiring trust and loyalty among their team members. The fear of being exposed as a fraud diminished, replaced by a recognition of their competence and the value they brought to their role.

Reflecting on the journey, the executive and their coach acknowledged the profound impact of psychoanalytic coaching strategies in facilitating this transformation. By confronting and working through the unconscious drivers of imposter syndrome, the executive was able to break free from the cycle of self-doubt and fear that had constrained their potential. This case study exemplifies the power of psychoanalytic coaching in not only overcoming imposter syndrome but also in fostering a level of self-awareness and personal growth that enhances leadership capacity and authenticity.

Case Study 4: Transforming Leadership Style through Understanding Unconscious Motivations

In a landscape where adaptability and collaboration are increasingly valued, a leader recognized for their rigid, autocratic leadership style faced the challenge of evolving. This leader, accustomed to directing with a firm hand, found themselves at odds with the dynamic needs of their team and the broader organizational culture. The desire to shift toward a more flexible and inclusive approach prompted them to seek psychoanalytic coaching, aiming to uncover and transform the underpinnings of their authoritarian style.

The psychoanalytic approach to coaching provided a nuanced framework for this exploration, focusing on the unconscious motivations that drove the leader's reliance on control and authority. This journey into the leader's psyche revealed that their leadership style was not merely a professional choice but deeply rooted in their personal history. By examining the influence of early authority figures, such as parents and early mentors, the coaching process uncovered a pattern of equating leadership with control, a strategy developed early in life as a means of gaining approval and a sense of security.

The coaching interventions were carefully designed to address these discoveries. Analyzing the leader's dreams became a key component of the process, offering insights into their fears, aspirations, and unconscious beliefs about power and leadership. Dreams where the leader felt challenged or undermined provided a particularly rich source of material, revealing underlying anxieties about vulnerability and loss of control. Additionally, the coaching facilitated a deep dive into the leader's experiences with early authority figures, exploring how these relationships shaped their understanding of leadership and authority.

The outcomes of this psychoanalytic coaching process were transformative. The leader emerged with a profound understanding of the unconscious motivations behind their autocratic style, leading to a significant shift in how they approached leadership. This newfound self-awareness enabled them to adopt a more flexible, collaborative leadership style, better aligned with the needs of their team and the organizational culture. The change was marked by increased openness to input from team members, a willingness to share decision-making, and a greater emphasis on fostering a supportive, inclusive work environment.

Reflecting on the coaching journey, the leader recognized the pivotal role of psychoanalytic coaching in facilitating this deep, lasting change. By bringing unconscious motivations into awareness and working through the influences of past authority figures, the leader was able to consciously choose a different path. This case study underscores the value of psychoanalytic coaching in transforming leadership styles. It highlights how understanding and addressing unconscious motivations can lead to more adaptable, effective leadership, ultimately benefiting the leader, their team, and the broader organization.

Conclusion

The case studies presented offer a compelling look at the diverse applications of psychoanalytic concepts in leadership coaching and underscore the profound transformations that can ensue from such deep, introspective work. Each story, unique in its context and challenges, illustrates the power of psychoanalytic coaching to facilitate significant change in leaders' professional behaviors, self-perceptions, and interpersonal dynamics.

In the first case, we explored the nuanced power dynamics within a family-owned business, where the blurring of personal and professional boundaries created complex leadership challenges. Psychoanalytic coaching enabled the leader to understand and reframe their unconscious beliefs about authority and power, inherited from family dynamics, leading to improved relationships and a clear succession plan. This case highlights the importance of addressing unconscious patterns that influence leadership styles and decision-making processes.

The second case centered on a leader in a high-tech company struggling with emotional intelligence. Through psychoanalytic coaching, the leader uncovered and worked through unconscious emotional blocks and past experiences, enhancing their empathy and relational skills. This transformation not only improved team dynamics but also increased the leader's effectiveness, demonstrating the critical role of emotional awareness in leadership.

In the third case, a corporate executive grappling with imposter syndrome underwent psychoanalytic coaching to explore the unconscious drivers of their anxieties. By examining early life experiences and familial expectations, the executive gained insights into their feelings of inadequacy, ultimately overcoming imposter syndrome and leading with increased confidence. This case underscores the value of understanding and addressing the deep-seated beliefs that contribute to leadership anxieties.

The fourth case involved a leader known for their autocratic style seeking to become more adaptable and collaborative. Psychoanalytic coaching delved into the unconscious motivations behind their need for control, facilitating a shift towards a more flexible, inclusive leadership approach. This transformation was achieved by exploring the influence of early authority figures and analyzing dreams, illustrating how psychoanalytic principles can guide leaders in evolving their leadership styles to meet changing organizational needs.

Collectively, these case studies illuminate the broad spectrum of leadership challenges that can be effectively addressed through psychoanalytic coaching. By engaging with the unconscious aspects of their personalities and behaviors, leaders can achieve breakthroughs that lead to more authentic, effective, and fulfilling leadership. The profound transformations detailed in these cases not only benefited the individual leaders but also had a positive impact on their teams and organizations, showcasing the transformative potential of integrating psychoanalytic concepts into leadership development.

The deep understanding of the unconscious is foundational to developing effective leadership qualities, marking a critical area where psychoanalytic coaching offers unique and invaluable contributions to leadership development. This approach goes beyond surface-level behavioral changes, delving into the intricate web of unconscious motivations, beliefs, and emotional patterns that underpin a leader's actions and interactions. By bringing these unconscious elements into awareness, psychoanalytic coaching facilitates profound and lasting transformation in leaders, enabling them to lead with greater authenticity, empathy, and effectiveness.

The significance of exploring the unconscious lies in its capacity to reveal the root causes of various leadership challenges, including communication breakdowns, decision-making difficulties, and interpersonal conflicts. Often, these challenges stem not from a lack of skill or knowledge, but from deeper, unresolved issues and internalized narratives that shape a leader's perception and behavior. Psychoanalytic coaching provides the tools and frameworks for uncovering these underlying factors, offering leaders a pathway to address and resolve them.

A deep understanding of the unconscious enriches leaders' emotional intelligence, a critical component of effective leadership. By becoming more attuned to their own unconscious emotional responses and those of their team members, leaders can enhance their empathy, improve their communication skills, and foster a more supportive and cohesive team environment. This emotional awareness also supports leaders in navigating the complexities of organizational dynamics, enabling them to respond to challenges with greater sensitivity and insight.

Psychoanalytic coaching also plays a pivotal role in helping leaders overcome common pitfalls such as imposter syndrome and leadership anxieties. By examining the unconscious beliefs and past experiences that fuel these feelings, leaders can develop a more secure sense of self-worth and confidence. This process not only impacts their personal growth but also translates into more assured and inspiring leadership.

The unique value of psychoanalytic coaching in leadership development lies in its holistic approach, addressing the leader as a whole person rather than focusing solely on professional competencies. This approach acknowledges the interconnectedness of personal history, psychological makeup, and leadership behavior, providing a comprehensive framework for growth and development.

The importance of a deep understanding of the unconscious in developing effective leadership qualities cannot be overstated. Psychoanalytic coaching offers a profound avenue for leaders to explore and transform the unconscious aspects of their personalities, leading to breakthroughs in leadership effectiveness. This exploration fosters not only the development of essential leadership qualities but also promotes personal well-being and fulfillment, underscoring the unique and transformative value psychoanalytic coaching brings to leadership development.

Coaches and leaders are strongly encouraged to engage with psychoanalytic principles and practices, recognizing the profound impact these can have on addressing leadership challenges and fostering both personal and professional growth. The exploration of psychoanalytic concepts provides a rich and nuanced understanding of the unconscious factors that influence leadership behavior, decision-making, and interpersonal dynamics. This deeper insight can catalyze transformative change, leading to more authentic, empathetic, and effective leadership.

The importance of case studies in this context cannot be overstated. Case studies serve as illuminating examples of how psychoanalytic principles can be applied in real-world scenarios, offering tangible evidence of the potential for growth and development. They provide both leaders and coaches with practical insights into the process of psychoanalytic coaching, including the identification of unconscious patterns, the exploration of their origins, and the integration of newfound understanding into more adaptive leadership practices.

For leaders, engaging with psychoanalytic principles and practices opens the door to profound self-discovery. It allows them to confront and work through the unconscious beliefs, fears, and motivations that may be hindering their effectiveness, paving the way for significant personal and leadership development. Leaders are encouraged to approach this journey with openness and curiosity, embracing the opportunity for deep reflection and growth.

For coaches, incorporating psychoanalytic principles into their practice enhances their ability to facilitate meaningful change in their clients. By drawing on psychoanalytic concepts, coaches can offer more comprehensive support to leaders, helping them navigate complex emotional landscapes and achieve breakthroughs that impact not only their professional lives but their personal well-being. Coaches are urged to continue their own education and development in psychoanalytic theory and practice, ensuring they remain well-equipped to guide leaders through this transformative process.

The engagement with psychoanalytic principles and practices represents a powerful avenue for leadership development. Case studies highlight the practical application of these concepts, providing both inspiration and guidance for leaders and coaches alike. By delving into the depths of the unconscious and addressing the root causes of leadership challenges, individuals can unlock unparalleled opportunities for growth, leading to more effective, authentic, and fulfilling leadership.

Chapter 10: Integrating Psychoanalytic Approach in Executive Coaching Programs

Chapter 10 delves into the strategic integration of psychoanalytic approaches into executive coaching programs, underscoring the profound impact that deep psychological insights can have on enhancing the effectiveness of coaching and the overarching process of leadership development. This chapter is designed as a comprehensive guide for coaches and program designers who seek to enrich their coaching methodologies with the nuanced depth of psychoanalysis. It aims to bridge the gap between traditional executive coaching practices and the transformative potential of psychoanalytic theory, providing a clear pathway for incorporating these insights into coaching frameworks.

The integration of psychoanalytic approaches offers a unique opportunity to explore the undercurrents of leadership behavior, decision-making, and interpersonal relationships through the lens of the unconscious. By tapping into this rich vein of psychological depth, coaches can facilitate a more profound and lasting change in executives, moving beyond surface-level adjustments to foster true personal growth and enhanced leadership capacity.

This chapter emphasizes the value of understanding the unconscious motivations, conflicts, and dynamics that drive leaders, highlighting how such understanding can lead to more effective and authentic leadership practices. Through detailed discussions on program design, ethical considerations, and the practical application of psychoanalytic concepts, the chapter provides a roadmap for coaches and program developers to integrate these principles into their work.

By exploring the integration of psychoanalytic approaches in executive coaching programs, this chapter not only advances the field of executive coaching but also contributes to the broader discourse on leadership development. It invites coaches and leaders alike to embark on a journey of deeper self-exploration, promising not just professional growth but personal transformation as well.

The successful integration of psychoanalytic approaches into executive coaching programs necessitates careful design, stringent ethical considerations, and a commitment to ongoing supervision and professional development for coaches. These foundational elements ensure that the deep, introspective journey facilitated by psychoanalytic principles is both effective and ethically grounded, offering a safe and transformative experience for leaders.

Careful design is paramount in creating coaching programs that effectively harness psychoanalytic insights. Programs must be structured to gradually introduce leaders to psychoanalytic concepts, allowing them to explore their unconscious motivations and behaviors in a supportive and structured environment. This involves tailoring the program's pace and interventions to suit the individual needs and readiness of each leader, ensuring that the exploration of deep psychological territories is both manageable and meaningful.

Ethical considerations are at the heart of integrating psychoanalytic approaches into coaching. Given the depth of personal exploration involved, it is crucial to uphold the highest standards of confidentiality, informed consent, and professional boundaries. Coaches must be diligent in creating a safe space where leaders feel comfortable to delve into sensitive areas of their psyche, knowing their vulnerabilities will be handled with respect and discretion. Ethical practice also involves being clear about the scope of coaching and recognizing when it is necessary to refer a leader to other forms of psychological support or therapy.

Ongoing supervision is essential for coaches employing psychoanalytic methods. Supervision provides a forum for coaches to reflect on their practice, discuss challenges, and gain insights from more experienced practitioners. It is a vital process that supports the coach's professional growth and safeguards the quality and integrity of the coaching provided. Supervision helps coaches navigate the complex transference and countertransference dynamics that can arise in psychoanalytic work, ensuring that these are managed in a way that benefits the leader's development.

A commitment to professional development is critical for coaches adopting a psychoanalytic approach. This field is rich and evolving, and staying abreast of the latest theories, research, and techniques is necessary for effective practice. Professional development may include formal education, workshops, reading, and personal psychoanalytic work. Engaging in continuous learning not only enriches the coach's understanding and skill set but also deepens their capacity for self-reflection and personal growth, which are crucial qualities in a psychoanalytic coach.

The integration of psychoanalytic approaches into executive coaching programs offers a pathway to profound leadership development. However, this approach demands careful program design, strict adherence to ethical standards, ongoing supervision, and a commitment to continuous professional development. These elements together ensure that coaches can provide safe, effective, and transformative coaching experiences, guiding leaders toward deeper self-awareness, personal growth, and enhanced leadership effectiveness.

Designing Psychoanalytically Informed Coaching Programs

Effective coaching programs that integrate psychoanalytic principles are underpinned by a deep understanding of several core concepts that are foundational to psychoanalytic theory. These principles provide a framework for understanding human behavior and change, making them essential for coaches aiming to facilitate profound and lasting development in leaders.

Exploration of Unconscious Processes

At the heart of psychoanalytic coaching is the exploration of the unconscious mind. This principle involves delving into the thoughts, feelings, and motivations that reside outside of an individual's conscious awareness but significantly influence their behavior and perceptions. Coaches guide leaders to uncover these hidden aspects of their psyche, revealing insights that can lead to transformative change. This exploration can uncover root causes of behaviors, decision-making patterns, and emotional responses that may be hindering a leader's effectiveness.

Transference/Countertransference Dynamics

Transference occurs when individuals project feelings, desires, and expectations from past relationships onto someone in the present, often unconsciously. In a coaching context, leaders may transfer feelings associated with authority figures from their past onto the coach. Countertransference is the coach's emotional response to the leader's transference, which can also be influenced by the coach's own unconscious processes. Understanding and managing these dynamics are crucial in psychoanalytic coaching, as they can significantly impact the coaching relationship and the leader's developmental journey. Recognizing and working through transference and countertransference can enhance the therapeutic alliance and provide rich material for insight and growth.

Use of Defense Mechanisms

Defense mechanisms are unconscious strategies employed by the ego to protect an individual from anxiety and internal conflict. Common mechanisms include denial, repression, projection, and rationalization. In psychoanalytic coaching, understanding and identifying these mechanisms in leaders can illuminate ways in which they may be avoiding confronting difficult truths about themselves or their situations. By bringing awareness to these defenses and gently challenging them, coaches can help leaders face and work through underlying issues, leading to more adaptive behaviors and thought patterns.

These foundational psychoanalytic principles offer powerful tools for executive coaching, enabling coaches to facilitate a deep level of personal insight and growth in leaders. By applying these concepts, coaching programs can move beyond surface-level changes to address the complex psychological underpinnings of leadership challenges, fostering lasting transformation in leaders' professional and personal lives.

A psychoanalytically informed coaching program is meticulously structured to navigate the depths of the unconscious mind, facilitating profound personal and professional development for leaders. This sophisticated approach is delineated into several key phases, each designed to build upon the last, guiding leaders from initial awareness to the integration of deep psychological insights into their leadership practice.

1. Initial Assessments: The program begins with comprehensive assessments to establish a baseline understanding of the leader's current challenges, strengths, and areas for development. These assessments might include psychometric tests, 360-degree feedback, and in-depth interviews. The goal is to gather a multifaceted view of the leader's psychological makeup, leadership style, and the dynamics within their professional environment. This phase sets the stage for targeted coaching interventions by identifying specific areas where psychoanalytic principles can offer valuable insights.

2. Goal Setting: With a clear understanding of the leader's starting point, the next step involves collaboratively setting goals for the coaching engagement. These goals are tailored to address the leader's unique challenges and aspirations, grounded in the insights gained from the initial assessments. Goal setting in a psychoanalytically informed program goes beyond surface-level objectives, aiming to explore and resolve underlying psychological barriers to effective leadership and personal fulfillment.

3. Exploration Phase: The core of the program is the exploration phase, where leaders are guided through a deep dive into their

unconscious processes, beliefs, and emotional patterns. This phase leverages psychoanalytic concepts such as the exploration of dreams, analysis of transference and countertransference dynamics, and examination of defense mechanisms. Through reflective discussions, guided introspection, and therapeutic techniques, leaders gain insights into the unconscious drivers of their behavior and decision-making. This exploration is crucial for uncovering the root causes of leadership challenges and for facilitating genuine self-awareness.

4. Integration of Insights into Leadership Practice: Armed with newfound insights into their unconscious motivations and behaviors, leaders are supported in integrating these revelations into their leadership practice. This phase focuses on translating psychological insights into actionable strategies for change, ensuring that the deep understanding gained through the exploration phase leads to tangible improvements in leadership effectiveness. Coaches work with leaders to develop personalized action plans that address specific areas of growth identified during the exploration phase. This might involve adopting new communication styles, reshaping relationships with team members, or redefining leadership values and priorities.

5. Ongoing Support and Evaluation: As leaders begin to implement changes in their leadership practice, ongoing support and periodic evaluations are essential to sustain progress and adjust strategies as needed. This support might include regular coaching sessions, check-ins, and reassessments to reflect on achievements and to refine goals. The evaluation process ensures that the coaching program remains responsive to the leader's evolving needs and challenges, facilitating continuous growth and development.

A psychoanalytically informed coaching program, with its structured approach to exploring and integrating unconscious processes into leadership practice, offers leaders a powerful pathway to transformation. By addressing the psychological underpinnings of leadership challenges, such programs not only enhance leadership effectiveness but also contribute to leaders' overall well-being and personal growth.

Tailoring a psychoanalytically informed coaching program to the individual needs of each leader is essential for maximizing its effectiveness and ensuring that it resonates with the leader's unique challenges, personality, development goals, and professional context. This customization process begins with a comprehensive exploration of the leader's personal and professional history, gaining insights into their career trajectory, pivotal life events, significant relationships, and previous challenges. Such an in-depth understanding helps to identify the psychological patterns and themes that may be influencing their current leadership style and interactions within the professional sphere.

The next step involves working collaboratively with the leader to pinpoint their core challenges and articulate both their immediate and long-term development goals. This requires a nuanced understanding of the leader's self-perception, aspirations, and the specific demands of their professional role, ensuring that the goals are aligned with personal growth as well as organizational objectives.

A detailed assessment of the leader's psychological dynamics is crucial. By employing psychoanalytic tools and techniques, coaches can uncover unconscious motivations, defense mechanisms, and potential transference or countertransference tendencies that underlie the leader's behavior. This understanding forms the basis for designing customized interventions that directly address the deeper issues at play.

The interventions themselves must be carefully chosen and adapted to meet the leader's specific needs. Whether the focus is on enhancing emotional intelligence, navigating complex power dynamics, or overcoming feelings of imposter syndrome, the techniques used—ranging from dream analysis to the exploration of early relational dynamics—should be tailored to facilitate meaningful insight and change.

It's also important to adapt the coaching communication and engagement style to match the leader's personality and preferences, ensuring the leader remains fully engaged in the psychoanalytic exploration process. Moreover, integrating an understanding of the leader's organizational context—including culture, team dynamics, and external pressures—into the coaching program ensures that interventions are not only personally relevant but also practically applicable.

Maintaining flexibility and an openness to ongoing reassessment throughout the coaching engagement is key. As leaders evolve and new insights emerge, it may be necessary to adjust the coaching goals and interventions to reflect the leader's changing needs and circumstances. This flexible, adaptive approach guarantees that the coaching remains responsive and continues to provide meaningful support for the leader's journey of personal and professional development.

By customizing the psychoanalytic coaching program in such a detailed and responsive manner, coaches can offer a deeply personal and impactful development experience, helping leaders to not only address their immediate challenges but also achieve enduring growth and satisfaction in their roles.

Ethical Considerations and Boundaries

Maintaining clear professional boundaries in coaching relationships is paramount, particularly when the coaching process delves into the deep psychological issues inherent in psychoanalytic approaches. These boundaries are essential for several reasons: they safeguard the professionalism of the coaching relationship, ensure a safe and supportive environment for the leader, and preserve the integrity of the coaching process.

When exploring the unconscious motivations, fears, and desires that influence a leader's behavior and decision-making, the coaching relationship can venture into territories that are intensely personal and potentially vulnerable. Clear boundaries help to define the roles and expectations of both the coach and the leader, creating a structured space within which such sensitive exploration can occur without compromising the leader's sense of security or the coach's objectivity.

Professional boundaries also serve to protect both parties from the potential complexities introduced by transference and countertransference dynamics. In the context of psychoanalytic coaching, where personal histories and unconscious patterns are brought to light, there's an increased risk of these dynamics affecting the relationship. By maintaining strict professional boundaries, coaches can more effectively manage these dynamics, ensuring that they contribute to the leader's growth rather than complicating the coaching relationship.

Clear boundaries are crucial for ethical practice. They ensure that the leader's confidentiality is respected, that the coach's interventions are appropriate and respectful, and that any personal information shared within the coaching context is handled with the utmost care and professionalism. This ethical framework is vital for building and maintaining trust, which is the cornerstone of any effective coaching relationship.

Establishing and communicating these boundaries from the outset of the coaching engagement is critical. It involves setting clear guidelines about the nature and limits of the coaching relationship, the confidentiality of the discussions, and the ways in which psychological insights will be explored and utilized. Coaches should also be mindful of maintaining these boundaries throughout the coaching process, regularly reflecting on their practice and seeking supervision when necessary to ensure that they navigate the psychoanalytic terrain ethically and effectively.

The maintenance of clear professional boundaries is fundamental to the success of psychoanalytically informed coaching programs. It ensures that the exploration of deep psychological issues is conducted in a manner that is safe, supportive, and conducive to the leader's development. By upholding these boundaries, coaches can foster a productive and transformative coaching relationship that respects the leader's vulnerability and promotes genuine personal and professional growth.

Confidentiality and privacy are foundational to establishing a trustful coaching relationship, particularly when psychoanalytic principles guide the exploration of deeply personal and sensitive issues. The assurance of confidentiality creates a safe space for leaders to openly share their thoughts, feelings, and experiences, some of which they may have never verbalized or fully acknowledged before. This level of openness is critical for the psychoanalytic coaching process to be effective, as it relies on uncovering and working through unconscious motivations, past experiences, and emotional patterns that influence the leader's behavior and decision-making.

The critical importance of confidentiality in coaching cannot be overstated. It underpins the entire coaching relationship, fostering an environment of trust and security. Leaders must feel confident that the insights, vulnerabilities, and personal revelations shared during coaching sessions will be protected and kept private. This confidence encourages them to engage more fully in the process, allowing for a deeper exploration of the issues at hand without fear of judgment, exposure, or repercussions in their professional or personal lives. Furthermore, confidentiality supports the psychological safety of the leader, which is essential for meaningful self-reflection and growth. Psychoanalytic coaching often involves delving into sensitive areas, such as early life experiences, family dynamics, and personal fears. Discussing these topics can be challenging and may bring up strong emotions. Knowing that these disclosures are confidential helps leaders to face these challenges more openly, facilitating a process of genuine discovery and transformation.

Maintaining confidentiality also reflects the coach's respect for the leader's autonomy and dignity. It acknowledges the leader's right to control over their personal information and reinforces the ethical responsibility of the coach to protect the leader's privacy.

This respect is crucial for building a strong, effective coaching relationship based on mutual trust and professional integrity.

To ensure confidentiality is upheld, coaches should establish clear agreements with leaders at the outset of the coaching engagement, specifying the boundaries of confidentiality, any exceptions (such as legal requirements or threats to safety), and how information will be stored and protected. Coaches should also be mindful of their own practices, ensuring they do not inadvertently disclose confidential information in supervision, professional discussions, or any other context.

Confidentiality and privacy are indispensable in creating a trustful coaching relationship. They enable leaders to explore personal and sensitive issues without fear of exposure, laying the foundation for a coaching process that can achieve deep psychological insights and foster significant personal and professional growth.

Obtaining informed consent from coachees is a fundamental ethical requirement in coaching, especially critical when the coaching process involves psychoanalytic techniques focused on exploring unconscious material. Informed consent ensures that coachees are fully aware of, and agree to, the nature, goals, and methods of the coaching process, including the exploration of deeply personal and potentially sensitive psychological aspects.

The necessity of informed consent is rooted in the principle of autonomy, respecting the coachee's right to make informed decisions about their participation in the coaching process. This is particularly pertinent in psychoanalytic coaching, where the exploration of the unconscious can reveal unexpected, and sometimes unsettling, insights into one's thoughts, feelings, and behaviors. Coachees must understand the potential depth and scope of this exploration, including the types of techniques that may be employed (such as dream analysis, examination of past experiences, and analysis of transference and countertransference dynamics), and the possible emotional and psychological terrain it may uncover.

Informed consent involves more than just a one-time agreement at the outset of coaching. It is an ongoing process of communication and agreement throughout the coaching relationship. Coaches should ensure that coachees have a clear understanding of the psychoanalytic aspects of the process, including the potential for uncovering deeply buried emotions and memories, and the impact this may have on their self-perception and behavior. This understanding allows coachees to make an informed choice about engaging in these processes and sets the stage for a collaborative, trust-based coaching relationship.

Informed consent includes discussing the limits of confidentiality, any exceptions where confidentiality might need to be breached (such as situations involving risk of harm), and how personal information will be recorded and stored. Coachees should also be informed about their right to withdraw consent at any time, to ask questions, and to raise concerns about the coaching process.

To facilitate informed consent, coaches can provide written materials outlining the psychoanalytic coaching process, hold initial discussions to explain and explore what psychoanalytic coaching entails, and check in regularly with coachees to reaffirm their understanding and consent as the coaching progresses. This practice not only upholds ethical standards but also reinforces the coachee's agency and comfort with the coaching process, contributing to a more effective and meaningful coaching experience.

Informed consent is a cornerstone of psychoanalytic coaching, ensuring that coachees are fully aware of and agree to the exploration of unconscious material. It underscores the ethical commitment to respect, transparency, and coachee autonomy, fostering a safe and productive environment for deep psychological exploration and growth.

Supervision and Continuing Professional Development for Coaches

Supervision plays a pivotal role in supporting coaches as they navigate the intricacies and challenges of psychoanalytically informed coaching. This essential component of professional practice offers coaches a structured framework for reflection, learning, and support, ensuring that their work remains ethical, effective, and attuned to the needs of their coachees. The complexity of delving into unconscious processes, coupled with the potential for transference and countertransference dynamics, makes supervision indispensable for coaches employing psychoanalytic principles.

Supervision provides a safe and confidential space for coaches to explore their own reactions, feelings, and thoughts that arise in the course of their coaching work. This reflective practice is crucial when dealing with the deep psychological material that psychoanalytic coaching can unearth. Supervisors, with their experience and expertise in psychoanalytic principles, offer invaluable insights and guidance, helping coaches to understand and navigate the emotional and psychological dynamics at play, both within themselves and their coachees.

One of the key benefits of supervision is its role in ensuring ethical practice. Supervisors help coaches to scrutinize their work from an ethical standpoint, ensuring that they maintain professional boundaries, confidentiality, and respect for the coachee's autonomy. This oversight is particularly important in psychoanalytically informed coaching, where the exploration of deeply personal and unconscious material could potentially blur boundaries or lead to ethical dilemmas. Moreover, supervision is instrumental in addressing countertransference issues. Psychoanalytic coaching opens the door to complex transference dynamics, where coachees may project onto the coach unresolved feelings or attitudes towards significant figures from their past. Countertransference, the coach's emotional reaction to the coachee's transference, if not recognized and managed, can hinder the coaching process and the coachee's development. Supervision helps coaches to identify their own countertransference reactions, understand their origins, and develop strategies for managing these effectively, ensuring that they can maintain an objective, supportive stance towards their coachees.

Supervisors also play a key role in fostering the professional development of coaches. Through supervision, coaches are encouraged to continuously expand their knowledge of psychoanalytic theory, refine their coaching techniques, and deepen their understanding of the psychological processes underlying leadership challenges. This ongoing learning and development are essential for coaches to remain effective in their practice and to provide the best possible support to their coachees. Supervision is an essential aspect of psychoanalytically informed coaching, providing coaches with the support, guidance, and oversight needed to navigate the complexities of this work. It ensures ethical practice, helps in managing countertransference issues, and fosters continuous professional development, all of which contribute to the effectiveness and integrity of the coaching process.

Supervision in psychoanalytically informed coaching can take various forms, each offering distinct advantages for enhancing reflective practice and professional growth among coaches. The primary models of supervision include individual and group supervision, each with its unique structure and benefits.

Individual supervision involves a one-on-one relationship between the coach and a supervisor. This model provides a personalized and focused environment where coaches can delve deeply into their coaching practice, exploring specific challenges, cases, and personal reactions in detail. The confidentiality and intimacy of the individual supervision setting allow for tailored guidance and support, making it an ideal space for coaches to address sensitive issues, including countertransference or ethical dilemmas, with a high degree of privacy and attention. The personalized feedback and targeted developmental strategies offered in individual supervision cater directly to the coach's specific needs, facilitating nuanced understanding and growth.

Group supervision, on the other hand, brings together multiple coaches under the guidance of one or more supervisors. This model fosters a collaborative learning environment where coaches can share experiences, insights, and challenges. Group supervision offers the benefit of collective wisdom, as coaches learn not only from their own cases but also from the experiences and perspectives of their peers. This diversity of viewpoints can introduce coaches to new strategies, broaden their understanding of psychoanalytic concepts, and offer varied approaches to common coaching challenges. Additionally, group supervision provides a sense of community and support, helping coaches to feel less isolated in their work and more connected to a professional network.

Both models of supervision support reflective practice, encouraging coaches to critically examine their work, understand their emotional responses, and consider the impact of their interventions. Reflective practice is central to psychoanalytically informed coaching, as it enables coaches to maintain awareness of their own processes and how these influence the coaching relationship. Supervision, whether individual or group, plays a crucial role in developing this reflective capacity, guiding coaches to become more self-aware, ethically attuned, and professionally competent.

Professional growth is another significant benefit of both models of supervision. Through ongoing supervision, coaches are exposed to advanced psychoanalytic theories, diverse coaching methodologies, and ethical considerations, contributing to their continuous learning and development. Supervision encourages coaches to challenge themselves, experiment with new techniques, and refine their practice in light of emerging insights and feedback.

In choosing between individual and group supervision, coaches may consider factors such as their personal learning style, the nature of their coaching practice, and their specific developmental needs. Some may find the personalized focus of individual supervision most beneficial, while others may thrive on the dynamic interaction and shared learning of group supervision. Many coaches engage in both models at different times in their careers, benefiting from the unique advantages each has to offer.

Engaging in supervision, whether individual or group, is essential for coaches employing psychoanalytic principles in their practice. It ensures that they receive the support, guidance, and professional development necessary to provide effective, ethical, and reflective coaching services.

Ongoing learning and development are vital for coaches, particularly those employing psychoanalytic principles in their practice. This commitment to continuous professional growth ensures that coaches remain at the forefront of their field, equipped with the knowledge, skills, and insights necessary to facilitate deep and transformative coaching experiences. Engaging in continuous professional development involves several key activities, each contributing to a coach's ability to understand and navigate the complex psychological landscapes of their coachees.

Training in psychoanalytic theory is fundamental for coaches integrating these approaches into their practice. Psychoanalytic theory offers a rich framework for understanding human behavior, emotions, and unconscious processes. By deepening their knowledge in this area, coaches can more effectively identify and work with the underlying psychological dynamics that influence a leader's actions and decisions. Training programs, whether formal academic courses or specialized training workshops, provide coaches with the theoretical foundation and practical tools to apply psychoanalytic concepts in their coaching.

Attending workshops and seminars is another crucial aspect of ongoing professional development. These forums offer opportunities for coaches to learn about the latest developments in psychoanalytic coaching, explore new techniques, and gain insights from leading practitioners in the field. Workshops and seminars also provide a platform for professional networking, allowing coaches to connect with peers, share experiences, and build supportive professional relationships.

Engaging in personal psychotherapy is particularly important for coaches working within a psychoanalytic framework. Personal psychotherapy not only supports the coach's mental and emotional well-being but also deepens their self-awareness and understanding of their own unconscious processes. This self-reflective work is invaluable, enhancing the coach's ability to manage countertransference, recognize their own biases and emotional responses, and maintain a clear, supportive presence for their coachees. Personal psychotherapy exemplifies the principle of 'practicing what you preach,' demonstrating a commitment to the introspective and developmental process that coaches facilitate for their leaders.

Participation in professional coaching associations and continuous reading of psychoanalytic and coaching literature can complement formal training and personal therapy. These activities keep coaches informed about emerging trends, ethical considerations, and best practices in psychoanalytic coaching, contributing to their overall professional competence and effectiveness.

Ongoing learning and development are essential for coaches integrating psychoanalytic principles into their practice. By committing to continuous training in psychoanalytic theory, attending workshops and seminars, engaging in personal psychotherapy, and staying connected with the broader professional community, coaches ensure they are well-prepared to guide leaders through the complex process of psychoanalytic coaching. This commitment to professional growth not only enhances the coach's practice but also ensures that they can provide the highest quality of support to their coachees, facilitating meaningful personal and professional transformation.

Case Examples and Best Practices

Integrating psychoanalytic approaches into executive coaching can yield profound insights and transformative outcomes for leaders. The following illustrative case studies showcase the successful application of these principles, highlighting the nuanced process, inherent challenges, and the significant growth experienced by leaders.

Case Study 1: Leadership and Vulnerability

Background: A senior executive in a multinational corporation struggled with delegating tasks and expressing vulnerability, impacting team trust and collaboration.

Process: Through psychoanalytic coaching, the executive explored unconscious beliefs linking vulnerability with weakness, rooted in early life experiences of high familial expectations. Sessions focused on understanding these deeply ingrained beliefs and their impact on the executive's leadership style.

Challenges: The executive initially resisted exploring personal history, viewing it as irrelevant to current leadership challenges. Overcoming this resistance required building a strong therapeutic alliance and gently guiding the executive to see the connections between past experiences and present behaviors.

Outcomes: The executive gained insight into how fear of vulnerability affected their ability to trust and empower their team. Acknowledging this allowed them to adopt a more open, collaborative leadership approach, significantly improving team dynamics and performance.

Case Study 2: Navigating Power Dynamics

Background: The CEO of a startup faced difficulties with assertiveness and decision-making, fearing that exerting authority would lead to conflict and disapproval.

Process: Psychoanalytic coaching delved into the CEO's unconscious association of authority with aggression, stemming from childhood experiences with authoritarian parenting. The coaching process involved exploring these associations and their influence on the CEO's leadership.

Challenges: A major hurdle was the CEO's discomfort with the emotions that surfaced during the exploration of childhood experiences. The coach worked to create a safe, supportive environment that encouraged emotional expression and processing.

Outcomes: The CEO developed a healthier relationship with power and authority, learning to assert themselves in ways that fostered respect without alienating team members. This shift led to more decisive leadership and a more cohesive, motivated team.

Case Study 3: Overcoming Imposter Syndrome

Background: A high-achieving female leader in the tech industry was plagued by imposter syndrome, doubting her accomplishments and fearing exposure as a fraud.

Process: The coaching engagement used psychoanalytic techniques to uncover the roots of the imposter syndrome, including exploring past experiences of being overlooked or underestimated because of gender biases.

Challenges: The leader's deep-seated beliefs about her own inadequacy were intertwined with societal messages about women in leadership, making it challenging to separate personal insecurities from external influences.

Outcomes: Through psychoanalytic exploration, the leader recognized the external origins of some of her self-doubts and learned strategies to affirm her value and achievements. This realization bolstered her confidence, enhancing her presence and effectiveness as a leader.

These case studies illustrate the power of psychoanalytic coaching in addressing complex leadership challenges by exploring the unconscious underpinnings of behaviors and beliefs. By confronting and understanding these deep-seated issues, leaders can achieve significant personal growth and develop more effective, authentic leadership styles. These transformations not only benefit the individuals but also have a ripple effect, positively impacting their teams and organizations.

Designing and implementing psychoanalytically informed coaching programs, while adhering to high ethical standards and ensuring effective supervision and professional development, involves a comprehensive approach that integrates deep psychological insights with practical coaching methodologies. The following summarizes best practices in these critical areas, ensuring that such programs are both effective and ethically sound.

Firstly, a strong foundation in psychoanalytic theory is essential for coaches. This requires rigorous training and education to understand the complexities of unconscious processes, transference and countertransference dynamics, and the role of defense mechanisms in shaping behavior and thought patterns. Coaches should possess a thorough grounding in these principles to apply them effectively in their practice.

When designing psychoanalytically informed coaching programs, customization is key. Programs should be tailored to meet the unique needs and goals of each leader, taking into account their specific challenges, personality, and professional context. Initial assessments and goal-setting are critical steps in this process, ensuring that the coaching is focused and aligned with the leader's development objectives.

Maintaining ethical standards is paramount in psychoanalytically informed coaching. This involves clear communication about the boundaries of the coaching relationship, confidentiality agreements to protect the leader's privacy, and informed consent to ensure that leaders fully understand and agree to the psychoanalytic aspects of the coaching. Ethical practice also requires coaches to be vigilant about their own biases and countertransference reactions, engaging in regular self-reflection and seeking supervision when necessary.

Effective supervision is another cornerstone of psychoanalytically informed coaching programs. Supervision provides coaches with a platform for professional reflection, learning, and support, helping them navigate the emotional and psychological complexities of their work. Both individual and group supervision models offer valuable opportunities for coaches to discuss cases, explore challenges, and receive feedback, enhancing their skills and ensuring the integrity of the coaching process.

Ongoing professional development is crucial for coaches to stay current with advances in psychoanalytic theory and coaching practices. This involves continuous learning through workshops, seminars, and professional networks, as well as personal psychotherapy to deepen self-awareness and understanding of unconscious processes. Engaging in professional development activities helps coaches to refine their techniques, expand their knowledge base, and grow both personally and professionally.

Best practices for designing and implementing psychoanalytically informed coaching programs involve a blend of solid theoretical understanding, customized program design, stringent ethical standards, effective supervision, and a commitment to ongoing professional development. By adhering to these practices, coaches can deliver impactful and transformative coaching experiences, facilitating deep personal growth and enhanced leadership effectiveness for the leaders they serve.

Conclusion

This chapter has articulated the profound value of integrating psychoanalytic approaches into executive coaching, presenting a compelling case for the depth and transformation such methodologies can bring to leadership development. At its core, the psychoanalytic approach offers a unique lens through which to understand and address the unconscious dynamics that underpin much of human behavior and interaction, particularly in the realm of leadership.

Key points highlighted include the necessity of a solid foundation in psychoanalytic theory for coaches. This deep understanding enables coaches to navigate the complex landscape of the unconscious, including the roles of transference, countertransference, and defense mechanisms. Such knowledge is crucial for identifying and working through the underlying issues that may be hindering a leader's effectiveness.

The chapter also emphasized the importance of tailoring psychoanalytically informed coaching programs to the individual needs of leaders. Customization ensures that the coaching engagement is relevant and impactful, addressing the specific challenges and goals of each leader within their unique professional context. This personalized approach is fundamental to the success of the coaching process, enabling leaders to achieve meaningful growth and development.

Ethical considerations were underscored as paramount in the practice of psychoanalytic coaching. Maintaining confidentiality, ensuring informed consent, and establishing clear boundaries are essential to creating a safe and trusting coaching environment. These ethical practices protect the integrity of the coaching relationship and the well-being of the leader, facilitating a space where deep exploration and transformation can occur.

The role of effective supervision was highlighted as critical for coaches employing psychoanalytic approaches. Supervision provides essential support and guidance, helping coaches to manage the emotional complexities of their work, ensure ethical practice, and navigate any countertransference issues that may arise. This support system is invaluable for maintaining the quality and integrity of the coaching process.

The chapter stressed the importance of ongoing professional development for coaches. Engaging in continuous learning, attending workshops and seminars, and participating in personal psychotherapy are all practices that contribute to a coach's ability to provide insightful, impactful psychoanalytic coaching. This commitment to growth ensures that coaches remain at the forefront of their field, equipped to facilitate deep, transformative change in the leaders they serve.

Integrating psychoanalytic approaches into executive coaching offers a powerful pathway to transformative leadership development. By exploring the depths of the unconscious, addressing the root causes of leadership challenges, and fostering a deep understanding of oneself and others, leaders can achieve unprecedented levels of insight, growth, and effectiveness. This chapter underscores the value of psychoanalytic coaching as a profound tool for personal and professional development, enhancing the capacity of leaders to navigate the complexities of modern organizational life.

Coaches are encouraged to approach the integration of psychoanalytic principles into their practice with a blend of diligence, ethical rigor, and an unwavering commitment to ongoing learning and self-reflection. This thoughtful and conscientious approach is essential for harnessing the full potential of psychoanalytic coaching, ensuring that it not only enhances the effectiveness of the coaching process but also significantly contributes to the holistic growth and development of leaders.

Diligence is foundational in understanding and applying psychoanalytic concepts accurately and effectively. Coaches must thoroughly grasp the depth and complexity of psychoanalytic theory, including the dynamics of the unconscious mind, transference and countertransference, and defense mechanisms. This requires a persistent pursuit of knowledge and skill, honing the ability to identify and work through the psychological underpinnings of leadership behaviors and challenges.

Ethical practice is paramount in psychoanalytic coaching, given its exploration of deeply personal and often sensitive areas of a leader's psyche. Coaches must uphold the highest standards of confidentiality, informed consent, and professional boundaries, creating a safe and trusting environment where leaders feel supported in their journey of self-discovery. Ethical integrity ensures that the coaching relationship remains a protective space for exploration and growth, respecting the vulnerability and dignity of each leader.

An ongoing commitment to learning and self-reflection is crucial for coaches integrating psychoanalytic principles. The field of psychoanalysis is continually evolving, with new insights and methodologies emerging that can enrich the coaching process. Coaches should engage in continuous professional development through workshops, seminars, and scholarly research to stay abreast of these developments. Additionally, personal psychotherapy and reflective practice are invaluable for coaches to explore their own unconscious processes, enhancing their self-awareness and ensuring they can navigate the complex dynamics of the coaching relationship without bias or countertransference issues interfering.

By approaching the integration of psychoanalytic principles with diligence, ethics, and a dedication to ongoing learning and self-reflection, coaches can significantly deepen their impact. This comprehensive approach not only enhances the coach's effectiveness but also fosters profound transformation in leaders. It encourages leaders to develop a richer understanding of themselves and their interactions with others, leading to improved leadership effectiveness, more authentic relationships, and an increased capacity to navigate the challenges of their roles. Coaches who embody these qualities and commitments are well-positioned to contribute meaningfully to the growth and development of leaders, ultimately benefiting individuals, teams, and organizations as a whole.

Conclusion

In this book, we have embarked on a comprehensive exploration of psychoanalytic approaches to executive leadership coaching, delving into the depths of foundational theories, their application in various leadership contexts, and the array of practical coaching strategies that emerge from this rich theoretical ground. This journey has illuminated the transformative power of psychoanalysis when applied to the realm of leadership development, offering a nuanced perspective on the psychological underpinnings of leadership behavior, decision-making processes, and interpersonal dynamics.

Beginning with an in-depth examination of psychoanalytic theory, we traced the origins and evolution of this profound body of knowledge, highlighting key figures and concepts that have shaped its development. This theoretical foundation set the stage for understanding the complex interplay between unconscious processes and leadership effectiveness, offering insights into how leaders can achieve greater self-awareness and emotional intelligence.

We then navigated the application of psychoanalytic principles in diverse leadership contexts, illustrating how these theories can be applied to address common leadership challenges such as navigating power dynamics, overcoming imposter syndrome, enhancing emotional intelligence, and fostering authentic communication and relationships. Through illustrative case studies, we showcased the practical impact of psychoanalytic coaching, revealing the depth of transformation possible when leaders engage in this introspective and exploratory process.

The book presented a range of practical coaching strategies informed by psychoanalytic principles, guiding coaches on how to integrate these approaches into their practice effectively. We emphasized the importance of ethical considerations, the role of supervision, and the necessity of ongoing professional development and self-reflection for coaches. These elements are crucial for ensuring that psychoanalytic coaching is conducted with integrity, sensitivity, and a commitment to fostering genuine growth and development in leaders.

As we conclude this exploration, it is clear that psychoanalytic approaches to executive leadership coaching offer a powerful avenue for achieving deep, lasting change. By engaging with the unconscious aspects of their personalities and behaviors, leaders can unlock new levels of insight, authenticity, and effectiveness. This book aims to inspire coaches and leaders alike to embark on this transformative journey, leveraging the profound insights of psychoanalysis to enrich their professional practice and personal growth.

The exploration of psychoanalytic theory within the context of executive leadership coaching offers a profound framework for understanding the intricacies of leadership behavior. At the heart of this exploration are several core psychoanalytic concepts that provide deep insights into the psychological underpinnings of leadership dynamics.

Psychoanalytic theory posits that much of human thought and behavior is influenced by unconscious processes—thoughts, feelings, desires, and memories that lie outside of conscious awareness. In the context of leadership, the unconscious can shape leaders' decisions, reactions, and interactions in ways that they may not be fully aware of. Recognizing the influence of the unconscious allows leaders to uncover the hidden drivers behind their actions and behaviors, offering a pathway to greater self-understanding and more intentional leadership practices.

Defense mechanisms are unconscious psychological strategies employed to protect individuals from anxiety and internal conflict. Common mechanisms include repression, denial, projection, and rationalization. Leaders might unconsciously use these mechanisms to cope with stress, conflict, or challenging emotions, impacting their decision-making and interpersonal relationships. By becoming aware of and understanding these defense mechanisms, leaders can learn to navigate their use more effectively, leading to healthier coping strategies and more adaptive leadership behaviors.

Transference refers to the phenomenon where individuals project feelings, desires, and expectations from past relationships onto someone in the present, often unconsciously. In leadership, this can manifest in how leaders relate to their team members, superiors, or other key stakeholders, potentially coloring their perceptions and interactions based on past experiences. Countertransference, on the other hand, involves the leader's (or coach's) emotional response to the transference, which can also influence the leadership or coaching dynamic. Understanding these dynamics is crucial for leaders and coaches alike, as it can help in managing personal biases and emotional reactions, fostering more objective and effective leadership and coaching relationships.

The relevance of these psychoanalytic concepts to leadership behavior cannot be overstated. They offer a lens through which to view and understand the complex emotional and psychological landscapes that leaders navigate. By integrating insights from psychoanalytic theory into executive coaching, leaders can achieve a deeper understanding of themselves and their behaviors, leading to transformative personal growth and enhanced leadership effectiveness. This deep, introspective work enables leaders to address the root causes of their challenges, fostering lasting change and a more authentic, emotionally intelligent approach to leadership.

Viewing leadership through a psychoanalytic lens reveals it as a deeply psychological phenomenon, shaped significantly by unconscious processes that influence leadership styles, decision-making, and leader-follower dynamics. This perspective offers profound insights into the complexity of leadership behavior, illuminating the often-hidden drivers behind leaders' actions and interactions.

Psychoanalytic theory suggests that a leader's style is not merely a product of learned behaviors or conscious choice but is deeply influenced by unconscious motivations and past experiences. For instance, a leader's preference for an authoritarian style may stem from an unconscious need for control or security, rooted in early life experiences. Alternatively, a collaborative leadership style might reflect an unconscious desire for acceptance and affiliation. Understanding these underlying motivations allows leaders to reflect critically on their preferred styles, potentially adopting more adaptive approaches that align with their conscious values and the needs of their organizations.

The role of the unconscious in decision-making is another critical insight gained from a psychoanalytic view of leadership. Leaders' decisions can be subtly swayed by unconscious biases, emotional reactions, and unresolved conflicts, leading to choices that may not always align with rational or objective criteria. By bringing awareness to these unconscious influences, leaders can strive for more balanced and reflective decision-making processes, incorporating both rational analysis and emotional intelligence.

Psychoanalytic theory also sheds light on the complex dynamics between leaders and their followers, emphasizing the role of transference and countertransference. Leaders and followers may unconsciously reenact past relational patterns in their interactions, with followers projecting parental or authoritative figures onto the leader, and leaders, in turn, projecting their own unresolved conflicts onto followers. This dynamic can significantly affect the nature of the relationship, influencing trust, communication, and collaboration. Recognizing and addressing these unconscious patterns can lead to healthier, more productive leader-follower relationships.

Viewing leadership through a psychoanalytic lens underscores the significance of unconscious processes in shaping leadership behavior. It provides a richer, more nuanced understanding of leadership as a deeply psychological phenomenon, where the inner world of the leader plays a critical role in their effectiveness and the dynamics they foster within their teams. By integrating psychoanalytic insights into leadership development, leaders can embark on a journey of self-discovery and growth, leading to enhanced leadership effectiveness, improved decision-making, and more positive leader-follower relationships. This approach not only benefits the individual leader but also contributes to the development of a more emotionally intelligent, adaptive, and resilient organizational culture.

In the exploration of psychoanalytic coaching, we delved into several specific techniques and tools that are pivotal for delving into the unconscious aspects of an individual's psyche, aiming to foster deep personal growth and enhanced leadership capabilities. One of the foundational techniques is listening with a third ear, which goes beyond the surface level of what is being communicated to understand the underlying, often unconscious, messages and emotions. This form of listening allows coaches to detect the subtle cues that indicate deeper issues or conflicts, facilitating a more profound level of dialogue and insight.

Exploring dreams and fantasies forms another critical aspect of psychoanalytic coaching. Dreams, with their rich symbolism and connection to the unconscious, provide invaluable insights into an individual's inner conflicts, desires, and fears. Similarly, fantasies can reveal latent aspirations and unresolved issues, offering another pathway to understanding the deeper layers of a person's psyche. Engaging with these aspects in a coaching context allows leaders to uncover and address the unconscious motivations that may be influencing their behaviors and decisions.

Navigating resistance and defense mechanisms is also integral to psychoanalytic coaching. Resistance often emerges as a natural response to the discomfort of exploring deeply personal or unconscious material, manifesting through avoidance, rationalization, or minimization. Defense mechanisms, such as denial, projection, or repression, serve to protect the individual from anxiety or psychological distress but can also hinder personal growth and self-awareness. Psychoanalytic coaching involves gently confronting these resistances and defenses, guiding leaders to recognize and work through them, thus facilitating a deeper understanding of themselves and enhancing their capacity for change.

These techniques and tools are not employed in isolation but are part of a coherent approach that views individuals holistically, considering the intricate interplay between their unconscious processes and conscious behaviors. By employing these psychoanalytic techniques, coaches can help leaders embark on a journey of self-discovery, enabling them to confront and transform the unconscious patterns that influence their leadership style, decision-making, and interpersonal relationships. The ultimate goal of psychoanalytic coaching is not only to address specific leadership challenges but to foster a level of self-awareness and emotional intelligence that supports sustained personal and professional growth.

Psychoanalytic approaches provide profound avenues for addressing common leadership challenges, fundamentally enhancing emotional intelligence, and offering effective strategies to overcome imposter syndrome and leadership anxieties. By delving into the unconscious motivations and unresolved conflicts that often underpin these challenges, psychoanalytic coaching enables leaders to achieve a deeper understanding of themselves and their behaviors, leading to significant personal and professional transformation.

Leadership challenges, such as difficulties in decision-making, conflict resolution, and team dynamics, are often manifestations of deeper psychological patterns. Psychoanalytic coaching helps leaders uncover the root causes of these challenges, whether they stem from past experiences, unconscious beliefs about authority and power, or internalized fears of failure. This deeper insight allows leaders to address not just the symptoms but the underlying issues, leading to more enduring and impactful changes in their leadership approach.

Emotional intelligence is crucial for effective leadership, encompassing self-awareness, empathy, and the management of one's own emotions and those of others. Psychoanalytic approaches enhance emotional intelligence by encouraging leaders to explore their emotional responses and understand their origins. This exploration fosters greater self-awareness and empathy, enabling leaders to navigate interpersonal relationships and team dynamics more effectively. Leaders learn to recognize and regulate their emotional reactions, improving communication and strengthening connections with team members.

Imposter syndrome and leadership anxieties, which can significantly hinder a leader's effectiveness and confidence, are also addressed through psychoanalytic coaching. By examining the unconscious beliefs and past experiences that contribute to these feelings, leaders can begin to challenge and reframe their self-perception. This process helps leaders build genuine self-confidence and reduce anxieties, allowing them to step into their roles more fully and authentically.

Psychoanalytic coaching offers a space for leaders to confront and work through resistance and defense mechanisms that may be blocking their growth. By recognizing and understanding these psychological barriers, leaders can develop new ways of thinking and behaving that are more aligned with their conscious values and goals.

Psychoanalytic approaches offer powerful tools for addressing leadership challenges, enhancing emotional intelligence, and overcoming imposter syndrome and leadership anxieties. Through a deep exploration of the unconscious and a focus on understanding the psychological underpinnings of behavior, leaders can achieve profound personal growth and significantly improve their leadership effectiveness. This process not only benefits the individual leader but also has a positive impact on their teams and organizations, contributing to a more emotionally intelligent, resilient, and effective leadership culture.

Ethical considerations, clear boundaries, and the necessity for ongoing supervision and professional development stand as pillars for coaches employing psychoanalytic approaches in their practice. These elements are crucial in maintaining the integrity, effectiveness, and safety of the coaching relationship, particularly given the depth of personal exploration involved in psychoanalytic work.

Ethical deliberations are paramount in psychoanalytic coaching, as the process often delves into deeply personal and sensitive areas of a leader's psyche. Coaches must navigate these explorations with the utmost respect for the coachee's privacy, autonomy, and well-being. This includes obtaining informed consent, where coaches clearly communicate the nature of psychoanalytic coaching, what it entails, and the potential emotional impacts it may have. Ensuring confidentiality is also essential, as it lays the foundation of trust that allows coachees to open up and engage fully in the process.

Boundaries are another critical aspect of ethical practice. Psychoanalytic coaching can blur the lines between professional and personal realms, making it essential for coaches to establish and maintain clear boundaries. This not only protects the coachee but also preserves the objectivity and professionalism of the coach. Boundaries help define the scope of the coaching relationship, preventing dependency and ensuring that the exploration of unconscious material is conducted in a safe and structured environment.

Ongoing supervision is indispensable for coaches using psychoanalytic techniques. Supervision provides a reflective space for coaches to discuss their cases, explore their own emotional responses, and receive guidance on managing the complex dynamics of transference and countertransference. It supports ethical practice by offering a venue for coaches to examine their work from an ethical standpoint, ensuring that they remain vigilant to potential boundary issues or ethical dilemmas. Supervision is also a key component of professional development, allowing coaches to continually refine their skills and deepen their understanding of psychoanalytic principles.

Professional development is essential in keeping coaches updated on the latest theories, research, and techniques in psychoanalytic coaching. The field is continuously evolving, and staying informed is crucial for effective practice. Professional development can take various forms, including formal education, workshops, seminars, and participation in professional coaching organizations. Engaging in personal psychotherapy is also recommended, as it enhances self-awareness and understanding of one's own unconscious processes, further enriching the coach's ability to facilitate deep transformational work.

Ethical reflections, boundaries, ongoing supervision, and professional development are integral to the practice of psychoanalytic coaching. They ensure that coaches can provide safe, effective, and ethically sound support to leaders, facilitating profound personal growth and enhanced leadership effectiveness. Coaches committed to these principles are well-equipped to navigate the challenges and complexities of psychoanalytic coaching, contributing to the development of insightful, self-aware, and emotionally intelligent leaders.

The landscape of leadership development is increasingly acknowledging the critical importance of psychological depth and self-awareness for effective leadership. This shift reflects a growing understanding that the challenges leaders face cannot be addressed through technical skills and knowledge alone but require a deep exploration of the leader's inner world. Psychoanalytic approaches, with their focus on uncovering unconscious motivations, beliefs, and emotional patterns, are uniquely positioned to meet this need, offering a pathway to transformative leadership development.

This growing recognition stems from the realization that many leadership behaviors, decision-making processes, and interpersonal dynamics are significantly influenced by factors that lie beneath the surface of conscious awareness. Emotional intelligence, resilience, and the capacity to inspire and motivate others are increasingly seen as foundational to leadership effectiveness. These qualities depend not just on what leaders know or do but on who they are at a deeper psychological level.

Psychoanalytic approaches to leadership development provide the tools and frameworks necessary for this kind of deep self-exploration. By engaging with the unconscious aspects of their personality and behavior, leaders can gain insights into the roots of their actions, preferences, and reactions. This process of self-awareness allows leaders to understand their strengths and vulnerabilities, fostering a leadership style that is more authentic, adaptive, and responsive to the needs of their teams and organizations.

Psychoanalytic coaching addresses the emotional complexities of leadership, such as the isolation many leaders feel, the stress of constant decision-making, and the challenges of managing diverse teams. It offers strategies for navigating these challenges that are grounded in a deep understanding of human psychology, enhancing leaders' capacity to manage their emotions and those of others effectively.

The emphasis on psychological depth and self-awareness also reflects a broader shift in organizational cultures towards valuing emotional intelligence, vulnerability, and authenticity. As organizations recognize the impact of these qualities on team cohesion, employee engagement, and overall performance, there is a corresponding increase in the demand for leadership development approaches that can cultivate these attributes.

Psychoanalytic approaches, with their rich tradition of exploring the depths of the human psyche, are well-equipped to respond to this demand. They offer a depth of insight and transformation that goes beyond conventional leadership training, addressing the very foundations of leadership behavior and effectiveness. By fostering a deeper level of self-awareness and psychological insight, psychoanalytic coaching helps leaders to not only navigate the complexities of their roles more effectively but also to contribute to the creation of more psychologically aware and emotionally intelligent organizational cultures.

As the importance of psychological depth and self-awareness in leadership continues to gain recognition, psychoanalytic approaches stand out as a powerful tool for meeting this evolving need. They offer a pathway to deep, lasting leadership development that is rooted in a profound understanding of the self, enhancing leaders' effectiveness and their ability to drive positive change within their organizations.

The integration of psychoanalytic approaches with other leadership theories and coaching models presents a promising avenue for creating a more holistic and comprehensive approach to leadership development. This fusion acknowledges that while psychoanalytic principles offer deep insights into the unconscious aspects of leadership behavior, combining these insights with other models can enhance the breadth and applicability of leadership coaching. Such integration allows for a multifaceted understanding of leadership that addresses both the inner psychological world of the leader and the external challenges they face in their roles.

One potential area for integration is with models that emphasize emotional intelligence and social skills, such as Goleman's Emotional Intelligence framework. Psychoanalytic approaches can deepen the understanding of how a leader's emotional patterns and unconscious dynamics influence their ability to manage emotions, empathize with others, and navigate social complexities. When combined, these models provide leaders with a roadmap for developing emotional intelligence grounded in a deep understanding of their own psychological makeup.

Integrating psychoanalytic principles with transformational leadership theory, which focuses on inspiring and motivating followers to achieve higher levels of performance, can offer insights into the unconscious motivations that drive a leader's ability to inspire and the psychological barriers that may hinder it. This combination can help leaders understand not just what behaviors inspire others, but why certain approaches resonate more deeply, both within themselves and their followers.

Psychoanalytic approaches can also complement coaching models that focus on goal setting and performance improvement, such as the GROW model. By incorporating an understanding of the unconscious beliefs and fears that may inhibit a leader's ability to set ambitious goals or take decisive action, psychoanalytic insights can add depth to the goal-setting process, making it more aligned with the leader's inner values and motivations.

The integration of psychoanalytic principles can enrich systems-oriented leadership models, which consider the complex interplay of individual, team, and organizational dynamics. Psychoanalytic insights into group dynamics, authority, and organizational culture can offer leaders a deeper understanding of the systemic forces at play within their organizations, enhancing their ability to lead change and navigate organizational complexities. This integration requires a nuanced approach that respects the unique contributions of each model while exploring the synergies between them. It demands a level of flexibility and openness from coaches, as well as a commitment to ongoing learning and development to effectively blend different theoretical perspectives.

In practice, integrating psychoanalytic approaches with other leadership and coaching models involves a dynamic and iterative process of application, reflection, and adaptation. It requires coaches to be adept at moving between different models, drawing on each as appropriate to the leader's needs and the specific challenges they face. This integrative approach not only enriches the coaching process but also offers leaders a more comprehensive toolkit for personal growth and leadership effectiveness.

The potential for integrating psychoanalytic approaches with other leadership theories and coaching models represents a frontier for innovation in leadership development. It offers a pathway to a more holistic understanding of leadership that combines the depth of psychoanalytic insight with the practical applicability of other models, equipping leaders to navigate the complexities of modern organizational life with greater awareness, adaptability, and impact.

The future of psychoanalytic theory and practice, particularly within the realm of leadership coaching, is poised for exciting advancements. As interdisciplinary research continues to flourish, insights from neuroscience, psychology, and even fields like artificial intelligence are likely to enrich psychoanalytic approaches, offering deeper and more nuanced understandings of the human psyche. These advancements promise to not only deepen the theoretical foundations of psychoanalytic coaching but also enhance its practical application in leadership development.

One area of potential advancement is the integration of neuroscience findings with psychoanalytic theory. Neuroscience has begun to uncover the biological underpinnings of unconscious processes, such as how memories are stored and retrieved and the neural mechanisms behind emotional responses. These discoveries could provide a scientific basis for many psychoanalytic concepts, offering a more integrated view of the mind that combines psychological depth with biological realism. For leadership coaching, this could mean more precise interventions aimed at modifying neural patterns associated with counterproductive behaviors or enhancing those linked to positive leadership qualities.

Another promising development is the application of findings from positive psychology, which focuses on the strengths and virtues that enable individuals and communities to thrive. Integrating positive psychology's emphasis on resilience, optimism, and well-being with psychoanalytic insights into unconscious motivations and conflicts could create a more balanced approach to leadership development. This integration could help leaders not only address their unconscious barriers to effectiveness but also build on their inherent strengths and capacities for positive leadership.

The growing field of cultural psychology, which examines how culture shapes psychological processes, offers another avenue for enriching psychoanalytic leadership coaching. As global interconnectedness increases, understanding the cultural dimensions of unconscious processes becomes critical for effective leadership in diverse organizational contexts. Psychoanalytic theory can be expanded to include a more nuanced consideration of how cultural norms and values influence unconscious motivations, identity formation, and interpersonal dynamics. This could lead to more culturally sensitive coaching practices that address the specific needs and challenges of leaders in a globalized world.

Advancements in technology, particularly artificial intelligence and machine learning, could also impact psychoanalytic theory and practice. While the deeply personal and introspective nature of psychoanalytic work cannot be replicated by machines, technology could assist in identifying patterns in language use, emotional expression, and behavior that hint at underlying unconscious processes. For leadership coaching, this might translate into tools that help coaches and leaders identify areas for exploration more quickly or track changes over time in a leader's emotional and psychological landscape.

The future advancements in psychoanalytic theory and practice are likely to be characterized by a greater integration of insights from neuroscience, positive psychology, cultural psychology, and technology. These developments promise to enrich psychoanalytic leadership coaching by providing a deeper, more nuanced understanding of the complex interplay between unconscious processes and leadership behavior. By embracing these advancements, psychoanalytic coaching can continue to evolve, offering leaders more effective tools for personal growth and organizational impact.

Adopting psychoanalytic approaches in mainstream leadership development presents a unique set of challenges, yet it also opens up significant opportunities for deeper, transformative change in leaders who engage with these methods. One of the primary challenges lies in the complexity and depth of psychoanalytic theory itself, which can be daunting for both leaders and coaches unfamiliar with its principles. The focus on unconscious processes, defense mechanisms, and the exploration of past experiences requires a level of introspection and vulnerability that may initially be uncomfortable for leaders accustomed to more conventional development approaches.

Another challenge is the potential resistance within organizational cultures to the deeply personal nature of psychoanalytic coaching. Organizations may hesitate to embrace methods that delve into the personal lives and psychological makeup of their leaders, fearing that this might cross boundaries or be deemed too invasive. There's also the issue of quantifying the outcomes of psychoanalytic coaching, as the changes it fosters, though profound, may not always translate into immediate, measurable results in the way that more traditional training metrics do.

Despite these challenges, the opportunities presented by psychoanalytic approaches for leadership development are immense. By engaging with the unconscious aspects of their psyche, leaders can gain insights into the root causes of their behaviors, attitudes, and emotions. This level of self-awareness facilitates transformative change that is not only deep but also lasting, enabling leaders to overcome long-standing barriers to their effectiveness and well-being.

Psychoanalytic approaches also offer the opportunity to address not just the symptoms of leadership challenges but their underlying causes. Whether it's improving communication, enhancing decision-making, or fostering better team dynamics, the changes achieved through psychoanalytic coaching are grounded in a profound understanding of oneself. This can lead to more authentic leadership styles, improved relationships with colleagues, and a greater capacity to navigate the complexities of organizational life.

As awareness grows of the importance of mental health and emotional intelligence in effective leadership, psychoanalytic approaches are increasingly recognized as valuable tools for developing these aspects. They align with contemporary emphases on authenticity, empathy, and resilience in leadership, offering a path to cultivate these qualities in a deep and meaningful way.

The integration of psychoanalytic principles with other leadership theories and coaching models presents additional opportunities for innovation in leadership development. By combining the depth of psychoanalytic insight with the practical applicability of other approaches, coaches can offer leaders a comprehensive development experience that addresses their needs on multiple levels.

While the adoption of psychoanalytic approaches in mainstream leadership development poses certain challenges, it also offers unparalleled opportunities for fostering profound personal growth and transformation. Leaders who engage with these methods can achieve a level of self-understanding and change that profoundly impacts their professional effectiveness and personal fulfillment. As the field continues to evolve, embracing psychoanalytic approaches can significantly enrich the landscape of leadership development, benefiting leaders, organizations, and the broader society.

Encouraging leaders and coaches to remain open to exploring the depths of their own and others' psychological landscapes represents a crucial pathway to achieving true leadership excellence. This exploration, while often challenging, offers a unique opportunity to uncover the underlying motivations, fears, and desires that influence leadership behaviors and decisions. By delving into these deeper aspects of the psyche, leaders and coaches can facilitate a process of transformation that extends far beyond surface-level changes, leading to more authentic, empathetic, and effective leadership.

The journey into one's psychological landscape requires courage and vulnerability. It involves confronting aspects of oneself that may be uncomfortable or difficult to acknowledge. However, this process of self-discovery is essential for personal growth and development. For leaders, understanding their own unconscious biases, emotional triggers, and defense mechanisms can lead to greater self-awareness and emotional intelligence, key components of effective leadership. It enables them to lead with greater authenticity, build stronger relationships with their teams, and navigate the complexities of organizational life with more resilience and adaptability.

For coaches, exploring their own psychological depths enhances their ability to facilitate meaningful change in others. It allows them to recognize and manage their own countertransference reactions, maintain professional boundaries, and approach each coaching relationship with empathy and insight. Coaches who engage in their own process of self-exploration are better equipped to guide leaders through the challenges and opportunities of psychoanalytic coaching, creating a safe and supportive environment for transformation.

The exploration of psychological landscapes also fosters a culture of openness and curiosity within organizations. When leaders and coaches model a commitment to understanding themselves and others at a deeper level, it encourages a similar openness among team members. This can lead to a more inclusive, supportive, and psychologically safe organizational environment, where individuals feel valued for their unique contributions and are empowered to grow and develop. Moreover, the insights gained from exploring psychological landscapes can inform more effective leadership strategies, enhance decision-making, and improve conflict resolution. By understanding the unconscious dynamics at play within themselves and their teams, leaders can adopt more nuanced and effective approaches to leading and managing others.

Remaining open to exploring the depths of one's own and others' psychological landscapes is not just a pathway to personal growth; it is a foundation for true leadership excellence. Leaders and coaches who embrace this journey can unlock unprecedented levels of insight, empathy, and effectiveness, benefiting not only themselves but also their teams and organizations. This openness to deep exploration represents a commitment to the ongoing process of learning and development that is at the heart of exceptional leadership.

The central message of this book emphasizes the profound impact that understanding and working with the unconscious can have on personal growth, leadership effectiveness, and the cultivation of authentic and emotionally intelligent leaders. At the core of this exploration is the recognition that much of our behavior, decision-making, and interpersonal dynamics are driven by processes that lie outside our conscious awareness. By bringing these unconscious elements to light, leaders can embark on a transformative journey, unlocking deeper insights into themselves and their interactions with others.

This journey into the unconscious is not merely an academic exercise but a practical tool with far-reaching implications for leadership development. It allows leaders to confront and resolve internal conflicts, understand their motivations, and address the root causes of their challenges. This process of self-discovery is essential for authentic leadership, as it enables leaders to align their actions with their true values and beliefs, leading with integrity and transparency.

The exploration of the unconscious enhances emotional intelligence, a key component of effective leadership. By becoming more aware of their own emotions and the unconscious biases that influence their perceptions, leaders can improve their empathy, communication, and ability to manage relationships. This heightened emotional intelligence fosters a more inclusive and supportive organizational culture, where team members feel understood, valued, and motivated.

The psychoanalytic approach to leadership development also offers a unique perspective on the dynamics of power, authority, and influence. By understanding the psychological underpinnings of these dynamics, leaders can navigate them more effectively, building trust and credibility with their teams and stakeholders. This deep understanding allows for more nuanced and adaptive leadership strategies, enhancing the leader's ability to inspire, motivate, and drive positive change.

The book underscores the powerful tool that understanding and working with the unconscious represents for leadership development. This approach not only offers a pathway to personal growth and improved leadership effectiveness but also supports the development of leaders who are more authentic, emotionally intelligent, and capable of navigating the complexities of modern organizational life. By embracing the insights offered by psychoanalytic theory, leaders can achieve a level of self-awareness and understanding that is foundational for true leadership excellence.

Embarking on the journey to explore the unconscious is a profound commitment to personal and professional transformation. This path, while challenging, is immensely rewarding, offering insights and growth that touch every aspect of your life. As you delve into the depths of your psyche, you uncover not just the roots of your leadership style and decision-making processes but also the essence of who you are. This exploration is not merely about becoming a better leader; it's about embracing a more fulfilling personal and professional life.

The journey into the unconscious invites you to confront fears, challenge long-held beliefs, and question habitual patterns of behavior. It requires courage, openness, and a willingness to face the unknown. Yet, with each step forward, you gain not only deeper self-awareness but also an enhanced capacity for empathy, resilience, and authenticity. These qualities are invaluable, enriching your relationships, enhancing your leadership, and ultimately leading to a more meaningful and satisfying life.

Remember, this exploration is a continuous process, a journey without a fixed endpoint. There will be moments of discomfort and revelation, but each offers an opportunity for growth and learning. Embrace these experiences with curiosity and compassion, both for yourself and others. The insights you gain from engaging with your unconscious can transform not only your approach to leadership but also how you relate to the world around you.

As you move forward, know that you are not alone on this journey. Seek out mentors, coaches, and peers who can guide, support, and accompany you along the way. Their perspectives can illuminate your path, offering encouragement and insight as you navigate the complexities of your inner landscape.

The exploration of the unconscious is a powerful route to not only better leadership but also a more enriching personal and professional life. It offers the promise of authentic self-expression, deeper connections with others, and a profound sense of fulfillment. May you approach this journey with an open heart and mind, ready to discover the limitless potential that lies within.